The Resonance of Dust

Edward Alexander

THE RESONANCE OF DUST

Essays on Holocaust Literature
And Jewish Fate

Ohio State University Press: Columbus

Library of Congress Cataloguing in Publication Data

Alexander, Edward.

The Resonance of dust.

Bibliography: p.

Includes index.

I. Holocaust, Jewish (1939–1945), in literature—Addresses, essays, lectures. 2. Israeli literature (Hebrew)—History and criticism—Addresses, essays, lectures. 3. American literature—Jewish authors—History and criticism—Addresses, essays, lectures. 4. Yiddish Literature—History and criticism—Addresses, essays, lectures. I. Title.

PN56.3.J4A4   809'.933   79-15515

ISBN 0-8142-0303-5

for Leah

נפשי קשורה בנפשה

TABLE OF CONTENTS

acknowledgements

In the course of writing this book, I have incurred many debts. Primary among them are my debts to the two scholars who were the earliest (and are still among the best) critics of that body of writing called "Literature of the Holocaust": Marie Syrkin and Irving Howe. To Robert Alter and Alvin Rosenfeld I am also greatly indebted for their many essays on Jewish writing in general and Holocaust literature in particular. From the writing of Cynthia Ozick and the conversation of Robert Loewenberg, I have received guidance that may even innocently reach into local tones of thought.

For help and suggestions of various kinds, I would like to thank Yehuda Bauer, Wayne Booth, Bruce Borrus, Hillel Daleski, Frederick Garber, Donald Kartiganer, Shirley Kaufman, Abba Kovner, Deborah Lipstadt, David Mesher, Asher Zelig Milbauer, and the staff of Yad Vashem.

For their support of my work in the form of fellowships and grants, I am indebted to the John Simon Guggenheim Foundation, the National Foundation for Jewish Culture, and the Agnes Anderson Fund of the University of Washington.

To the secretarial staff of the Department of English at the University of Washington and especially to Jane Cornell, who is at once typist and editor, I am indebted for typing much of the manuscript.

Several of the essays in this book originally appeared in *Judaism* and *Midstream* magazines, and I am grateful to their editors for permission to use them here.

Lionel Trilling once suggested that a primary reason for the apparent decline of the novel as a form of art was the fact that ever since Hitler's destruction of European Jewry the task of revealing and articulating man's depravity, an activity that had been a chief occupation of the human mind for four hundred years, had been rendered unnecessary:

> Society's resistance to the discovery of depravity has ceased; now everyone knows that Thackeray was wrong, Swift right. The world and the soul have split open of themselves and are all agape for our revolted inspection. The simple eye of the camera shows us, at Belsen and Buchenwald, horrors that quite surpass Swift's powers, a vision of life turned back to its corrupted elements more literal and fantastic than that which Montaigne ascribed to organized society. A characteristic activity of mind is therefore no longer needed. Indeed, before what we now know the mind stops; the great psychological fact of our time which we all observe with baffled wonder and shame is that there is no possible way of responding to Belsen and Buchenwald. The activity of mind fails before the incommunicability of man's suffering.[1]

Trilling was writing in 1948, shortly after the war; and however true his denial of the possibility of responding to the fact of genocide was at that time, it no longer seems an accurate description of our situation with respect to the Holocaust. After a lengthy silence on the subject, a substantial body of literature dealing with the Holocaust has come into being: novels, poems, memoirs, histories, diaries, biographies.

Not all of these responses, to be sure, are admirable or even worthy of the label "activity of mind." Many of them, including one or two used in this volume for purposes of illustration and comparison, even make one wish that the famous doctrine of "silence" regarding the Holocaust had been observed rather than written about so abundantly. Some of our historians and biographers have so taken to heart Oscar Wilde's doctrine that "the one duty we owe to history is to re-write it"[2] that they have created what amounts to a Hitler hagiography.[3] In fact, this enterprise has become a kind of right-wing equivalent to the left-wing historians' "revisionist" view of Stalin as a gruff but kindly fellow driven to excesses by the intransigence of Harry Truman. At the present time, Europe is being swept by a "Hitler-*welle*," a tidal wave of literature, subliterature, and films devoted not merely to de-demonizing Hitler but to making him into an object of hero worship. Indeed, to minimize or altogether to deny the Holocaust has now become, along with "anti-Zionism," the main business of those who wallow in the filth of antisemitism.[4]

But of course what Trilling really meant to say was not that there is no possible, but that there is no *adequate*, way of responding to the spectacle, enacted in full view of much of the world, of a genocidal campaign that had engaged the human and material resources of the German people for over six years, until its murderous work had been completed or else interrupted by invading armies. When Matthew Arnold, whose great modern disciple Trilling was, demanded "adequacy" of literature in his Oxford University lecture of 1857 "On the Modern Element in Literature"[5] he wanted a literature that could give to his contemporaries an intellectual deliverance from their doubts and confusions by providing them with the complete intelligence of their historical situation. For Arnold modern experience seemed so disordered and intractable that he doubted the ability of the literary imagination to assimilate it and give it coherence.

But our experience and our historical situation are not Arnold's; neither perhaps are our aspirations for literature. Even if one could have a literature that appeared adequately to represent and adequately to comprehend the spectacle of the concentration camps and death factories, would one be satisfied with it? I doubt it. When you wrestle with an angel, it is probably better to lose than to win; and this is more especially the case when you wrestle with the angel of death who visited the Jews of Europe. We are, in other words, dealing here with one of those problematic human enterprises in which some degree of failure or inadequacy is almost a precondition of success, in which we can expect no more than a shattered majesty and a noble imperfection. To say this is not to make of the Holocaust a license for literary nuttiness and "absurdity" or a rare and splendid occasion for demonstrating the infinite elasticity of the literary image. Rather, it is to acknowledge that literary works (like many of those dealt with in this book) that are characterized by uncertainty, paralysis, and ambivalence may provide a more adequate response to the Holocaust than works controlled by a tangible voice committed to the traditional transmutation of suffering into beauty and chaos into tragic significance.

What Trilling called "the incommunicability of man's suffering" during the Holocaust seems at first but an extreme version of a problem that has always troubled writers: how authoritative can the imagined life of a fictional creation be about historical events? This problem was troubling Wordsworth when in *Preface to Lyrical Ballads* (1800) he said that the poet, in order to overcome the "slavish and mechanical" situation of those who only imitate what others act and suffer, was compelled "for short spaces of time perhaps, to let himself slip into an entire delusion, and even confound and identify his own feelings with theirs. . . . " Dickens was addressing the same dilemma when he claimed, in his preface to *A Tale of Two Cities* (1859), a novel describing the butchers and the butchered of the Reign of Terror, that "I have so far verified what is done and suffered in these pages, as that I have certainly done and suffered it all myself."

Fewer than half of the writers dealt with in this book had actual experience of the ghettos, death camps, and outdoor killing centers of the Holocaust. If some readers are unwilling to grant to those writers who were neither victims nor eyewitnesses of the great destruction the authority that they readily allow Dickens to derive from a suffering he did not himself experience, this is because they sense that what happened to the Jews of Europe is so different from anything else in human history that it cannot be merely imagined. Terrence Des Pres, in his profoundly humane and intelligent work *The Survivor: An Anatomy of Life in the Death Camps*, deliberately stays as close as he can to the testimony of survivors because "radical suffering transcends relativity."[6] Nothing is more common in the accounts by survivors of their experiences than the remark that they had been not merely in a strange place but on another planet altogether. Generalizing from such accounts, Hannah Arendt remarked: "There are no parallels to life in the concentration camps. Its horror can never be fully embraced by the imagination for the very reason that it stands outside of life and death."[7] But many of the survivors have also admitted that they have very little confidence in the substantial relation between their own reports and the actuality of the camps, precisely because, once having returned to this planet and the world of the living, they can hardly believe in their own past experiences. Even Elie Wiesel, who is to the general public perhaps the best-known reporter of personal experience and loss in the Holocaust, has said, "The event seems unreal, as if it occurred on a different planet. . . . Did it really happen? I often wonder."[8] We need not deny a certain advantage to the novelist or poet who works from experience and observation; but we must remember that the greatest imaginative writers have not been directed exclusively or even primarily by observation. No matter how much they were "protected" from experience, little of experience was protected from them.

With few exceptions, the writers discussed in this book were moved to composition by extraliterary motives. What the Yiddish critic S. Niger said of the postwar Yiddish poets is true also of many who have written of the Holocaust in other languages: "Insofar as [they] are conscientious—and they are—they no longer want to be reckoned with as artists or 'mere' artists. It is as if they feel guilty that their people's and their own tragedy has become no more than a 'theme' for their poems and stories."[9] It should be readily apparent to all, and will be objectionable to some, readers of this book that I share the view of these writers that in the aftermath of the Holocaust the historical situation of the Jewish people is so desperate that an evaluation of Holocaust literature in merely literary terms is an unaffordable luxury.[10] I have tried at all times to keep in mind T. S. Eliot's dictum that "the 'greatness' of literature cannot be determined solely by literary standards; though we must remember that whether it is literature or not can be determined only by literary standards."[11]

Since the Holocaust, in which one-third of the world Jewish population and the spiritual center of Jewry were destroyed, it is the merest commonplace to say that the very fate of the Jewish people is in question. The oldest Jewish communities of forty years ago—in Germany, in Poland, in Yemen, in Iraq (where Jews had lived for 2,500 years)— today are no more. Unless there is an abrupt reversal both of the laws of probability and of the character of world politics, the last remaining coherent center of the historic Jewish civilization, the State of Israel, may not long survive. If, as Irving Howe has said, "the central premise of Jewish survival is a defiance of history,"[12] that spirit of defiance will have to overcome nearly insuperable difficulties if the miracle of Jewish survival is to be perpetuated.

From the time that Hitler launched his genocidal campaign against them up until the present moment, the Jews, a tiny and in most ways insignificant people, have been at the storm center of world history, apparently unable to extricate themselves from the front of the stage. This simple yet incredible fact has been uppermost in my mind as I considered the literature that came out of the Holocaust, which let loose against the Jews a primordial energy of destructiveness that has by no means spent itself. The more I read of the novels, poems, memoirs, and diaries discussed in the essays that comprise this book, the more I felt that I was reading not of a past finished and dead but of one continuous (though not, of course, identical) with the total form of our present life. "There is," says the philosopher Joseph Dan, "no reason whatsoever to expect that the twentieth century will treat Jews any better in its concluding quarter than it did during its second and third quarters."[13]

The "simple yet incredible" fact just referred to is but one of many that confront us when studying the Holocaust. If there is a recurrent theme of the essays in this volume, it is the danger to the Jewish people of incredulity, an incredulity that has been induced by that congeries of ideas we call by the names of liberalism or modernism or worldliness. "Worldliness," says Cynthia Ozick, is "the gullibility that disbelieves everything."[14] The Jews, once a holy people defined and disciplined by a belief that they had been chosen by God for a special destiny, have since the Enlightenment become by and large a worldly people, which is to say a people that denies its own transcendent reason for being, its own life-principle. The several critiques of the Enlightenment and its varied offspring that appear in this book contend that their historical situation now requires the Jews to choose between their attachment to liberalism, modernism, the seductions of commonsensical knowingness, and their survival as a people.

The fact that most of the writers dealt with in this book view the Holocaust from the point of view of Jewish religion or Jewish historical destiny may give to readers unfamiliar with the Holocaust as a historical phenomenon two misleading impressions. One is that the German criminals, who in many of the works here treated are disembodied and shadowy figures, were merely fulfilling a role previously assigned to them by Jewish history. The other is that the Jews brought their terrible fate upon themselves and even abetted the Germans in their murderous work.

To guard against the first misconception, one must remember the difference between the metaphysical and the historical realm. To view the German perpetrators of the Holocaust, as some Jewish writers do, as the modern continuators of Pharaoh, Haman, and Titus is to view them under the aspect of sacred history, as an instrument of the divine will in His tragic struggle with the chosen but refractory people. It is not to exonerate them of full responsibility for the crimes they committed as active agents in secular history. The standards of literature, moreover, are not those of a court of justice. Even if they were, it is hard to see why the literary transformation of Hitler into Satan, of Mengele and Eichmann into devils, should exculpate them for their monstrous crimes. (They themselves, to be sure, anticipated that the unprecedented, the "inhuman," scale of their crimes would itself render all existing forms of legal punishment absurd and therefore inapplicable.)

Strong as is the modern liberal instinct to exculpate the criminal, the modern liberal tendency to inculpate not only society but the victim himself is yet stronger. The poet Abba Kovner refers to this tendency when he writes acidly of those who betrayed Jews to their German executioners: "Perhaps they were not guilty— / there is always someone more guilty: / (the victim) / (the victim)." It is for this reason that I offer my second caution in the form of a disclaimer. Especially in the first essay in this book, and to a lesser extent elsewhere, criticism of Jewish gullibility is leveled not only at "modern" Jews in general but at some of the victims of the Holocaust in particular. This criticism, which is usually made by the authors I have been trying to interpret, but sometimes also by the interpreter himself, is not intended to blame the victims for being victimized or to accuse them of significantly cooperating in their own destruction. Distinctions between those who believed in the stated intentions of the Germans and those who did not are important and must be made. The Jewish religious tradition that makes of all Hitler's Jewish victims martyrs who died for *Kiddush Hashem* (sanctification of the [divine] name) cannot obliterate the knowledge that they were fallible human beings or remove the subject of their state of mind from critical discussion. But we must keep in mind always the distinction between the killers and their victims, the fact that it was a central intention of the killers to turn their victims into helpless sheep before slaughtering them, and the fact that other groups and nations (all of whom had more arms and experience of armed conflict than the Jews) failed equally with the Jews to offer substantial physical resistance to the German death machine.

This book makes no claim to being a comprehensive and exhaustive treatment of the literature of the Holocaust. I have included for discussion mainly those writers who seemed to me primarily concerned with the relationship between the Holocaust and the course of Jewish history, the fate of the Jewish people. I have, for the most part, excluded those writers for whom the destruction of European Jewry affords primarily a stunning example and ultimate revelation of man's inhumanity to man, or the occasion for apocalyptic excursions in thought or in literary mode. I have also been forced to exclude writers—such as Uri Zvi Greenberg, Aharon Appelfeld, and Abraham Sutzkever—who, although immediate to my concerns in this book, are not readily available to English readers in translation. Even so, I have been obliged at times to be more expository and less allusive than criticism requires in presenting some relatively unknown writers who are included here.

In the first two chapters of the book, writers have been grouped according to theme. In chapters three and four, they have been grouped according to nationality, not merely for classificatory purposes, but in order to compare the rival claims of Israeli and American Jewry to the inheritance of the historical Jewish culture destroyed in Europe. The fifth and sixth chapters concentrate on two contemporary Jewish voices, I. B. Singer and Saul Bellow, whose power and distinctiveness cannot be subsumed under thematic or national categories, even though their work touches on much that is broached in the earlier essays. The two final chapters treat the theological dimensions of the Holocaust. The seventh chapter discusses the impact of the Holocaust upon the covenantal structure of Jewish religion. The eighth and concluding chapter analyzes a little-known Yiddish novella by Chaim Grade that sums up and brings forth with startling lucidity and intellectual power most of the quandaries that the Holocaust has created in the imagination of the Jewish writer and for the future of the Jewish people.

1.   "Art and Fortune," in *The Liberal Imagination* (New York: Viking, 1950), pp. 264–65.

2.   Oscar Wilde, "The Critic as Artist," in *The Artist as Critic*, ed. Richard Ellmann (New York: Vintage, 1969), p. 359.

3.   See, e.g., John Lukacs, *The Last European War* (New York: Anchor Press, 1976); John Toland, *Adolf Hitler* (New York: Doubleday, 1976); and David Irving, *Hitler's War* (New York: Viking, 1977).

4.   For a description and analysis of this "new" antisemitism, see Yehuda Bauer, *The Holocaust in Historical Perspective* (Seattle: University of Washington Press, 1978), especially the chapter "Against Mystification: The Holocaust as a Historical Phenomenon."

5.   Matthew Arnold, *On the Classical Tradition*, ed. R. H. Super (Ann Arbor: University of Michigan Press, 1960), pp. 18–37.

6.   *The Survivor* (New York: Oxford University Press, 1976), p. vi.

7.   Hannah Arendt, *The Origins of Totalitarianism*, 3 vols. (New York: Harcourt, Brace & World, 1951), 3:142.

8.   "Jewish Values in the Post-Holocaust Future: A Symposium," *Judaism* 16 (Summer 1967): 285.

9.   *A Treasury of Yiddish Poetry*, ed. Irving Howe and Eliezer Greenberg (New York: Holt, Rinehart & Winston, 1969), p. 52.

10.   The best-known example of a relentlessly literary critical study of Holocaust literature is Lawrence L. Langer's *The Holocaust and the Literary Imagination* (New Haven and London: Yale University Press, 1975). In this ambitious survey of the European literature of the Holocaust, the fate of the Jews is most often discussed as an aesthetic instrument that "catalyzes the imagination as it expands to symbolic dimensions" (p. 61). Langer deals with the poems and novels of his authors (none of whom, it should be noted, wrote in Yiddish or Hebrew) in the phenomenological manner, "enlarging" on what the literary works say about the Holocaust in order to add to their ultimate significance. His own touchstone of value in judging Holocaust literature is "its ability to evoke the atmosphere of monstrous fantasy that strikes any student of the Holocaust, and simultaneously to suggest the exact details of the experience in a way that forces the reader to fuse and reassess the importance of both" (p. 30).

11.   T. S. Eliot, "Religion and Literature," in *Selected Essays: New Edition* (New York: Harcourt, Brace & World, 1950), p. 343.

12.   *A Treasury of Yiddish Poetry*, p. 58.

13. Joseph Dan, "Will the Jewish People Exist in the 21st Century?", *Forum* 23 (Spring 1975): 61.

14. "On Living in the Gentile World," in *Modern Jewish Thought*, ed. Nahum N. Glatzer (New York: Schocken Books, 1977), p. 172.

The Resonance of Dust

That they could all be murdered, the Jews of Vilna, Kovno, Bialystok, Warsaw, the millions with their wives and children—hardly a single one wanted to believe that. What was the meaning of this? Was it just blindness?—Abba Kovner

There is a great temptation to explain away the intrinsically incredible by means of liberal rationalizations. In each one of us, there lurks such a liberal, wheedling us with the voice of common sense.—Hannah Arendt

chapter 1

The Incredibility of the Holocaust

In 1951 the incredibility of the Holocaust and the un-
imaginativeness of normal people were made themes of
Hannah Arendt's classic study *The Origins of Totalitarianism.* In that book, she stressed the extent to which
the Nazis relied on the likelihood that the wild improbabili-
ty of the scale of their crimes, their very immensity, would
guarantee that, should they lose the war, they and their
preposterous lies would be believed, whereas their victims
would be derided as fantasists. "The Nazis did not even
consider it necessary to keep this discovery to themselves.
Hitler circulated millions of copies of his book in which he
stated that to be successful, a lie must be enormous—which
did not prevent people from believing him as, similarly, the
Nazis' proclamations, repeated *ad nauseam*, that the Jews
would be exterminated like bedbugs (i.e., with poison gas)
prevented anybody from *not* believing them."[1]

Critical studies of the Holocaust and its literature since
1951 have often repeated Hannah Arendt's observation but
rarely modified or amplified it. My primary purpose in this
essay is to raise the question of whether the undeniable
phenomenon of general refusal to credit the intrinsically
incredible horror of the Holocaust[2] can be usefully discussed or fully understood without concentrating attention
on the Jewish identity of the victims. In other words, I want
to suggest that the inability of the victims themselves to
credit the threat and then the actuality of destruction was a
function not only of human psychology and the mad
inventiveness of the Germans but of Jewish history and
Jewish sensibility. My secondary purpose is too polemical
to be stated explicitly at the outset of a scholarly essay without creating the effect of Stendhal's proverbial pistol shot at
a concert, but will, I hope, make itself felt as I proceed.

I would like to begin with a few examples of pre-Holocaust Jewish literature that impute to the Jewish people a deep-seated unwillingness to credit the fact that they have enemies, and that these enemies are capable of murder; a deep-seated unwillingness, ultimately, to credit the existence of evil. It has been said that the Holocaust casts its black shadow not only over everything that has followed it but also over much that preceded it, especially in modern Jewish history and literature.[3] There can therefore be no such thing as a "pure" and unbiased reading of pre-Holocaust Jewish literature by any of us who live in the post-Holocaust epoch, no dispassionate observation of the literary and social fact. I can only ask that each reader test my "subjective" reaction to these stories by returning to the texts themselves, which always retain their integrity and wholeness.

The fictional capital of folly in the Jewish imagination of the nineteenth century was the city of Chelm. Many Chelm folktales are directed against the folly and innocence of Jewish intellectualism when faced with actual and practical problems. But whereas the folktales about Chelm gave exaggerated and apparently incredible examples of blindness to actuality, I. L. Peretz made his Chelmites exemplary of very recognizable Jewish traits drawn out into extreme or radical form.

A good example of this technique is the story "The Shabbes-Goy," a consciously literary tale based upon the Chelm folk materials. The story is about a Chelm rabbi who specializes in explaining away the brutality of the *Shabbes-goy* (a non-Jew hired to do small chores forbidden to Jews on the Sabbath) toward a Jew named Yankele. Each time Yankele reports to the rabbi that he has been beaten by this "murderer," the rabbi responds not by blaming the *goy* but by discovering in Yankele's actions or appearance some provocation to the violence. All his ire is directed against Yankele for maligning "one of God's creatures" as a murderer. " 'Murderer . . . is not necessarily the proper word. I explained that to you once before, if it were so, the world would not be permitted to exist. There are no murderers!' " When Yankele returns to report a third beating, the rabbi " 'can't possibly believe that the *Shabbes-goy* . . . should, just like that, without a reason, be a murderer. The concept lacks reality.' " Finally, when Yankele is beaten a fourth time, the rabbi's intellectual ingenuity is exhausted and he must confess that the mere existence of the Jew, his desire to live and not to die, is a provocation to murder. At last, therefore, he proposes practical action. And what is that practical action? Nothing else than to appease the criminal by buying him off. Faced with the prospect of imminent violence against the whole Jewish community of Chelm, the rabbi proposes: " 'Now, in order to appease his resentment, and with the object of redeeming the entire community from dire peril, let us give the *Shabbes-goy* a raise: a larger portion of the Sabbath loaf and *two* drinks of brandy instead of one. . . . Perhaps he'll have compassion!' "

From Chelm it is geographically and chronologically a long way to the unnamed capital city of Kafka's story "An Old Manuscript"; but in another sense, it is no distance at all. The inhabitants of this town, who have never concerned themselves with problems of self-defense, awake one morning to find themselves surrounded by nomadic soldiers "from the North." These ferocious nomads are totally alien to the city's inhabitants. Speech with them is impossible; and "our way of living and our institutions they neither understand nor care to understand." The nomads are savage brutes who take what they need from the local merchants without making payment. But the narrator, who is one of these merchants, performs intellectual calisthenics in order to deny the enormity of the threat. "They do it because it is their nature to do it. . . . You cannot call it taking by force." True, he is being robbed, but when he sees how much worse the butcher across the street is treated, he "cannot complain." The narrator and his fellow merchants, like the Chelm rabbi, hit upon a solution to this threat from barbarian invaders. They agree to contribute money to the butcher so that he can keep the savages amply supplied with meat. "The butcher is nervous and does not dare to stop his deliveries of meat. We understand that, however, and subscribe money to keep him going. If the nomads got no meat, who knows what they might think of doing. . . . " Robert Alter remarks of this passage that nothing could be more characteristically "Jewish" than that the tradesmen in this community "should answer the terrible challenge only by pooling resources to subsidize the principal victim of the invaders."[4]

By another Kafka story, "The Great Wall of China," we are brought still closer to the phenomenon of Jewish denial of empirical reality, especially when it takes the form of an organized political threat to Jewish existence. Kafka's story tells of a tribe in south China that lives in physical and spiritual isolation from its neighbors and from contemporary life. It is faithful to an emperor who lives at an infinite remove, and whose precepts, though eternally true, remain shrouded in fog. Its people pay homage to the distant city of Pekin, which is "far stranger to the people in our village than the next world." They lead a life "that is subject to no contemporary law, and attend only to the exhortations and warnings which come to us from olden times."

In order to obliterate the present, these south Chinese will go to extraordinary lengths. On one occasion, a beggar interrupts the celebration of a feast day by bringing news of a violent revolt in a neighboring province. The villagers react to this distressing news first by laughing at it, then by destroying the beggar's written evidence of the revolt, and finally by driving the beggar out with blows. "And though . . . the gruesomeness of the living present was irrefutably conveyed by the beggar's words, we laughed and shook our heads and refused to listen any longer."

What makes this story of Kafka, in which Jews are never mentioned, a Jewish story? More than anything else, I believe, it is the stress on the villagers' refusal to credit tangible evidence that disaster is about to befall them, and their seeking refuge in "ancient history told long ago, old sorrows long since healed." They beat the bearer of bad tidings not only because of the ostrich impulse to shield themselves from knowledge of unpleasant truth but also because of a feeling, given them by awareness of their long history of survival, that they are superior to politics. They have survived until now because they were a people who attended *only* to the exhortations and warnings that came from olden times, and who did not allow present exigencies to weaken their loyalty to the ancient faith and the distant city. Why should they interrupt a feast day they were ordered to observe by that "high command" which "has existed from all eternity" in deference to a messenger bringing news of horrors such as they have experienced and survived a thousand times?

If Kafka's south Chinese are not exactly to be identified as Jews, at least they act in ways that Sholom Aleichem, for one, thought characteristic of the Jews of Eastern Europe. In his story "Dreyfus in Kasrilevke," Sholom Aleichem describes the unwillingness of the Jews of Kasrilevke to credit the report of the Dreyfus trial, which is not merely a miscarriage of that equal justice upon which France, above all European nations, prided herself but a denial of the divine promise. When Zaidle, the town's only newspaper subscriber, reads them the bad news of Dreyfus's conviction, they express outrage—"not against the judge who had judged so badly . . . not against the generals who had sworn so falsely nor against the Frenchmen who had covered themselves with so much shame"—but against Zaidle, the bearer of bad tidings. For them the empirical evidence collected in a newspaper is as nothing compared with the divine promise that "the truth must always come out on top, just as oil comes to the top of water!" The more credible the divine promise, the less credible (to them) is the evidence that denies it. The Kasrilevkites, like Kafka's south Chinese, lay claim to a supernal knowledge that makes them superior to all merely political considerations. Hence they too seek refuge from the historical present by declaring it (and its newspaper reflection) incredible: " 'Paper!' cried Kasrilevke. 'Paper! And if you stood here with one foot in heaven and one foot on earth we still wouldn't believe you. Such things cannot be! No, this cannot be! It cannot be! It cannot be!' "

Sholom Aleichem concludes the story on an ironic note that expresses sympathy more than criticism. In effect, he endorses the *shtetl*'s invincible faith in divine justice by asking, "Well, and who was right?" Ruth Wisse has remarked that the story "contains a double irony. The ideal pits itself against reality but is finally vindicated by that same reality. Were Dreyfus not finally acquitted in the human courts of law, the schlemiel insistence on God's justice would have been less convincing."[5]

But just how convincing is this insistence? At the time Sholom Aleichem wrote the story (1902), Dreyfus had gained pardon rather than acquittal. Yet if Sholom Aleichem derived any satisfaction from the apparent resolution of the "affair," he was involving himself in as grave an indulgence of Jewish political innocence as any he imputed to his schlemiels. For Hannah Arendt has demonstrated that the willed Jewish innocence of the political character of the Dreyfus Affair foreshadowed yet more spectacular denials of a grim actuality.

French Jews—despite the fact that their countrymen had everywhere taken up the cry "Death to the Jews"—could not believe that anything more was at stake in the Dreyfus Affair than their social status. Sophisticated French Jews, who had none of Kasrilevke's faith in divine justice and who in fact traveled in those circles "in which," according to Proust, "one's intelligence was understood to increase with the strength of one's disbelief in everything,"[6] interpreted hostility toward themselves as resentment of their un-assimilated brethren from the East (from, so to speak, Kasrilevke). These "emancipated" Jews refused to cooperate with French political figures who wanted to wage a political struggle against antisemitism precisely because, according to Arendt, they "failed to see that what was involved was an organized fight against them on a political front." They maintained their proud and innocent superiority to political considerations in the face of "a huge dress-rehearsal for a performance that had to be put off for more than three decades," a dress-rehearsal, that is, for the Nazi movement. Only one small group of Jews broke from the ranks of the politically innocent and incredulous: these were the Zionists. The only visible result of the "affair," she concludes, "was that it gave birth to the Zionist movement—the only political answer Jews have ever found to antisemitism and the only ideology in which they have ever taken seriously a hostility that would place them in the center of world events."[7]

If indeed the Jews in general did not at this time take seriously the threat that antisemitism, in the form of a pan-European campaign against them, posed to their survival, what was their reasoning? Among the assimilated, belief in liberalism approached so nearly the condition of religious faith that any departure from the ideals of the open society and equal justice in Western liberal democracies could seem no more than an aberration, a temporary digression from the inevitable movement toward liberty, equality, and fraternity. The religious, for their part, knew that despite the terrible massacres inflicted upon the Jews for thousands of years, despite the destruction of a large part of European Jewry during the Chmielnicki massacres, the most widespread and terrible of European history, the Jewish people had always survived—and survived not through political action but through accommodation and waiting. The religious, at least as indifferent to a political struggle on behalf of the Jews as their assimilated brethren were, received endless reminders from their prayers that they were indestructible as a people. The Jebusites, the Girgashites, the Perizzites—all were gone; but the Jewish people remained.

Scholarly opinion varies on the question of whether the plan to destroy the Jews of Europe (and not only of Europe) was uniquely a product of "modern" antisemitism or a logical culmination of the age-old phenomenon of Jew-hatred deeply embedded in the culture of Christian Europe. There is at least ample documentation of the advocacy of genocide of the Jews in the century previous to Hitler, both in the predictable German and Austrian sources as well as in the (to some) less predictable French sources, like Proudhon.[8] But the very fact that Jews themselves were (and are) so numerous among Proudhon's admirers shows how little seriousness was attached to the utterance of this allegedly unthinkable thought.

When they launched their campaign of genocide against the Jewish people, the Germans relied not only on the indifference of the nations of the world to the fate of the Jews but on the inability of most people to credit reports of genocide, and to believe that in the midst of the twentieth century the most cultivated nation of Europe would devote all its energies and much of its resources to the production of Jewish corpses.[9] Thus, on 18 June 1943, the Reichskommissar for the Ostland wrote to the Reichsminister for the occupied Eastern Territories about the mass killing operations then in progress against the Jews: "Just imagine that these events were to become known to the enemy and were being exploited by them! In all probability such propaganda would be ineffective simply because those hearing and reading it would not be prepared to believe it."[10] This was the expected bonus for committing crimes on a scale beyond what the ordinary human imagination could conceive. The unexpected bonus was that the victims themselves were "not prepared" to believe what was happening to them.

For some of these victims were spiritual descendants of Peretz's rabbi of Chelm and of Kafka's beleaguered tradesmen, who thought to forestall calamity by bribing its agents. If anyone doubts that a shared body of themes unites modern Jewish writers of the most diverse backgrounds, let him compare "The Shabbes-Goy" and "An Old Manuscript" with the entry in Chaim Kaplan's *Warsaw Diary* that tells how the Jews of the Warsaw Ghetto interpreted the Nazi decree of forced labor as "some hint for an enormous financial contribution instead." The Jews, whom Kaplan prefers to call "the People of Hope," "did not believe that the decree of forced labor for Jews would be put into effect." Moreover, Kaplan himself, like the Chelm rabbi, at first took the reports coming from Lublin less as warnings of the wrath to come than as slanders against human nature. "What they reported was so horrifying that we began to wonder if they too were exaggerating, for surely human beings created in the image of God would be incapable of such evil deeds." To move from Peretz and Kafka to accounts of the Warsaw Ghetto is to return from shadows to that which casts them, and to recognize, as Kaplan soon did, that "reality surpassed imagination by far."[11]

One of the most sustained attempts to analyze and evaluate the Jews' unpreparedness for believing in the reality of the horror directed against them is Alexander Donat's memoir of Warsaw, Treblinka, Radom, and Auschwitz: *The Holocaust Kingdom.* The central premise of Donat's analysis of the destruction of Polish Jewry is that it was not only hunger and disease, terror and treachery that achieved the Germans' monstrous aim: Jews had also increased their vulnerability by hallucinating moderation in their enemies. Hitler's victims, like the rabbi of Chelm, did not believe in evil: "What defeated us, was Jewry's unconquerable optimism, our eternal faith in the goodness of man." The inhabitants of the Warsaw Ghetto witness roundups of 6,000 to 10,000 people a day who are shipped to Treblinka. Some of these escape from the trains or from the death camp itself and return to the Ghetto to tell their story. But the Jews of Warsaw, although bombarded by eyewitness reports about the boxcars, the unloadings, the selections, the gas chambers disguised as showers, are just as incredulous as the "Chinese" in Kafka's story or the Kasrilevkites of Sholom Aleichem's. "Those eyewitness reports were hard for us to believe. Surely the Germans, even the Nazis, were not capable of such utter inhumanity?" Despite his criticism of them, Donat does not sharply distinguish himself from the majority of Jews who refused to believe in empirical evidence. He admits that it was only after 300,000 people had been deported to Treblinka and he had heard the story from an escapee whom he knew personally that he recognized "the incredible was a matter of fact. . . . The nation of Kant and Goethe was deliberately and systematically murdering defenseless men, women, and children in its gas chambers."[12]

Donat's repeated references in *The Holocaust Kingdom* to the demigods of Western culture leave the reader with the strong impression that the faith that was shattered in the Holocaust was not Judaism but various surrogates for it that have attracted Jews ever since the Enlightenment. When, for example, in a passage filled with anger toward himself, Donat bemoans the fact that "we were . . . stripped of all we had held sacred," he enumerates among the articles of exploded faith Polish nationalism, two thousand years of Christianity, "silent in the face of Nazism," and devotion to modern Western civilization. Judaism, however, is not mentioned.

When Donat deplores the opposition of the Jews to physical resistance, however, he blames their psychological paralysis on both secular humanism and traditional Judaism. The emancipated Jews had for generations "looked to Berlin as the symbol of law, order, and culture." "We fell victim," he admits, "to our faith in mankind. . . . "[13] But those who had never placed their faith in mankind—a notion of whose blasphemy Donat does not seem fully aware—but in God were also, in his view, to blame for the failure to act. The religious believed in *Kiddush Hashem*, sanctifying God's name by a martyr's death. Their policy, therefore, was to counsel against resistance and violence as descrating the purity of martyrdom: " 'For two thousand years we have served mankind with the Word, with the Book. Are we now to try to convince mankind that we are warriors?' " Those who did eventually undertake armed resistance were the ones who were emptied of all hope of whatever kind, secular or religious. "There is no precedent for the eventual uprising of the Warsaw Ghetto because it was undertaken . . . without the slightest hope of victory in life."[14] Only when, in mid-1943, Donat and his friends came to believe in the genocidal intentions of the enemy could they believe in the possibility of Jewish armed resistance. "In this Dantesque atmosphere nothing seemed impossible, for nothing was more fantastic than reality."[15]

But Maidanek went beyond anything Dante imagined, or could imagine. It gave proof that although modern secular man can do without a heaven, he must have a hell, even if self-created. "Maidanek was hell. Not the naive inferno of Dante, but a twentieth-century hell where the art of cruelty was refined to perfection and every facility of modern technology and psychology was combined to destroy me physically and spiritually." Donat, who had been a journalist, now feels it his primary duty to survive in order to tell about the murder of the Jewish people, for who but a survivor could convey the unimaginable reality of a factory whose purpose was "the destruction of the greatest number of prisoners in the shortest time at the lowest cost."[16]

In Maidanek, Donat talks frequently with an inmate named Dr. Ignacy Schipper, who disputes his view that the resistance was the most important fact in the destruction of Warsaw and a turning point in Jewish history. Schipper, a historian, denies that the present events mean the destruction of the Jewish people. They are, of course, terrible, but from the historian's point of view still comparable to other disasters in Jewish history. Yet even he worries most about whether future generations will believe the story of Maidanek. If the murderers are victorious, they will write the history books and either celebrate their achievement or else wipe out the memory of the Jews as thoroughly as they had wiped out their lives. " 'But if *we* write the history of this period of blood and tears—and I firmly believe we will— who will believe us? Nobody will *want* to believe us, because our disaster is the disaster of the entire civilized world. . . . We'll have the thankless job of proving to a reluctant world that we are Abel, the murdered brother. . . .' "[17] For Schipper, the problem is not that the Holocaust is intrinsically incredible but that the world, a sizable portion of which believes itself to be hewn from the Jewish rock, has a vested interest in not believing it. It will be too frightened to accept the implications of the fact that a member of the family of nations has been removed from its midst.

In the final section of his narrative, Donat describes internment at Auschwitz, the march of Jewish slaves to

Dachau, and finally the liberation by Patton's Third Army. He deplores the inability of the newly liberated Jews to take revenge upon their German masters through an act of collective punishment. "We had the souls of slaves, of cowards; we were crippled by two thousand years of pogroms and ghettos, two thousand years of the Sixth Commandment had tamed and blunted in us that natural virile impulse of revenge. The sublime words, 'Thou shalt not kill,' which had been our shield against murder and persecution became the shield and protector of a nation of murderers and our alibi for our own cowardice and weakness."[18] This element of bitterness toward Jewish religion comes as something of a surprise in a book that records the author's disillusionment not with Jewish religion but with the various idolatrous substitutes for it that Jews have embraced ever since the Enlightenment. But it sounds the note that has now, over a decade later, become dominant in Donat's utterances about the Holocaust.

In a long paper entitled "The Voice of the Ashes," which he delivered in 1975 to the New York Conference on the Holocaust sponsored by the Institute of Contemporary Jewry, Donat lays upon Jewish religion all blame for the Jews' inability to respond effectively to the threat of destruction. Announcing—perhaps to the considerable surprise of those who know him only as he reveals himself in The Holocaust Kingdom—that he is "Jewish to the tips of my fingers," Donat defiantly declares that "because I am Jewish, I reject God." Jewish religion in general and Hasidism in particular, he charges, blinded the Jewish people to the real existence of both evil and suffering. His own memoir of the Warsaw Ghetto explicitly blamed the failure to offer physical resistance to the Germans on Jewish history in the Diaspora, on physical circumstances and on "our faith in mankind," as well as on religious quietism. But now Donat appears not only to accept the cruel and stupid image of the Jewish population going as sheep to the slaughter but to say that the faith that paralyzed the Jews into inaction was not at all the secular faith in man but Torah itself: "Due to the moral dis-

armament and quietist conditioning of the orthodox and
Hasidic teachings the religious Jewish masses were
passive. . . ."[19]

It is possible that some of the disparity between *The
Holocaust Kingdom* and "The Voice of the Ashes" is
attributable to the inevitable difference between a memoir
and a lecture. We assume the first—especially in Donat's
case, where it probably bears some relation to a lost diary—
to have greater subjective honesty and less polemical
manipulativeness than an ideological lecture. Yet ultimately the disparity lies in Donat's own hesitation in deciding
whether the Jews' failure to turn into knowledge the
fact of the destruction process was due to their belief in man
or in God. At one point in his 1975 lecture, he includes as
part of his lengthy indictment of the rabbinic power for self-
deception in the face of Jewish suffering the stories of rabbis
who prior to entering the gas chambers of Auschwitz and
Treblinka expressed joy at their imminent ascent to God
and urged other Jews to express this joy by singing, even as
they were being led to death, *"Ani Maamin,"* (I believe).[20]
But later in the same lecture he denies the very thing for
which he blames them: "I was two steps away from the gas
chamber of Maidanek and looked death many times in the
face. Never have I heard anyone intone *Ani maamin* (one of
the postwar legends)."[21]

Although Donat now believes that the centrality of God
for the Jewish people has been replaced by the centrality of
the State of Israel, he does not believe that this transformation will in any way lessen the hatred of the nations for the
Jews. "The holocaust is not yet history. . . . We are alone
in our historical struggle, and we can count only on
ourselves." Having disparaged religious faith as both
partly responsible for, and incredible after, the Holocaust,
Donat finds himself in the position of affirming a willed
belief in the permanence of what for him is a man-made
entity: "We must believe that Israel is a guarantee against
another Holocaust."[22]

If the Holocaust was the supremely incredible experience
for the Jews, and their reaction to it the most fatal

indulgence of their traditional political innocence, then the destruction of the Hungarian Jewish community and the acquiescence of the Hungarian Jews in their own destruction provided the single most incredible episode of the Holocaust. Raul Hilberg, in his book *The Destruction of the European Jews*, lays great stress upon the fact that the Jews of Hungary had survived until mid-1944, so that Hungary was the only country in which the Jews had full warning and full knowledge of what was to come while their community was still unharmed. Dr. Rudolf Kastner later testified that "at the moment of the occupation of Hungary, the number of dead Jews amounted to over five million. We knew very well about the work of the *Einsatzgruppen*. We knew more than it was necessary about Auschwitz. . . . We had, as early as 1942, a complete picture of what had been happening in the East with the Jews deported to Auschwitz and the other extermination camps."[23]

But apparently the Hungarian Jews would not or could not credit what they knew. Eichmann, the man who arranged deportation to the death camps, no sooner arrived than, in the words of the historian Levai, "he virtually hypnotized the Jewish Council and through that body, the whole of Hungarian Jewry."[24] Offered the "opportunity" to establish a Judenrat that would publish all German orders to the Jews, and assured that they had nothing to fear if they cooperated, the Jews repressed the empirical knowledge they had about the five million already dead and acquiesced in the process leading to their own destruction. They did their best to ignore all evidence of danger and to resist all intimations of impending death. The question of whether they were deceived or self-deceived must inevitably be uppermost in our thoughts when we read accounts of the experience of Hungarian Jewry.

One such account is the posthumously published *Diary of Eva Heyman*. Eva Heyman came from a family in which assimilation was not merely a device but a principle. Although not a remarkably perceptive child, she recognized with clarity that her parents really wanted to *be* Aryans. Once she heard one of her relatives say that although Eva was still pretty, her "racial character" was bound to show when she grew up.[25] The meaninglessness of her suffering—for she would not have hesitated a moment to escape into conversion if that could have helped her—was not an added burden to her; for despite her entire lack of Jewish identity, she never was troubled by the question "Why me?"

Only one person in the whole family understood and referred to the "final solution." This was Uncle Lusztig, the most disliked person in the group. He did not know the full story of the destruction process, but he did know about the deportations to Poland, and about the horrible conditions in the cattle cars. To Eva's mother he said that "I, Soma Lusztig, [am] the man whom you all consider to be a nasty old pessimist, but all I am is a very old man and I do not bury my head in the sand the way all of you do."[26] But Eva's mother was convinced that since the Germans already knew the war to be lost they were hardly likely to expend their flagging energies and meager transport on the destruction of Jews.

Eventually Eva's mother and stepfather saved themselves with forged papers validating their Christian-Aryan identity. But Eva herself was left behind in the comforts of home and the care of her governess Juszti. As a result, the thirteen-year-old girl was deported to Auschwitz on 6 June, the day of the Allied landing in Europe, and killed after the very last "selection" carried out by Dr. Mengele, who personally shoved her onto the truck going to the crematorium (the intervening "mercy" of gas chambers having by this point in the war been dispensed with for children).

The most remarkable document in this book is not the diary itself but the appended letter by the Christian governess Juszti to the mother Agi in 1945, after the war. It is a letter of accusation and of self-accusation. She blames Eva's mother for "having lulled yourself with excuses that looked real . . . and for not having fought to have Eva with you, even in more modest circumstances." If the mother had not been so adept in deceiving herself with the belief that Eva's danger was not so great that she needed to be uprooted from her ordinary life in order to be rescued, the girl would still be alive. Agi had indulged herself with the comforting notion that it would be more "practical" to keep the girl in the beautiful, spacious apartment than to subject her to the terrors and uncertainties of flight. "That," says Juszti, "was reality, but unfortunately it was not the truth."

If the Christian governess's accusation, which may have been a contributing factor in Eva's mother's suicide in 1949, seems harsh, then it is at least not so harsh as what she says of herself. Her own failure, she says, lay in adhering to conventional bourgeois morality, in failing to imagine that for which her own experience supplied no precedent. Why did she herself not disobey her employers, abandon everything and go off into hiding with Eva? Forged papers could have been obtained with money. But "the problem wasn't money, but my lack of imagination. . . . And here, dear Agike, is where I failed. This is a greater failure than yours! . . . because I was a petty *petite bourgeoise*, an old ass, an early-morning churchgoer."[27] This untutored woman recognized, belatedly to be sure, that the failure to rescue Eva Heyman was, above all, a failure to imagine the fantastic quality of actuality itself.

The classic presentation of this phantasmagoric reality, and the most famous account both of Jewish suffering during the destruction process generally and of the destruction of Hungarian Jews in particular, is Elie Wiesel's nonfictional novel *Night*. This small book demonstrates how what we complacently call "reality" has now become more incredible than anything previously dreamt of by the most imaginative writer of fiction. It merits a place in literary history if only for rendering a final verdict on the ancient debate over the nature of "reality" in literary characters and situations. It has, or certainly ought to have, taught a generation of literature teachers that the actual world is so fantastic, especially in its capacity for evil, that no literary work can be so resistant to reason and "common sense" as the actuality it purports to describe, and that books by even the most wildly fantasizing writers will fall short of breath in the effort to keep pace with reality. In this

connection Des Pres has commented on "the oddly 'literary'
character of experience in extremity . . . as if amid the
smoke of burning bodies the great metaphors of world
literature were being 'acted out' in terrible fact."[28] Rolf
Hochhuth speaks for those writers who have learned at
least the literary lesson of the Holocaust when he insists
that "anyone in this day and age who . . . does not 'openly
and honestly declare war on naturalism in art,' must
capitulate in the face of every newsreel. . . . "[29]

It is precisely the inability of the mature, rational,
worldly, and commonsensical characters in *Night* to encompass the phantasmagoric quality of reality itself that
delivers them to their doom. Their failure is one of imagination. When Eliezer laments the fact that his parents "had
lacked the courage to wind up their affairs and emigrate [to
Palestine] while there was still time," the courage referred
to is of the sort required to imagine disaster and contemplate extreme action. The very first character introduced in
Night is Moche the beadle, who initiates Eliezer, Wiesel's
alter ego, into the mysteries of the Cabbala. As early as
1942, the barefoot Moche, a foreigner in Hungary, is deported along with other foreign Jews from the town of
Sighet. At the end of the year, he returns, talking no longer
of God or of Cabbala but wanting only to tell his story and
plead with everyone to "prepare yourself while there [is]
still time." But people refuse not only to believe his stories
of mass executions by shooting but even to listen to them.
"I did not," confesses the narrator, "believe him myself."[30]
Rather, the boy occupied himself with Talmud and Cabbala
and took it for granted that better days would not be long in
coming. Moche, like the beggar in Kafka's story or Zaidle in
Sholom Aleichem's tale, is taken for a madman.

The people of Sighet fail to imagine what is, in fact,
required to grasp the actuality of their situation. The
situation Wiesel describes illustrates perfectly Hannah
Arendt's assertion, quoted earlier, that the Nazis'
proclamations that the Jews would be exterminated like
bedbugs did not prevent anybody from *not* believing them.
Certainly it did not prevent the Jews of Sighet from seeking

refuge in incredulity. "Yes, we . . . doubted that he wanted
to exterminate us. Was he going to wipe out a whole
people?"[31] It is not fantasy but reality that overwhelms the
power of imagination. Illusion thus continues its absolute
rule over Sighet, until the Jews find themselves in
hermetically sealed cattle wagons leaving Hungary.

Having failed to listen to Moche, whose "madness"
outraged their realism and incurable optimism, the Jews
now find themselves harangued by still another "mad"
person, Mme Schachter, who screams: " 'Jews, listen to me!
I can see a fire! There are huge flames! It is a furnace!' " By
way of response, the young men tie her up and gag her.
When this fails to silence her, "they struck her several times
on the head—blows that might have killed her." Kill the
bearer of bad tidings! Mme Schachter has no empirical
foundation for her vision, but her nightmare is borne out in
actuality: "In front of us flames. In the air that smell of
burning flesh. . . . We had arrived—at Birkenau, reception
center for Auschwitz."[32] The Jews of Sighet had called
Moche mad, and Mme Schachter (apparently with more
justification) as well. They had denied the witness both of
the messenger who had already seen as well as of the one
who foresaw. The insidious and "knowing" voice of
common sense blinds them to actuality, so that only those
who are "mad" can credit the existence of a world in which
madness has become the normal condition.

At Auschwitz, Eliezer sees and experiences for himself
what had once been thought the visionary fancies of great
imaginative poets. He learns that it is not only in the Book
of Daniel (3:12-30) that men are thrown into furnaces; and
not only in *King Lear* that men are brutally forced to
acknowledge that "unaccommodated man" is no more than
a poor, bare, forked animal: "For us, this was the true
equality: nakedness. Shivering with the cold." Not alone in
Brueghel's paintings does the last judgment of religious
tradition become an obscene, degrading travesty: as Dr.
Mengele made his selections, "all the prisoners in the block
stood naked between the beds. This must be how one stands
at the last judgment." Nor, finally, is it only in a Dante's

Inferno that babies are thrown alive into a burning ditch. The Holocaust remains incredible and unimaginable even to those who see it with their own eyes:

> I pinched my face. Was I still alive? Was I awake? I could not believe it. How could it be possible for them to burn people, children, and for the world to keep silent? No, none of this could be true. It was a nightmare. . . . Soon I should wake with a start, my heart pounding, and find myself back in the bedroom of my childhood, among my books. . . . [33]

"Among my books"—that is to say, back in the comforting realm of credible fiction rather than the horrific one of incredible reality.

It must be stressed that Wiesel's own intention in depicting the incredibility of the destruction of the Jews is not to criticize the Jews for imaginative failure, or for taking refuge in religious belief or for assuming the mask of political sophistication or for clinging to the subterfuge afforded by "common sense." Rather, he believes that the Holocaust, having no precedents or analogues in history, was irrational, unique, intrinsically incredible, and remains so today, even to those, like himself, who experienced it. "The event seems unreal, as if it occurred on a different planet. . . . The Holocaust defies parallels. Did it really happen? Maybe not. I often wonder."[34] Even after he had published a very substantial number of books dramatizing and interpreting his Holocaust experience through fictional characters, Wiesel could express skepticism about whether the writings of survivors and witnesses had any "substantial relationship with what they have seen and lived through."[35]

Although he never tried to blur the fact that the Holocaust experience is primarily a Jewish experience, Wiesel often denied that there lay in it some lesson for the Jews that should cause them to alter their accustomed ways of doing things. "I do not believe the Holocaust teaches us anything in our daily life or in our political and practical attitudes. I do not believe that another Holocaust is possible. Not for the Jews." Wiesel made this rash statement in March 1967, about seven weeks before Egypt closed the Straits of Tiran in order to strangle the Jewish state and a host of Arab armies moved toward the borders of Israel while their leaders loudly announced their intention to turn the Mediterranean red with Jewish blood. In the aftermath of the ensuing Six-Day War, Wiesel was forced to acknowledge that he, the keen analyst of the Jewish unwillingness to credit explicit threats to destroy the Jewish people, had himself fallen pray to that traditional blindness. Nasser of Egypt, rather like the *Shabbes-goy* of Peretz's story, had often declared that "Israel's existence is itself an aggression," but sophisticates knew better than to believe him. "During the Six-Day War we witnessed a repetition in history. Only the setting had changed, the mechanism had remained the same. The shadow of Auschwitz finally enveloped Jerusalem."[36]

The Six-Day War seems to have demonstrated to Wiesel that the Holocaust was, is, and will continue to be, an event of Jewish history. To say this is to call into question one of the pieties of Holocaust scholarship: namely, the "revelation" that all things are now possible, that the genocide successfully carried out against the Jews may now be directed against other peoples. Piotr Rawicz ironically comments on this tendency to transfer Jewish moral capital to others in a novel that insists relentlessly on that sign of the Covenant indelibly inscribed on every Jewish male. Rawicz concludes *Blood from the Sky* by declaring: *"This book is not a historical record. If the notion of chance (like most other notions) did not strike the author as absurd, he would gladly say that any reference to a particular period, territory, or race is purely coincidental."*[37]

But the convergence of probabilities that we name the Holocaust was not coincidental. To "universalize" it by saying that it shows all things are now possible is to evade the shocking and incredible particularity of Jewish experience in the way that universalism always does.[38] "We have, " insists Cynthia Ozick, "to think of the Holocaust as an organism, not as a snowflake. . . . It cannot be said that a snowflake has a 'history.' But the Holocaust, though what it births is death, nevertheless is like a biological birth: it produces itself, it renews itself, *out of a similar ancestry*"[39] (italics mine). The horror renews itself not precisely because antisemitism is eternal or inevitable. Nevertheless it seems futile to explain this renewal merely by social and political causes, the thousand accidental configurations of world politics producing, over the span of centuries, the identical effects. We would be guilty of that "prohibition of questioning" which Eric Voegelin imputes to Marxism and naturalism [40] if we did not consider at least the possibility that the desire to remove the Jewish people from the world, a desire that today finds ready expression in the U.N. as well as in the U.S.S.R., is in some way connected with the reason why the Jewish people was called into existence in the first place. The Jews believe themselves to be a covenanted people called into being thousands of years ago for the purpose of redeeming a corrupted world; why, then, should they find it so difficult to believe that so long as the world is unredeemed the Jewish idea and the Jewish people will provoke this murderous hate?

If, as is sometimes charged, the Jews who were caught in Hitler's trap clung to the delusions of disbelief in order to salvage whatever comfort lay in false hope, what moved the Jews who lived in relative safety to deny credence to the reports of horror flooding in upon them at least as early as August 1942? Professor Yehuda Bauer has pointed out that the "Bund," the Jewish Socialist Party of Poland, transmitted to London in May 1942 a detailed report showing that the Germans had "embarked on the physical extermination of the Jewish population on Polish soil." The report was taken very seriously by the Polish National Council in London, which included two Jewish representatives, Szmul Zygielbojm and Ignacy Schwarzbart. But, despite considerable publicity in the London *Daily Telegraph* and the Jewish press in England, neither the Allies nor the Jewish leadership could be roused from disbelief and complacency. Thus the Polish Government in Exile's *Bulletin for Home Affairs* remarked that "if the Polish reports from the Homeland do not find credence with the Anglo-Saxon nations and are considered to be untrustworthy, they surely must believe the reports from Jewish sources." The crucial fact was that, according to Bauer, "the Jews themselves either did not believe the reports or did not want to believe them"[41]

Marie Syrkin has acknowledged that the Bund report reached the desk of the *Jewish Frontier*, of whose editorial board she was a member, in August 1942. "After reading this detailed account of the functioning of the extermination centers we rejected it as the macabre phantasy of a lunatic sadist." But they did not wholly reject it. Something in them was skeptical of skepticism itself. Therefore they hit upon a solution that cannot but remind us of the way in which the Jews of Chelm and Kasrilevke and south China responded to reports of monstrous evil: "We decided to print a portion of the report in small type in the back of the issue. . . . Our notion was that the atrocity tale, surely untrue, should not be emphatically publicized; that is why we chose small type."[42]

Eight months later, with the fall of the Warsaw Ghetto in April 1943, the extermination of virtually the whole of Poland's three and a half million Jews had been completed. In London, Zygelbojm, in despair over his inability to rouse either the Allies or the Jewish leadership from the seductive comforts of skeptical "common sense," "published" his report in the largest type available to him: he killed himself. He made of his death, in his suicide note, "an energetic cry of protest against the indifference of the world which witnesses the extermination of the Jewish people without taking any steps to prevent it."[43] It is as if the messenger of bad tidings, after repeatedly being spurned as a fabricator of atrocities, has no alternative to futility but to feel upon his own pulses the suffering endured by those in eastern Europe. Only so can he declare his identity with those who suffer the atrocities rather than with the rest, among whom he dwells, who disbelieve them. His death, Zygelbojm believed, would more eloquently testify to his belief in the "incredible" reports than anything he had ever said or written.

Some have seen in the historic inability of the Jews to credit the enormity of the horrors planned and unleashed against them a proof of Jewish moral superiority to the nations of the world. Yitzhak Katznelson insisted that every Jew in the Warsaw Ghetto knew for a certaintly that he was destined to be transported to a place from which he would never return. "Young and old knew that they would be murdered." Yet they somehow could not believe what they knew, or should have known, from evidence. Hence they "actually began to believe that they were travelling to some labour camp." But this willed self-deception, this refusal to believe that the Germans were carrying out the systematic slaughter of the whole Jewish people, was, in Katznelson's view, a proof that the Jews retained their spark of divinity and therefore also their humanity. "Blessed are we," he wrote in his *Vittel Diary*, "that could not believe it! We could not believe it because of the Image of God that is in us. Only a heart tainted with villainy could comprehend or imagine the possibility of such an abomination! We did not believe it could happen because we are human beings."[44]

But is it really true that naïveté and incurable optimism are proof of moral superiority? Is the belief that one is entitled to a morally better existence than is available to those who enter the mire of political life anything other than arrogance parading as purity? Today, the Jewish people still—"incredibly"—finds itself at the storm center of world politics, besieged from without by Amalek and Edom and Ishmael, and weakened from within by those who rest their claim to superior wisdom upon their inability to credit the sincerity of the nations that "have consulted together with one consent" and said: "Come, and let us cut them off from being a nation; / That the name of Israel may be no more in remembrance" (Psalm 83). Those who believe that Jewish chosenness must be validated by a living reality as well as by the memory of innocent martyrdom will find a "lesson" in the phenomenon of Jewish disbelief in the Holocaust. They will recognize that the warfare between brutal actuality and self-deluding hope is today as real and living as ever it was for the Jewish people. They will recall with clarity that the first Jew who organized armed resistance to the Nazis was a man who was distinguished from his fellow Jews not by his physical courage or by his political acumen, but by his willingness to believe the incredible: "In November 1941 a young girl crawled up over the thousands of bodies in the pits at Ponar and made her way twenty miles through a frozen forest back to the Vilna ghetto. No one could believe her story, forty thousand Jews dead in a ditch. But Abba Kovner listened and believed. He was twenty-two years old. He wrote the first Jewish call to arms in the Vilna ghetto. . . . "[45]

"The Incredibility of the Holocaust" first appeared in the March 1979 issue of *Midstream: A Monthly Jewish Review.*

1. Hannah Arendt, *The Origins of Totalitarianism,* 3 vols. (New York: Harcourt, Brace & World, 1951), 3:137.

2. One of the earliest comments on the incredulity of the general public with regard to the Holocaust is Arthur Koestler's essay of January 1944 in the *New York Times Magazine* called "The Nightmare That Is a Reality." In it he claimed that a number of people, including himself, had already been screaming for ten years about atrocities to an unbelieving world, but to no avail: "We started on the night when the epileptic van der Lubbe set fire to the German Parliament; we said that if you don't quench those flames at once, they will spread all over the world; you thought we were maniacs. At present we have the mania of trying to tell you about the killing, by hot steam, mass-electrocution and live burial of the total Jewish population of Europe. . . . The facts have been published in pamphlets, White Books, newspapers, magazines and what not. But the other day I met one of the best-known American journalists over here. He told me that in the course of some recent public opinion survey nine out of ten average American citizens, when asked whether they believed that the Nazis commit atrocities, answered that it was all propaganda lies, and that they didn't believe a word of it" (reprinted under the title "On Disbelieving Atrocities," in *The Yogi and the Commissar* [London: Hutchinson, 1965], p. 90).

3. Dan Jacobson, "The Problem of Isaac Bashevis Singer," *Commentary* 39 (February 1965): 49.

4. Robert Alter, *After the Tradition* (New York: E. P. Dutton, 1969), p. 33.

5. Ruth R. Wisse, *The Schlemiel as Modern Hero* (Chicago: University of Chicago Press, 1971), p. 49.

6. Marcel Proust, *Swann's Way.*

7. Arendt, *Origins of Totalitarianism,* 1:118, 45, 120.

8. J. L. Talmon, "European History—Seedbed of the Holocaust," *Midstream* 19 (May 1973): 12.

9. Abundant evidence that Hitler's foreign policy was an instrument of his racial policy, of his plan for "the destruction of the Jewish race in Europe," is provided in Lucy Dawidowicz's aptly named book, *The War against the Jews: 1933-1945* (New York: Holt, Rinehart & Winston, 1975).

10. Quoted in Gerhard Schoenberner, *The Yellow Star* (New York: Bantam, 1973), p. 124.

11. *The Warsaw Diary of Chaim Kaplan*, trans. and ed. Abraham I. Katsh (New York: Collier, 1973), pp. 116, 312.

12. *The Holocaust Kingdom: A Memoir* (New York: Holt, Rinehart & Winston, 1965), pp. 8, 73, 95.

13. Ibid., p. 103. Cf. Abba Kovner: "The Jews who lie in the mass grave of Minsk did not owe their deaths only to German bullets; they were betrayed by their faith, the faith they had held so dear for two decades [i.e., since 1917] in the fraternity of peoples and the solidarity of the builders of freedom, their faith in the new man" ("Threnody for a Movement," unpublished typescript). See the discussion by Des Pres (who also quotes this passage from Donat) of the extent to which Holocaust victims were imbued with this "faith in humanity" (*The Survivor*, p. 83).

14. *The Holocaust Kingdom*, pp. 103-4.

15. Ibid., p. 150.

16. Ibid., pp. 167-68, 202.

17. Ibid., p. 211.

18. Ibid., pp. 290-91

19. "The Voice of the Ashes," unpublished MS, pp. 42, 15.

20. Ibid., p. 13. A similar indictment is made, from a much more detached perspective, by Ruth Wisse: "Throughout the process of annihilation, the majority of Jews refused or were unable to face reality. The hymn of the concentration camps was the Ani Maamin: 'I believe with perfect faith in the coming of the Messiah' " (*The Schlemiel as Modern Hero*, p. 66).

21. "The Voice of the Ashes," p. 40.

22. Ibid., pp. 50-52.

23. Raul Hilberg, *The Destruction of the European Jews* (Chicago: Quadrangle Books, 1961), p. 529.

24. Ibid.

25. *The Diary of Eva Heyman*, ed. Judah Marton (Jerusalem: Yad Vashem, 1974), p. 26.

26. Ibid., p. 99.

27. Ibid., p. 113.

28. Des Pres, *The Survivor*, p. 70. For a shrewd discussion of Wiesel's fiction see Frederick Garber, "The Art of Elie Wiesel," *Judaism* 22 (Summer 1973): 302.

29. Rolf Hochhuth, *The Deputy* (New York: Grove Press, 1964), p. 288.

30. Elie Wiesel, *Night* (New York: Avon, 1969), pp. 62, 16.

31. Ibid., p. 17.

32. Ibid., pp. 35, 38.

33. Ibid., pp. 45, 82, 42-43.

34. "Jewish Values in the Post-Holocaust Future: A Symposium," *Judaism* 16 (Summer 1967): 285.

35. *One Generation After* (New York: Avon, 1972), p. 57.

36. Ibid., pp. 287, 175.

37. *Blood from the Sky* (London: Secker & Warburg, 1964), p. 316. Elsewhere Rawicz has stressed how genuine "Holocaust books" deal not only with the process of destruction, "but also with the object of the destruction in all its uniqueness and holiness—the old life of the annihilated Jewish communities" (*From Bergen-Belsen to Jerusalem: Contemporary Implications of the Holocaust*, ed. Shulamit Nardi [Jerusalem: Institute of Contemporary Jewry, 1975], p. 27).

38. Carried to its extreme form, this becomes the habit—as in I. F. Stone—of appropriating the language and specter of the Holocaust as if it were in prospect for nearly everybody—except, of course, the Jews themselves.

39. "What, Then, Must We Do?" (New York: Jewish Education Press, 1975), p. 4.

40. Eric Voegelin, *Science, Politics, and Gnosticism* (Chicago: Henry Regnery Co., 1968), pp. 21-27.

41. Yehuda Bauer, "When Did They Know?" *Midstream* 14 (April 1968): 56.

42. Marie Syrkin, writing in reply to Bauer, *Midstream* 14 (May 1968): 62. It is only fair to add that Marie Syrkin and Hayim Greenberg, the editor of *Jewish Frontier*, soon recognized their error and devoted the entire issue of November 1942 to a detailed report on "Jews under the Axis: 1939-1942." In their preface to this forty-page documentation, they wrote that "we have paid Nazi spokesmen the compliment of not believing their monstrous professions. The reports in this issue, however, substantiate the Nazi claims."

43. *Anthology of Holocaust Literature*, ed. Jacob Glatstein et al., (Philadelphia: Jewish Publication Society, 1969), p. 330.

44. Yitzhak Katznelson, *Vittel Diary* (Beit Lohamei Hagettaot: Hakibbutz Hameuchad Publishing House, 1972), pp. 83-84.

45. Shirley Kaufman, Introduction, *A Canopy in the Desert*, by Abba Kovner (Pittsburgh: University of Pittsburgh Press, 1973), p. xiv.

Far more than the Zionists have done to provide the Shield of David with the sanctity of a genuine symbol has been done by those who made it for millions into a mark of shame and degradation. The yellow Jewish star, as a sign of exclusion and ultimately of annihilation, has accompanied the Jews on their path of humiliation and horror, of battle and heroic resistance. Under this sign they were murdered; under this sign they came to Israel. If there is a fertile soil of historical experience from which symbols draw their meaning, it would seem to be given here. Some have been of the opinion that the sign which marked the way to annihilation and to the gas chambers should be replaced by a sign of life. But it is possible to think quite the opposite: the sign which in our own days has been sanctified by suffering and dread has become worthy of illuminating the path to life and reconstruction. Before ascending, the path led down into the abyss; there the symbol received its ultimate humiliation and there it won its greatness.—Gershom Scholem, "The Star of David: History of a Symbol"

chapter 2

Holocaust and Rebirth:
Moshe Flinker, Nelly Sachs, and Abba Kovner

My subject is the link between the Holocaust and the rebirth of Israel in the imaginative and spiritual life of the Jewish people, insofar as that life has been conveyed to us in modern literature. That these two events are the most important in modern Jewish history is unquestionable. It is likewise unquestionable that there is a causative link between them, and that, as Yehuda Bauer has written, "the Holocaust is the central factor not only in Jewish history in the twentieth century in general, but also . . . in the period of the struggle for a Jewish state in particular."[1] Yet it is noteworthy that in the 1973 Yad Vashem symposium on *Holocaust and Rebirth*, in which Professor Bauer's statement appeared, there was no sustained attempt to deal with the superhistorical connection between Holocaust and Rebirth. The sole exception was J. L. Talmon, who, in his lecture "European History as the Seedbed of the Holocaust" expressed his horror at those who profess to see the Holocaust as the price exacted by the God of history for Jewish redemption; if there is "some terrible majesty and magnificence to the Holocaust," he argued, it is in its dramatic symbolization of the conflict between the two permanently opposed world views of morality and paganism.[2]

Yet the sense of an intimate and mystical connection between holocaust and rebirth is deeply embedded in Jewish sacred literature and in Jewish historical consciousness. In the book of Ezekiel, the prospect that God will make "a full end of the remnant of Israel" is inseparable from the promise that "I will even gather you from the peoples, and assemble you out of the countries where ye have been scattered, and I will give you the land of Israel." (Ezekiel 11:13, 16). The legend that the Messiah was born on the very day that the Temple was destroyed is deeply embedded in Jewish tradition, as is the Talmudic notion that the Messiah will come only in a generation totally innocent or wholly guilty.

That the relation between the religious idea of redemption through catastrophe and actual historical events may take grotesque forms is well known. Long before 1492, Kabbalistic writers proclaimed that year as the one in which catastrophe would bring the redemption of the Jews; the catastrophe came, but where was the redemption? The attachment of a large part of the Jewish world to the false messiah Sabbatai Zevi in the seventeenth century arose from the desire to fathom the catastrophe of Chmielnicki's massacre of a very large part of the Jewish population of Poland in relation to the tradition of catastrophic apocalypse. But this plunge into mysticism led to a Jewish catastrophe as horrendous, in its own way, as the one it attempted to explain. The facile and even cruel "explanations" of the Holocaust, which have come from rabbis as well as priests, as God's punishment of Jews for deserting true religion, should serve to remind us that religion, like all other things that are potentially good (and perhaps more than most), is capable of being distorted to malignant usages. But they should not prevent us from listening to those whose imaginations have led them to ask, if not to answer, the question of whether there is a transcendent meaning in the relation between the destruction of the Jews of Europe and the establishment of a Jewish state in Palestine.

In 1938, Gershom Scholem, in the last of his famous series of lectures "Major Trends in Jewish Mysticism," spoke of "the mystical course which, in the great cataclysm now stirring the Jewish people more deeply than in the entire history of Exile, destiny may still have in store for us. . . . "[3] At the time, Hitler's war against the Jews was well under way, but the "Final Solution," i.e., the plan to remove the Jews of Europe from the face of the earth, had not yet been conceived, much less implemented. I propose, in the following essay, to examine three of the writers who have entered the dangerous area of imagining what this mystical course has been. My aim is not to define this mystical course, for this, as Scholem said in the same lecture, "is the task of prophets, not of professors."[4] But I hope to show that a rich vein of literary speculation has been opened into the relation between those tremendous events which have involved the entire world in the fate of the Jews.

Moshe Flinker

My first text expresses more passionately than any I shall touch the conviction that the rebirth of Israel from the ashes of the Holocaust represents a divine scheme of redemption. But it was written in 1942–43 by a sixteen-year-old Dutch boy who was murdered in Auschwitz in 1944, four years before the state was created. The diary of young Moshe Flinker,[5] written in Hebrew and first published in 1958 at the recommendation of S. Y. Agnon, is perhaps the most intensely inward and spiritual of all the diaries written by victims of the Holocaust. Although Moshe was in hiding in Belgium with his parents, five sisters, and a brother, we learn very little indeed (barely the names) of the other members of the family and get little circumstantial detail about their lives or those of the Jews of Brussels. In the mind of this extraordinary boy, grief could not be merely personal or familial, but extended to the whole of the Jewish people. In his diary, therefore, we witness the internalization of the awful drama of the Holocaust in the form of a struggle of the religious will to keep alive the idea of a just and benevolent God in the face of a terrible evil.

Moshe felt that by his determination to find a divine meaning in the cataclysm that was befalling his people, he had so isolated himself from his family that he could express his thoughts only to his diary. The inability to speak of his quandary to those around him aggravated his sense of frustrating paralysis and inaction. He began the diary precisely because he hated "being idle." Yet the diary is more than an anodyne; it is a spiritual diary, an account of the state of his soul. "The truth is that yesterday I hadn't the cheek to report to myself what I had done during the day, because I did nothing. By that I mean that I did nothing to better my soul or to elevate my spirit." It is a measure of how far Moshe falls in spirit during the nine months of keeping the diary that by its end he is assailed by the suspicion that spiritual action is no action at all.

The diary's most constant impulse is the passion for redemption. Moshe desires two things above all others: that he may, by imaginative sympathy and by killing all joy in his own heart, share in the sufferings of the Jewish people who have already been shipped to the East; and that messianic redemption may at last not only end the age-old suffering of the Jews but prove that the suffering had some meaning. Throughout the diary Moshe asks, sometimes explicitly, sometimes implicitly: "If not now, when wilt Thou help Thy chosen people, O Lord?" " . . . What can God intend by all these calamities that are happening to us in this terrible period?" He senses, with a shrewdness that few adult Jews in Europe (or elsewhere) possessed in 1942, that the present calamity of the Jewish people is not merely the latest in the long series of afflictions of the Exile but has its unique enormity, universality, and finality: "I find it very hard to believe that what we are going through today is only a mere link in a long chain of suffering . . . today it is quite possible to destroy the entire people of Israel." Although Moshe never for a moment doubts God's existence or the chosenness of the Jewish people, he is disturbed and infected by those around him who say that there is no God because, if He existed, he would not have allowed such calamities to befall His people.

Moshe's answer to the question of God's purpose in the unprecedented suffering of the Jews comes a few days later, in the form of a terrifying paradox that is one of the diary's distinguishing characteristics. Moshe decides that messianic redemption, which assuredly is long overdue, is now being retarded only by the desire of the Jews and the Allies for a victory over the German scourge. If the war against the Jews marks the end of Jewish Exile, and it does, then the war and the horrible sufferings it brings are none other than the "birthpangs" of the Messiah. Salvation, then, cannot possibly come from a victory by the Allies, which would merely preempt and delay the triumph of the Messiah. Those Jews, including Moshe's family, whose highest hope is to return to the life they knew before Nazism naturally desire the victory of the Allies. Such Jews thereby prove to Moshe that what they seek is not salvation but merely a return to the Exile, from the Land and from God. Such Jews do not understand that the extremity of their physical plight represents also the extremity of their spiritual hope—for it is unthinkable that the Jews will ever be visited with a greater evil than that of Nazism. Their suffering has been so fearfully prolonged and horrible because "the prophet foretold that we would not return [to Eretz Israel] because of our righteousness but as a result of the evildoing of our enemies and our agony at their hands. . . . " The evil force of the world has not yet burned itself out, but for Moshe it is not conceivable that the force of evil or the magnitude of Jewish suffering will ever be greater than they are in Hitler's Europe.

Moshe can never be easy with his paradoxical solution to the question of why the principle of evil is in the ascendancy in the world or with the practical consequence of his solution, which aligns him with the author of his people's suffering in the war raging through Europe. But the possibility that God has no part in what is happening is to Moshe even more horrible than the possibility that He does. With that spiritual modesty which is one of the diary's most poignant features, Moshe admits: "Obviously my outlook is a religious one. I hope to be excused for this, for had I not religion, I would never find any answer at all to the problems that confront me." His explanation of the Holocaust is apocalyptic and cataclysmic in a distinctly religious way. But he does not attempt to hide the undercurrent of skepticism that always threatens this paradoxical faith. Thus he looks forward to Hanukkah as a likely occasion for redemption, yet on the eve of the holiday confesses, "I have the feeling that this Hanukkah will pass, as have so many others, without a miracle or anything resembling one."

Moshe's longing for redemption, for the end of the world

as we have known it, coexists in the diary with an ambition that is both a function of this hope and yet in conflict with it. This is his decision, "after much deliberation," to prepare himself for a career as a Jewish statesman in the Land of Israel. "Even though it would take a miracle to free us now, the rest of my idea—living in our land—isn't so far-fetched." Although we may be tempted to smile condescendingly at Moshe's belief that the success of the messianic era will be contingent on Jewish statesmanship in the New Jerusalem, it is also true that because normative Judaism never separated celestial from earthly Jerusalem, it made of Jerusalem a unique symbol of orderly civilized life.[6] Moshe's choice of career is also influenced by some practical concerns, such as the unavailability of books. "Statesmanship," he remarks with his usual combination of innocence and perspicacity, "as opposed to science, does not demand systematic study, an activity which is impossible for me these days."

Having chosen to prepare for the career of a Jewish statesman, Moshe undertakes to prove to himself the seriousness of his intentions by plunging into the study of Arabic, for the very good reason—one that had not occurred to all potential Palestinian statesmen in 1942—that "a large part of the inhabitants of the land of Israel and the surrounding countries speak it." Moshe's decision to study Arabic is one of many examples of the mysterious combination of the wildly messianic and the shrewdly practical in the character of this sixteen-year-old boy. Belgian Jews of a "practical" strain of mind believe that their salvation will come with an Allied victory, but Moshe sees with a lucidity that is wholly unempirical that the slogan of Allied propaganda—when the Allies decided not to extend help to the Jews of Europe—of "rescue through victory,"[7] was a fraud. Thus, despite the apparent perversity of Moshe's desire that the Germans win every battle short of absolute victory because only such an extremity would ignite redemption, he was entirely right in his expectation that the Jews of Europe were doomed unless rescue came from a source other than the Allies for whose victory they yearned.

The diary's turning point comes on 22 December 1942, when Moshe learns from his father that 100,000 Jews have already been murdered in the East. Hearing this, he wishes to join his brothers in death, and finds that the Bible, which formerly had soothed and consoled him, can offer sustenance only through the Book of Lamentations, that is, through evocations of Jewish agony, not Jewish glory. In spite of his deeply felt belief in cataclysm as the necessary antecedent to redemption, Moshe feels a rising anger toward God and a diminishing ability to draw nourishment from His word. "I have done what I said I would do—study the Bible each day—but I have found nothing in it."

As the sufferings of his people multiply and the tarrying of the Messiah entails ever more destruction, Moshe undergoes a spiritual agony whose causes are at once national and personal. It is not only that the God of history has abandoned His people but that the God of the heart has abandoned young Moshe. "During recent days an emptiness has formed inside me. Nothing motivates me to do anything or write anything, and no new ideas enter my mind; everything is as if asleep. . . . When I pray I feel as if I am praying to the wall and am not heard at all, and there is a voice inside me that says: 'What are you praying for? The Lord does not hear you.' . . . I think that the holy spark which I always felt within me has been taken from me, and here I am, without spirit, without thought, without anything, and all I have is my miserable body." This deeply felt sense of God's withdrawal from the soul into a region so distant that from it He can neither hear nor be heard has afflicted many religious people in the last century. But Moshe stands forth as the symbol of the hundreds of thousands, perhaps the millions, who during the Holocaust suffered the double affliction of the absenteeism or withdrawal of the God of history and the God of the heart, each withdrawal reenforcing the other to overwhelm the individual afflicted by both. For such people, Moshe thinks, "their spiritual anguish . . . may well be greater than their physical pain."

The intensity of Moshe's messianic longing is constantly threatened by the enormity of the afflictions of the Jews.

How much more pain, how many more victims, must be expended before redemption comes? The birth pangs of the Messiah have magnified to an "extent that I would almost say that the cure is worse than the disease." But throughout his agony, he doggedly and assiduously pursues his study of Arabic. He encounters enormous difficulties in obtaining books, which are anyhow in German, a language he does not know well. He reports to his diary his advancement to the "*maza*" verbs despite the fact that his efforts to obtain the requisite textbook—in French—have failed. Although he belittles his Arabic study as "merely an expression of idleness, " it is clear that it is actually a token of his faith that he and the Jewish people both have a future, and that this future will have meaning only if it is a distinct break with the past.

Yet despite his study of Arabic in order to become a Jewish statesman in the land of Israel, Moshe's messianic longing is not, at first, translated into Zionism. In fact, in this very entry where he reports his progress in Arabic, he declares that "for me Zionism cannot now remedy our weakness. Only through the troubles that are now approaching can we attain complete salvation and redemption." But a few months later, when he feels that "the emptiness has spread within me and now fills me completely," he receives something like a revelation, a letter from God. This letter is in the form of a Palestine school almanac that he finds in a Hebrew library. Although he had read the book once before, in a less barren period of his life, it had made little impression on him. But now, in the depths of his loneliness and isolation "from all my brothers, from everything nationally Jewish," the almanac appears to him in a wholly different light. "It now seemed like a letter to me, as a sign of life of the rest of my people. I love it so much that I can hardly bring myself to return it to the library. The name of the almanac is 'My Homeland.' How many times have I not said this word to myself in the last week, and each time it comes into my mind I am filled with yearning for it, and my soul longs for my country that I have loved—and still love—so much."

This moving entry carries implications for the spiritual life of the Jewish people (and for the political life of the modern world) that are not adequately conveyed by the old quip that when a man is no longer capable of being a Jew, he becomes a Zionist. For it shows how, at the deepest level of Jewish religious experience, the will to create meaning out of the terror of history leads or is led to the idea of a national home that will end the Exile of the Jewish people, not only from the promised land but from God. It is not merely that Moshe feels, under the pressure of the genocidal campaign against the Jews, "how much we need a country in which we could live in peace as every people lives in its country." Such a passion, deriving from such a religious crisis, could hardly be satisfied by the Zionist ideal of "normalization." The Jewish homeland, as he conceives it, must redeem the terrible burden of Jewish history, of which Moshe has the fullest imaginative grasp. He sees the Holocaust as (what it is called in Yiddish) the *khurbn*, the culminating final event in "the chain linking the destruction of the Temple with the present day; I see the rivers of blood shed in the name of the sanctification of our holy faith. . . . "

The way in which the land of Israel is to represent an end to Jewish history as it has existed for two thousand years is not purely "spiritual." In Moshe's vision, the actual Jewish *yishuv* in Palestine is an integral part of the redemptive process. This comes out most clearly in the contrast that it poses in Moshe's mind to the Jews of Europe. Moshe, we recall, had begun his diary in order to overcome his sense of helpless inaction through spiritual means. But as the diary approaches its end, Moshe increasingly feels that purely spiritual action—prayers, beseechings, diaries—"cannot reestablish our continually violated honor. Action alone is of any use." He comments bitterly on the paradox of chosenness that the Jewish people has been chosen indeed—to be persecuted. "Is it a nation of soldiers or farmers? No—it is a nation of victims, and a people well suited to being victims. . . . " The powerlessness and inaction of the Jews of Europe threaten even Moshe's writing, for like them he feels "hemmed in on all sides, like a bird in a cage," and wonders "What use is thought without action. . . . ?" His thirst for action can be quenched only by the sole counter-example to the passive suffering of Europe's Jews: namely, the Jews of Palestine. He learns from the papers how they, "when they suffer . . . will die as Jews who have defended themselves, as free Jews—and not like those of my brothers who are now suffering under the atrocious Germans, who lead them like sheep to be slaughtered."

Moshe wrote these words on 3 September 1943. The very next words in the diary, written on 6 September, announce his intention "of emigrating to the Holy Land to help my brothers in their struggle." In this, the last dated entry of the diary, Moshe expresses an unwonted confidence, not so much in his own future as in that of the Jewish people: for he is "absolutely sure that all the sufferings that we have undergone have given us certain rights, and by the general spiritual elevation of our people we have managed to raise the question of the Jews to the status of a problem for all mankind." Thus what was to have been the first notebook of Moshe's diary ends with an upsurge of national feeling, confirmed by the new will of the Jewish people to end its victimization and make its own destiny.

This feeling of confidence is not wrought into consistency with Moshe's previously expressed feeling that it is not through human action that Jewish deliverance will come. Perhaps, if he had lived, Moshe would have seen in these human actions not denial of faith in the promise of deliverance but man's acting out of the redemptive process. For the final (albeit undated) entries in the diary express simultaneously the belief that the Jewish disaster has attained a cosmic dimension, and that passionate desire to give at least a human meaning to this suffering by returning, with the remnant of his people, to rebuild the homeland.

As he contemplates (from afar, he thinks) the suffering of his people, Moshe envisions two ways in which this suffering may be related to something beyond itself and so given meaning. He sees from his window a blood-red sky, and becomes convinced that these "bleeding clouds" are the cosmic reflection of the Jewish sea of blood in the European inferno. Presently, this sky is a reproach to him for having "forgotten" his people and their tragedy; but its future destiny is to intercede, for the very last time, with the Ruler of the Universe to redeem His people.

In a gigantic pathetic fallacy, Moshe imagines the blood-red clouds ascending to the throne of heaven and posing the accusatory questions that dominate his own mind: "How long will He vent his wrath upon the people He chose, who have been suffering for Him for two thousand years? . . . Two thousand years have we been persecuted. Two thousand years have we brought into this world children who are doomed to suffer. Lord our God is this still not enough?"

But the very final note of the diary is one not of accusation of God but of self-accusation. His anguished desire to join his fellow Jews as a victim or to go to Palestine as their avenger ("—the return of our beloved people to their homeland. That will be the greatest revenge that could ever happen.") is thwarted. He therefore berates himself for withdrawing from his people and concludes the diary with an expression of a paralysis that feels to him like death itself.

Moshe's agony of separation from his tortured brethren was soon to end, with his capture by the Gestapo and ultimate execution in Auschwitz. We may be sure the irony of his being arrested on the eve of Passover (7 April 1944) was not lost on Moshe Flinker. Would the loathsome Germans prove, after all, through the alchemy of tragedy, to be the instrument for realizing the promise of redemption celebrated on the holiday? Would he and his people indeed find themselves, as a result of this monstrous paradox, "next year in Jerusalem"? Who can doubt that Moshe asked himself these questions, perhaps continued to ask them throughout his deepest degradation and suffering.

Moshe Flinker's is the purest example of the natural connection between the Jewish religious quandary caused by the Holocaust and the resolution offered by the establishment of a Jewish state. Passionately religious, wholly innocent of politics and contemptuous of human action to bring redemption, Moshe was irresistibly driven by the plight of his people, whose terrible fate he was to share, to seek hope and meaning in Zion. In the passion with which he storms the heavens themselves, in his intense imaginative desire to break through the bonds of this world to a new one, Moshe stands forth as a figure of tragic intensity and dimension. He forces us to ask, as he himself did, whether such suffering, magnified six million times, can conceivably have been inflicted and endured without leaving its permanent mark in heaven and on earth.

Nelly Sachs

One of the most ambitious attempts to answer this question, and in a language that would have seemed perfectly natural to Moshe Flinker, is the poetry of Nelly Sachs. Her sense of the intimate relation between Exile and Return, degradation and exaltation, suffering and redemption, national destruction and national rebirth, is remarkably like Moshe's. She too imagines the sufferings of the Jewish people to have been "constellated" in the heavens themselves. If Moshe sees the very sun turning "as red as blood" because it has been wounded with Jewish suffering, then Nelly Sachs says to the crying Job, symbol of the Jewish people, that "one day the constellation of your blood / shall make all rising suns blanch." The final vision of Moshe's diary, that of a blood-red sun about to set, is the vision that reigns at the outset of the imaginative drama that is enacted in Nelly Sachs's poetry, when she sees the Germans marching across a red carpet that is "the setting sun of Sinai's people."

Although Nelly Sachs's physical situation when she wrote her poems—that is to say, safely out of her native Germany and the inferno of Europe and looking back on the wreckage and carnage—was far different from Moshe's, they were alike in their desperate quest to place themselves imaginatively within the suffering of their people. By the time Nelly Sachs came to compose her massive threnody,

Moshe was himself among those "dead brothers and sisters" to whom she dedicated all of her work.

The poetry of Nelly Sachs is one of the most elaborate and sustained attempts to assimilate the Holocaust into the poetic imagination and into Jewish history. Between 1946, when her first volume of poems—*In the Habitations of Death*—appeared, and her death in 1970, she published volume after volume in the attempt to penetrate what she called "a mystery that begins with night." She has been taken to task by some for illuminating this mystery too well and by others for illuminating it too feebly or not at all. On the one hand, it is charged that the themes and symbols of her poems so thoroughly integrate the Holocaust into the long history of the Jewish people that they "diminish the uniqueness of the horror and . . . turn the murderers into impersonal and abstract forces."[8] On the other, she is faulted for never saying with adequate specificity what the mystery is or where, exactly, the resurrection toward which her heart and verse surge and strain is to be realized.

The first charge would be legitimate if, indeed, it had been Nelly Sachs's primary intention to convey, with the immediacy of an eyewitness or the concrete particularity of the novelist, the phenomenal reality of the destruction of European Jewry. But she assumes from the outset that this greatest of crimes has so disoriented the universe, of which the poet's vision is one part—she speaks of writing with one eye ripped out—that realistic description is the least likely way to capture its reality, which is, in truth, even beyond fantasy. Images of physical dismemberment, as in the poem "Ebb and Flood Strike a Chord," are as rife in her poetry as in Picasso's paintings; they are an aspect of that starting point in night which challenges the integrating power of her imagination. If, in her work, the German murderers are disembodied and without personal identity, it is because that is, in metaphysical (but not legal) justice, their due for turning millions of Jewish victims into smoke.

The second charge—that for all her stress on rebirth, the kind of resurrection she envisions is not fully articulated— seems to ignore an axiom of Holocaust literature: namely, that in the aftermath of the most terrible event of modern, if not all, history, we must live and act without certainties. In seeking meaning in the Holocaust, especially in seeking, as Nelly Sachs does, a divine meaning, one is prohibited from confusing one's own certainty with absolute certainty. Browning's paradox—that in art perfect realization means spiritual stagnation—applies more forcefully here than anywhere else. A tentative resolution of theological doubts is the only resolution men will tolerate.[9]

I believe that in the imaginative universe that Nelly Sachs created the rebirth of the Jewish people in their ancient homeland played a crucial role, even if it never provided her with a conclusive answer to questions intrinsically unanswerable. In every volume, she wrestles with the paradoxical link between the destruction of the Jewish people in Europe and their rebirth, especially (though not exclusively) in Israel. This link never becomes an article of faith, but it is the sole recurring concrete expression of her faith in the possibility of resurrection.

The theme of resurrection—of flesh as well as spirit—is sounded in the very first poem of the first volume, but sounded with irony and bitterness. In "O the Chimneys" the poet collapses the massive physicality of millions of Jewish corpses into a collective image of "Israel's body" drifting as smoke through the air, to be welcomed in heaven by a star turned black because it is now "a chimney sweep." "Or," asks the poet, "was it a ray of sun?" The chimneys of the death factories, through which the smoke that was all that was left of the Jewish people escaped, may from some transcendent point of view be seen as "Freedomway for Jeremiah and Job's dust." But the image (strikingly similar to images in the poetry of Glatstein and Zeitlin and Kovner) seems too spiritualized and etherealized to represent the calamity that is the poem's subject. Even more upsetting is the question "Who devised you and laid stone upon stone / The road for refugees of smoke?" The skeptical reader is inclined to answer, "the Germans, of course." But the poet does not answer. Here it would seem that the very attempt to place the Holocaust within the framework of

Jewish history leads to thoughts that frighten the poet herself, who ends with an exclamation, a cry of pain. The implied question of whether the physical resurrection of the flesh described in her epitaph from Job is possible to these "refugees of smoke" also remains unanswered in the concluding lament: "O you chimneys, / O you fingers / And Israel's body as smoke through the air!"

The next poem, "To you that build the new house," offers more concrete, material images of rebirth. It exhorts the survivors, in putting up their walls, *not* to "hang your tears for those who departed, / Who will not live with you then." Memory will make not only building but sleep impossible. The poem's many imperatives are summed up and generalized in its final one:

> Build, when the hourglass trickles,
> But do not weep away the minutes
> Together with the dust
> That obscures the light.

If read literally, this poem can seem an insensitive injunction to forget the victims lest that memory paralyze efforts of rebuilding and obscure the light that still exists behind the dust (an obsessive image in Nelly Sachs's poems for the Jewish dead). The skeptical reader we imagined for "O the Chimneys" might also be tempted to remark about this injunction to the surviving Jews to ignore their stricken brethren that it is urging people to do more abundantly that which they already do excessively. But in fact, the poem is addressed by Nelly Sachs to herself and to all those burdened by their own inescapable immersion in the Holocaust. For her and for them, there is no question of forgetting; what they seek is the most useful expedient for keeping the dead alive and for rescuing an ancient people before "the hourglass trickles." This expedient is not weeping but building. This is the true memorial because, as Rabbi Nachman said (in the epigraph to the poem): "*There are stones like souls.*"

To speak of stones, in such a context, is to think of Jerusalem, especially if we keep in mind that for Nelly Sachs stones are like "a satchel full of lived life." But historical Eretz Israel first appears in the poetry in the image of the sand of Sinai. This sand, originating in the distant past, has been carried by the Jewish people throughout its long history of transformations, has "Mingled with throats of nightingales, / Mingled with wings of butterflies," and was in the "deathly shoes" taken from the victims of Auschwitz. These victims were themselves turned to dust, which also will become sand, just as the murderers who turned them into dust "will be dust / In the shoes of those to come."

Such a poem as "But who emptied your shoes of sand?" illustrates the impregnation of Nelly Sachs's poetic imagery with the physicality of Eretz Israel. These images suggestively rather than discursively demonstrate that the Diaspora was not a mere rupture in Jewish historical continuity and that the Jews in Exile were still "Sinai's people," whose inherited memories of their homeland became an integral part of their life. The mystery of suffering attendant on the transformation of Jewish "dust" back into Sinai sand is as great as that by which the suffering of Philomela was transformed into the beautiful song of the nightingale referred to in the poem.

The Holy Land, endowed with a voice by Nelly Sachs, contemplates the fate of her children among the nations. The vessels of her holiness were squandered abroad, where Death "Painted *Israel* red on all the walls of the world." Now the Holy Land, much diminished in majesty, asks only:

> What shall be the end of the little holiness
> Which still dwells in my sand?

She receives from the voices of the dead the injunction not to seek revenge. But, unsatisfied with this merely negative counsel, she repeats her question. This time she is answered by the action of a single child, "murdered in sleep," who rises from the dead, "bends down the tree of ages / And pins the white breathing star / That was once called Israel to its topmost bough." By this act she retrieves from its depths of degradation the "badge of shame" that the Nazis affixed to her in the ghetto, forcing the ancient tree of life to stoop to the realms of death so that it may renew itself through the grafting of this old-new branch called Israel. "Spring upright again, says the child, / To where tears mean eternity."

But it is one thing to observe the paradoxical relationship between degradation and exaltation, another to assert their necessary and causal link. To say that the end of the world of European Jewry brought about the rebirth of the Jewish people in Israel is not necessarily to assert that a higher power than man willingly presided over the death of European Jewry for the purpose of resurrecting the Jewish people in their homeland. Yet sometimes Nelly Sachs seems to assert precisely this. As the epigraph to one poem in this volume, she cites the statement from the Zohar that "the sinking occurs for the sake of the rising." In another she urges her audience to learn again "how to listen" so that "on the day of destruction" they will be able to hear "how in death / Life begins."

Ordinarily, to assert that life arises only from death (as when childbirth causes a mother's death) is to assert a gloomy view of existence. Our uneasiness with this conjunction in Nelly Sachs, however, arises from the fear that it is too sanguine. If we have forced ourselves to see the Holocaust in its full horror, we cannot blink the fact that for the Jews of Europe this calamity was indeed—as Hannah Arendt says—"the end of the world."[10] The great, perhaps insuperable, challenge that Nelly Sachs took upon herself was to join a full recognition of this fact to a celebration, however hedged and tentative, of the birth she believed to have been caused by this death. In many ways, this was a more formidable task than that of the elegist who traditionally undertook to triumph over death through the power of language, perception, and poetic tradition; such triumphs cannot be gainsaid by historical events. What is so daring in Nelly Sachs's poems relating Holocaust to rebirth is that her elegiac response to the death of a people keeps straining toward a historical validation and will not rest content with the easy resolutions of what Irving Howe calls "*Geistesgeschichte*: the encapsulation of an extremely complex group of historical events by a theory so nebulously inclusive that it leaves no possibility for refutation."[11]

In some poems, the breakthrough to the new world of rebirth seems to depend not merely on catastrophe but on the extent of the catastrophe: had fewer been killed, "Chorus of the Wanderers" appears to imply, the enormous distance between Exile and Return could never have been encompassed. The homeless wanderers, "clad in the rags of the land / In which we rested," trod the dust of Exile until it began "to stir our grandsons' blood." Then, by their death, they build a path to the new world: "Like measuring rods our bodies lie on the earth / And measure out the horizon—." The wanderers died in the wilderness, but their corpses laid the road to the promised land: "Our death will lie like a threshold / Before your tight-shut doors."

Eclipse of the Stars, published in 1949, a year after the establishment of the State of Israel, is the most explicitly "Zionist" of Nelly Sachs's volumes. Here the hopes so tentatively set forth in the first volume are allowed to flourish, and the generalized theme of rebirth is vivified and particularized by the nourishment of a living reality.

The volume takes as a given the inability of the nations to accept the People Israel in their midst: "Why the black answer of hate to your existence, Israel?" This people, which always in the family of nations "sang / one note lower / or one note higher," has, despite the unique blessing it brought to the world as "the source of the living God," at last been abandoned by angels and mortals. The European survivors of this people, those who have not been "turned to ashes," can never return to their former dwelling places. The nations who ask where the survivors plan to go do not see that "they are always going to their graves." Terror creates a homelessness for which "all ways wither like cut flowers—."

But, paradoxically, just because we inhabit an era when chaos and darkness have reestablished their empire more firmly than ever, "Time roars with our longing for home." Exile is not eternal—that, after all, had been the definitive prophecy of Jesus regarding the Jewish people—and there is still a way homeward that has not withered. In a recurring image, the sand of the hourglass has nearly run out for the Jewish people. But the sand actually runs not into the bottom of the hourglass but ultimately back to the desert from whence it came, and from whence the people of Israel came as well. In the astonishing metaphysical image that holds the meaning of "Women and girls of Israel," the sand of the desert, accumulating through the centuries since Jewish expulsion, is also the sand of the hourglass that measures the little remaining time of the Jewish people. Paradoxically, this process of dissipation both resulted in, and was halted by, the blooming of the desert:

> the desert, the great bend in the road to eternity,
> which had already begun to fill with its sand
> the hourglass of lunar time,
> breathes above the filled-in footsteps
> of those who go to God, and its parched veined springs
> fill with fertility—

The transformation of Jewish existence in the Diaspora into Jewish existence in Israel is symbolized by the transformation of the "hourglass of dust" in which exiled time itself, the "homeless millennia," has roamed since the destruction of the temple, into the sand of the desert from which both dust and glass were created.

Perhaps the most affirmative of the poems in this volume, and the one in which the feeling of imminent return is strongest, is "Now Abraham has seized the root of the winds":

> Now Abraham has seized the root of the winds
> for home shall Israel come from dispersion.
>
> It has gathered wounds and afflictions
> in the courtyards of the world,
> has bathed all locked doors with its tears.
>
> Its elders, having almost outgrown their earthly garb
> and extending their limbs like sea plants,
>
> embalmed in the salt of despair
> and the wailing wall night in their arms—
> will sleep just a spell longer—

But youth has unfurled its flag of longing,
for a field yearns to be loved by them
and a desert watered

and the house shall be built
to face the sun: God

and evening again has the violet-shy word
that only grows so blue in the homeland:
Good night!

This poem is an encapsulated history of Jewish Exile in all its bitterness, a poetic realization of the Zionist dream of making the desert bloom, and a celebration of homecoming. But, if read as a discrete unit, the poem's affirmation appears to come at the cost of keeping the Holocaust decently out of view. It needs (as is often the case with individual poems by Nelly Sachs) to be complemented by another poem in this volume, which recalls that the wonders of Abraham are inescapably those "which we with our bodies must consummate."

The overriding metaphysical premise of Nelly Sachs's poetic universe is a sense of the world's unity and integrity, in the sense of wholeness, oneness, a vast assemblage of organic parts each one of which impinges on every other, so that no part of the whole system can be removed or changed without every other part being affected. Therefore, in *Eclipse of the Stars* as everywhere in Nelly Sachs's poetry the images of transformation, metamorphosis and resurrection abound. "Ending flows to beginning / like the cry of a swan" and "the soul, folded, waits / to be born again / under the ice of the death mask." But here the images are given a habitation and a name; the generalized desire for rebirth is attached, albeit with full consciousness of the risk of doing do, to a living, struggling reality.

"Land of Israel," the first of two poems so titled in this volume, pictures a people "seared by dying" moving back into the valleys of Eretz Israel. Such a picture, the poet believes, must surely evoke "the patriarchs' blessing / for those returning." The image of the patriarchs, complemented by the poem's subsequent allusions to Elijah and to the imminent appearance of "a new Ruth," is meant to remind us that the scheme of redemption in which disaster is the necessary prelude to apocalypse, is not the desperate invention of the poet responding to an otherwise meaningless modern history, but a scheme inherent in the ancient Covenant between God and His chosen people. The survivors of the Holocaust have "come home from the corners of the world with tear-stained eyes" not merely for the purpose of establishing themselves in a normal homeland such as all other people have but "to write the psalms of David anew" in a reconsecrated land.

To read such lines is to recognize at once that the poetic solace which Nelly Sachs offered her people, the poetic embrace in which she sought to enfold them, aspires to more than rescue and relief. She does indeed desire, as the second "Land of Israel" poem says, to "stanch the blood / and thaw out the tears / which froze in the death chambers." But she instinctively recognized that to restore the human image to so tortured and humiliated a people as the Jewish survivors of Hitler's Europe, more was required than merely to return them to the status of tolerated aliens that they had formerly held. They had, rather, to be returned to "the lost memories / which smell prophetically through the earth / and sleep on the stone" in the land of Israel, and only there. The restoration of the human status to the survivors could not, she knew, be achieved without the restoration of nationality; nor could the poet herself, speaking for the Jews who remained outside the land of Israel, be born again unless the national center of her people was reborn, and "out of the desert sand" Israel "thrust up . . . trees again."

These poems celebrating the idea of national redemption for a shattered people represent Nelly Sachs's most determined effort to penetrate what in one poem she calls "the mystery overgrown with forgetting," a mystery that contains the relationship between degradation and exaltation, and between an exiled people and its homeland. Yet the very title of her next volume—*And No One Knows How to Go On* (1957)—shows how fragile and tentative was her Zionist affirmation. Several poems return to the dark prospect that life, in the aftermath of the Holocaust, has become impossible on this planet. If it is indeed the case that, as she says in one poem, "all lands are ready to rise / from the map," then it can hardly matter whether the Jewish people resides in Israel or in Uganda.

Yet the volume does continue to explore the possible link between the great Jewish death in Europe and the great Jewish rebirth in Israel. The figure of Daniel becomes the symbol of the poet herself in his ability to recover "forgotten dreams even from behind the last slope of coal." He gathers fragments and preserves what has been torn down. Nelly Sachs emulates Daniel's own courage by entering the space "between hangman and victim" in order to retrieve the possibility of a new life. Her Israel is both the land and the people, the latter being nourished in Exile by its memories but also nourishing what is remembered by its remembering and suffering. "Israel," she cries, "is not only land!" Its desert sand took wing in prophecy, and its "eternity-snorting mountains" were transmuted into "the milk-white foam / Of children's prayers." Yet the physicality of Israel has outlasted the Holocaust and now awaits that birth of its new self whose precondition has been the death of the old. By the intensity with which she perceives them, the bloodletting of the People Israel and the peeling of corpse-skin from the dead become for Nelly Sachs part of a homeward movement and enable the elegiac transformation of death into new life:

> Late firstborn!
> You have come home with the spade
> into the unexcavated,
> the unconstructed,
> but into the line
> that leads again
> through the synagogue of longing
> from death into birth.

Death Still Celebrates Life (1965) makes clear in a number of ways that the healing process for the Jewish people cannot be a simple reversal of the process of destruction and Exile, "for entrance can never be / the same as exit where farewell and return are parted by the incurable wound of life." Biblical prophesy, which always points "from graves / into the next dawn," does prepare us for the paradox that a new dawn is always the gift of night. But Nelly Sachs could never rest comfortably in this paradox. Her work consistently yearns toward consolation and transcendence, but declines finally to lay hold of them, for fear that they may not be real. The image of an Israel reborn from ashes is her particular example—powerful as a symbol because it is first an actuality—of the more general desire, of a poet "on the track of my rights of domicile," for a homeland that will offer refuge to those who were cast out— from country, from life, from the human status itself.

In Nelly Sachs's poetry the land of Israel is both itself and the crossroads where the poet's desire for, and disbelief in, redemption meet. In "I do not know the room," she insists with certainty that nothing is lost, that somewhere "the smile of the child / who was thrown as in play / into the peeling flames is preserved." In a poem explicitly labeled as one of mourning entitled "Everywhere Jerusalem," she says that ultimately everything is, indeed, saved, but "saved for the devouring fire / of His absence—." The Jerusalem that is said in the title to be everywhere is never mentioned in the body of the poem, for in the absence of God it has become the only enduring and universal presence in Jewish life.

Abba Kovner

My place of work is a wooden hut between the graveyard and the children's house. There I am writing something that has no beginning and no end. But if there is a central thread that goes through the empty pages, it is the leitmotif of those who survived, those who were destroyed and those who come after them. (Abba Kovner, 7 March 1975)

Abba Kovner's work and life have been attempts to join together what has been separated by history, especially by the Jewish history of expulsion, dispersion, oppression, Holocaust. He himself has located the source of his creative work in a tension between two loves, his love of the Jewish people and his love of the land of Israel. He has sought to bring together, as completing counterparts, those Jews who attached themselves to the Jewish people but had no experience of the living reality of the land, and those Israelis who saw themselves "as the first of a new humankind—."[12] During the first half of his life, he gained honor and fame as a resistance fighter in Vilna and the surrounding forests and then as a leader in the Brichah movement that brought the pitiful remnant of European Jewry to the homeland in Palestine. In this period, he sought to bring the Jewish people to the land of Israel. But in his work as a creative writer, he has initiated a vast backward movement of recovery that is intended to carry the imagination of his contemporaries in Israel back to the Jewish people, back to a buried life they thought they had forgotten or, perhaps, never even known.

To understand Kovner's poetry, we must recognize that it is based on the impulse to join people with land, matter with spirit, the living with the dead, past with present, life with literature. At any particular moment in his poems, we may be simultaneously at the foot of Sinai and at the edge of the shooting pits of Ponary, circling the walls of Jericho and the walls of a European convent or ghetto, defending Vilna (the "Jerusalem of Lithuania") and the Jerusalem of modern Israel, receiving the Covenant and giving it back. He is a writer whose imagination, like his life, may rise from the material to the spiritual, but may also return, for renewal, from the spiritual to the physical. Two examples of this forward and backward movement from Kovner's life may help to underscore its centrality in his poetry.

At the war's end, Kovner felt powerfully the need not only for rescue but for transformation of the Jewish people. He was shocked by the apathy of those small segments of the European Jewish population that had not suffered in the Holocaust, people who had lived through an event of biblical enormity without even noticing it. "There blew in our faces a chill cellar-wind of a community that goes on living as if nothing had happened, as it did before the deluge, as if there had been no deluge."[13] His immediate goal was physical rescue, a task made difficult enough by allies as well as enemies in Europe, and by the British Mandatory Government in Palestine; but he could not conceive of physical rescue apart from spiritual renewal. Physical rescue of European Jewry might perhaps take place if the survivors could be moved from the displaced persons camps to America, but spiritual renewal required their reunion with the Jewish land. Yet it was not only the European survivors who needed spiritual rebirth after the great catastrophe: "We want," he said in a speech of 1945, "to come to the Land of Israel, to its people, and by the force of our conviction, of our inquietude, our sense of the danger that hovers over us and is also latent within us, to change its ways of thinking . . . which is also largely the outcome of detachment, distance and indifference."[14] If the Jewish people were one—and, Kovner believed, they were—then Palestinian Jewry could not achieve its mission unless it absorbed into its consciousness the central experience, grim and oppressive though it had been, of modern Jewish history. Just how true this was even Kovner could not know until the traumatic war of 1967 dramatically revealed how "young Israelis . . . in the most critical hours of their lives, found that their deepest feelings came into contact with that forgotten chapter . . . that seemingly repressed chapter, the destruction of our people in Europe."[15]

But sometimes it is important, even essential, that spirit renew itself at the source, that literature revitalize itself through contact with life. Kovner is fond of pointing out that in classical Hebrew there was no single word for literature; rather, literature was called *hayim she-bi-khtav*—life in writing. The rightness of this apparently cumbersome phrase was proved to Kovner by his experience in commanding resistance fighters in the Vilna ghetto. On 1 September 1943, the Germans surrounded the ghetto in order to remove the last thousands of Jews to the death camps. It was necessary to build defense positions with sandbags, but—irony of ironies—the people whose forefathers had for a thousand years built their homes of drifting sand could now find none with which to protect themselves against German bullets. Their salvation (temporary, to be sure) lay in "the great volumes of the Talmud in their brown leather binding," which were taken from the famous Jewish library of Vilna to serve in place of sandbags. The event has remained with Kovner as a revelation of the complex possibilities of renewal in the interactions between matter and spirit, life and literature. From one point of view, the Talmud was here degraded from a spiritual to a physical role; yet in the process it enabled a preservation of Jewish life through a transformation of the traditional Jewish passivity in the face of violent threat. "I propped up my rifle on the back of the books. Were the books a support for the rifle with its ten bullets? Or, at that hour, were they a support for something else?"[16]

The desire to overcome geographical and chronological discontinuity by joining Israel with Diaspora, present with past, is apparent in Kovner's account of the genesis of *My Little Sister*, published in 1967, that is, almost a quarter of a century after the events of the Holocaust that form its center. He was, he has said, walking late at night through the streets of a section of Tel Aviv when he heard the shrieks of a woman coming from a high window. Although his own attention was riveted on the terrible screams, neither the other passersby in the street nor the people behind the neighboring windows seemed to pay any attention. Kovner was at once carried back to the Holocaust years when the collective death rattle of the Jews of Europe failed to disturb the placidity or even attract the attention of the outside world.

> A cloister's wall is high.
> A wall of silence
> still higher.
>
> (Section 8)*

This gave the first impulse toward recovery of the past. The second came from Kovner's discovery of the truth behind the appearances. In actuality, he had been hearing the cries of a woman in labor coming from a maternity hospital; those who knew the neighborhood paid no attention

*Subsequent parenthetical references for verse quotations should be understood to be to section and not page numbers.

because they were familiar with such cries and knew their cause. Stirred by recollections of the past, of the sense of isolation and abandonment, by the particular memories of the agonies of mothers and children during the Holocaust— "I never thought a woman who had her child taken out of her arms had gone like a sheep to the slaughter"[17]—and by the paradoxical relation between torture and birth, Kovner set himself to what he has called "an enduring attempt to turn ashes into an eternal light."[18]

The incident in Tel Aviv is specifically reflected in *My Little Sister* in several ways. The Dominican convent in which the little sister receives (temporary) shelter is shown to be out of touch with the true human actuality and the horrors raging through Europe among the Jews by virtue of the fact that here "No woman has crouched to give birth / on the floor." (11) The convent's mother is the Mother Superior, its ideal of motherhood the virginal mother of the infant Jesus, over whose image the nuns lovingly fuss. The contrasted ideas of motherhood give rise to the poem's contrasts between the sanctified Christian image of the crucified Jesus and "my crucified memory / outside the fence!" (10), a memory of images themselves crying for sanctification: "ashes that speak" (5) and "heaps of small shoes."(35)

The mother's agony of which the cries from the lying-in hospital reminded Kovner is in *My Little Sister* illustrated in ways that, if considered logically, are mutually inconsistent; yet this inconsistency gives us a clue to the organizing idea of the poem. In the opening section of Part Four, the poet looks back "from the promised land" upon the carnage in Europe and searches among heaps of small shoes for his sister-bride. He then imagines all the little sisters who were killed, before their parents could say good-bye to them or explain to them that they had not really resented the extra burden of weight on the road to death. He wishes that he could have

> even in one word
> whispered
> that you were no burden to us.

> On the way. Mother walked heavy.
> I.
> All your brothers.
> And the desperate convoy.
>
> (35)

In Part Five of the poem, however, the mother's agony is not that she was separated from her child on the way to execution in the mass graves evoked in part iii of Section 35 but that her infant never survived the maternity hospital that was the starting point of Kovner's imaginative journey:

> The Bikur Ḥolim Hospital
> walls soaked
> with the smell of sour urine
> and dying hopes.
>
> In the old hospital
> among walls of red brick
> my sister died.
> She was two hours old.
>
> (45)

In the following section, the suffering mother is said to have mourned eight years (1940-48, when the State of Israel was established) "a daughter / who never came into the world."

This factual inconsistency in the narrative indicates clearly enough that we are dealing not with a single sister-bride or a single mother but with a generalized account of the Holocaust. Kovner's mode of generalizing is something like Milton's; that is, he eschews abstract, generalized language and limits himself to specific images and concrete details, but says that the occurrence might have happened this way *or* that way *or* yet a third way; except that (unlike Milton) he omits the *or*. A hint of Kovner's intention is given in the poem's title itself. In grammatical strictness, the Hebrew title should be *Aḥoti Haktana* rather than, as it is, *Aḥoti Ktana*; the grammatical anomaly indicates that it is not a single little sister we are recalling but all the little sisters, born and unborn, who were swallowed up by the Holocaust. Long before Kovner heard the shrieks from the Tel Aviv maternity ward, his imagination was captured by a little girl who had died, yet lived. She was one of the 47,000

Jews taken from Vilna to the shooting pits of Ponary. Incredibly, she managed to crawl out from among the thousands of dead and dying bodies to tell her story. Like a myriad of such survivor-witnesses whom we now know from the history and literature of the Holocaust, she was believed by no one—except for Abba Kovner, who proceeded to organize the armed resistance. " . . . The central fact in Kovner's life," according to Shirley Kaufman, "is his confrontation with the half-dead, half-crazed girl from the mass grave at Ponar. Her face haunts every line he writes."[19]

The little sister of the narrative finds refuge in the convent but also "betrayal / —no island. / Only a folded sail in a storm." (15) Unlike the group that took her to the convent and was itself later shot by the mobile killing units of the *Einsatzgruppen*, the little sister was "not privileged to be condemned to death" and "did not enter a covenant of blood" (just as later she is said to be "not privileged to see / the light of the day!" [46] But Section 39 seems to say that she was turned over to the Germans by the nuns and eventually turned into ashes. Her "shorn head" (40) is both that of a nun and a death-camp inmate.

The little sister's varied and contradictory fate is most fully explored in Section 28, which describes the preparations for her wedding. The brother-narrator here stresses her identity as the "sister-bride" of Song of Songs. Many of the central images and motifs of Kovner's poem are to be found in Solomon's song, especially in its eighth and concluding chapter, where the speaker wishes that the beloved could be "as my brother, / That sucked the breasts of my mother!" The speaker subsequently says of the sister that "thy mother was in travail with thee, / There was she in travail and brought thee forth." Finally, he asks: "What shall we do for our sister / In the day when she shall be spoken for?" (a line quoted from in Section 36).

If, as traditional religious interpretation of Song of Songs holds, the sister-bride is no mere figure of romantic love poetry but a symbol of the people of Israel, then the little sister's wedding would be a reaffirmation of the covenantal relationship between God and his Chosen People. Every

Jewish wedding, to be sure, is to some extent such a reaffirmation, since there is "No man without a wife, neither a woman without a husband, nor both of them without God" (Genesis Rabbah 8:9). Kovner describes many of the customary appurtenances of the wedding ceremony, including the braided challah, the dish of honey, and the golden chicken soup. But an anomalous element intervenes. "The whole world drinks / kosher chicken soup:" Chicken soup, however, is not supposed to be drunk until *after* the ceremony, and then only by the bride and groom. Yet the canopy, the covering that symbolizes the consummation of the marriage, is not present at all, and therefore the "whole world" would seem to be celebrating an event that has not taken place. The mystery of the world's presence at the prematurely celebrated Jewish wedding is resolved in the following lines:

> Our father took his bread, bless God,
> forty years from one oven. He never imagined
> a whole people could rise in the ovens
> and the world, with God's help, go on.

The world flocks to celebrate a Jewish marriage precisely because it is a marriage with death. The Covenant that was given at Sinai has been returned in Europe as the whole Jewish people returns—in smoke—to the God who did them the dubious favor of choosing them as his special people. The feeling at this point in Section 28 is similar to that in Glatstein's famous poem "Dead Men Don't Praise God": "We received the Torah on Sinai / and in Lublin we gave it back." But Kovner goes beyond Glatstein. Both feel the immediacy of the biblical past and its painful and paradoxical continuity with the Holocaust present, but Kovner feels, and indeed embodies, the future, as well; after the givingback in Lublin, there is to be a retrieval in Sinai. Although "the marriage contract will be written in stone" for multitudes of little sisters, the canopy missing from this wedding of death will again be raised, and raised in the very place from which the seemingly dissolved Covenant came, the desert of Sinai.

The marriage contracts are written in stone, the whole

vanished Jewish world has become "a choir of stones" (40),
a huge cemetery. After such material and spiritual ravages,
is it possible to rebuild,

> to wipe from the lips
> the taste.
> To bring back
> a world of innocence,
> as if to its socket a bone
> from the foot of the dead.
>
> (32)

The contrast between the wholeness, unity, and coherence
of the Dominican convent and the "Jerusalem of
Lithuania," Vilna, "a city thrust on its back / like a horse
in blood, jerking its hooves / unable to rise" (17), like the
contrast in *Canopy in the Desert* between Saint Catherine's
Monastery with its 3,000 steps to Sinai and "the kind of
stuff / Jacob's ladder was made of" (Eighth Gate), is at first
dispiriting to the poet. He stands amidst the ruins of his
world and asks,

> With what—
> with what, little sister,
> shall we weave and draw the dream
> now?
>
> (34)

The question faced by Kovner was not very different from
the one put to Martin Buber in 1933 by a Christian
polemicist who asked whether the fulfillment of Jesus'
prophecy that Jerusalem would be destroyed and never
again come under Jewish rule did not prove that the
Covenant between God and the Jews had been abrogated.
Buber replied as follows:

> I live not far from the city of Worms, to which I am bound by the
> tradition of my forefathers; and, from time to time, I go there.
> When I go, I first go to the cathedral. It is a visible harmony of
> members, a totality in which no part deviates from perfection. I
> walk about the cathedral with consummate joy, gazing at it.
> Then I go over to the Jewish cemetery consisting of crooked,
> cracked, shapeless, random stones. I station myself there, gaze
> upward from the jumble of a cemetery to that glorious
> harmony, and seem to be looking up from Israel to the Church.

Below, there is no jot of form; there are only the stones, and the dust lying beneath the stones. The dust is there, no matter how thinly scattered. There lies the corporeality of man, which has turned to this. There it is. There it is for me. There it is for me, not as corporeality within the space of this planet, but as corporeality within my own memory, far into the depths of history, as far back as Sinai.

I have stood there, have been united with the dust, and through it with the Patriarchs. That is a memory of the transaction with God which is given to all Jews. From this the perfection of the Christian house of God cannot separate me, nothing can separate me from the sacred history of Israel.

I have stood there and have experienced everything myself; with all this death has confronted me, all the dust, all the ruin, all the wordless misery is mine; but the covenant has not been withdrawn from me. I lie on the ground, fallen like these stones. But it has not been withdrawn from me.

The cathedral is as it is. The cemetery is as it is. But nothing has been withdrawn from us.[20]

Kovner's answer, albeit it in far more secular terms, is also that the Covenant has not been withdrawn from the People Israel; but the covenantal relationship must be held in abeyance until the remnant of the Jewish people returns, spiritually as well as physically, from the Diaspora to the original source and site of the Covenant.

> There was no one
> with me there who spoke
> or understood my tongue
> cleaving to the roof of my mouth
>
> (if I forget thee Oh canyon!
> if I forget thee)
>
> On all my roads
> I imagined I'd find the road
>
> to you

(69)

As this passage from *A Canopy in the Desert* suggests, the canopy missing from the little sister's wedding is to be found only in the homeland. The feeling with which we are left at the conclusion of *My Little Sister* has much in common with what we feel near the end of the book of Leviticus, when God announces that although he will bring his Chosen People to nearly total destruction in the lands of their enemies, while their own land "shall lie forsaken without them," he will not even then break his Covenant with them, or theirs with the land. They have rejected his ordinances and abhorred his statutes; "And yet for all that, when they are in the land of their enemies, I will not reject them, neither will I abhor them, to destroy them utterly, and to break My covenant with them. . . . " When Kovner returned to the liberated—and destroyed—Vilna, he found amidst the ruins only the eastern wall of the old synagogue, and on it an ancient inscription: "Lift up the miracle-banner for the ingathering of our exiles."[21] Already at the end of *My Little Sister* the poet seems to be embarking, with the imagined bier of his dead mother, on a ship that cracks through the ice floe of the vast cemetery of Europe on its journey south, out of exile and toward a renewal of life and the Covenant. The First Gate of *A Canopy in the Desert*, published three years later, is entitled "The Return to the South," suggesting both the trip to southern Israel, the Negev and Sinai, but also the larger return of the Jews of Europe from Exile to their homeland.

That the rebirth in the homeland is to be no clear and unambiguous resurrection of life and rediscovery of the Covenant is already implicit in *My Little Sister*. Part Four begins with the poet-survivor-brother calling from Israel to the unanswering corpse of his sister in Europe:

> From the promised land I called you,
> I looked for you
> among heaps of small shoes.
> At every approaching holiday.

Part Five concludes with the mother who both mourns her children and is herself mourned by the son who carries his mother's bier away from the ice fields of the European cemetery. The mother figure here represents Rachel weeping for her children, the centuries-old pain of the Jewish mother who bled and suffered in childbirth so that murderers should be amply supplied with victims for their knives, the shrieking mother in the Tel-Aviv hospital, the Israeli mother who mourns her sons fallen in battle, and—

not least of all—the poet's memory of his own mother, who when he ordered the headquarters of the Vilna resistance sealed off, fell against the gate and asked her son in terror whether she should remain in Vilna or flee with him into the forests: "And I, the commander of the ghetto fighters, could not look into her eyes as I answered, 'Mother, I don't know!' And so to this very day I don't know whether I am worthy of the honor of a ghetto resistance fighter, or the curse of a son who abandoned his mother and did not go with her on her last road."[22]

In Section 46 of *My Little Sister* the mother whose memorial candles "ran out in the ghetto" carries her memories of the little sister elsewhere, kindling her "on all the seas." Her mourning continues until 1948, when the State of Israel is established. The speaker from the promised land asks her how she can mourn indiscriminately both her sons "who were cut down," apparently in the War of Independence, and the daughter "who never came into the world." Here "never came into the world" seems to mean not only never was born but never entered into history, died, that is to say, from the point of view of many native-born Israelis, a death both passive and meaningless because it was not an integral part of world history.[23] In *Canopy in the Desert*, the poet himself speaks of the Sinai desert as "The one place in the world / where a man will not die alone" (79), presumably because here one fights and dies for the survival of the Jewish people. But here the mourning mother turns aside the accusatory question and repeats, with significantly altered words, her earlier reply: "my son—she was not privileged to see / the light of the day!" The little sister never saw either the literal light of the day or the light of the new dawn that emerged in 1948 after the darkest night in Jewish history; yet the mother insists that her aborted life and her many deaths in the Holocaust are inseparable from the life that seems to be starting *ab initio* in the homeland, in Israel.

In yet another story of mothers and sons disputing over the ashes of their destroyed past, Kovner has told of

a great fire in the house of the parents of the Maggid of

Mezeritch, when he was only a child of ten. His father was not there. He saw his mother standing in the yard, wringing her hands as she watched the conflagration and weeping bitterly. "Mother," he said to her, "do this wooden house and this wooden furniture deserve to have you weep over them?" "Son," the mother replied, "it is not for the house or the furniture I am weeping. The scroll of our family pedigree has been left behind there in the fire." "Don't cry, mother," said the ten-year-old boy. "I'll write you a new pedigree, starting with me." . . .

It is said of the Maggid of Mezeritch that later when he was a grown man, he would hide his face in his hands, whenever he remembered what he had said to his mother.[24]

Part of Kovner's poetic effort to reunite what time and history have separated has been his repudiation of what he calls the "infantile" Israeli myth of "It starts with me." The creative reunion of the People Israel with the land of Israel toward which *A Canopy in the Desert* moves cannot be realized unless those memorial candles of Section 46 of *My Little Sister* are replanted in the new soil. The dead sister who in the earlier poem was berated for the "offense" of her "scalding silence" at holidays now speaks in the desert:

> Don't hand me over to a mute wall
> embalmed in the sounds of words—
> I am the threshold of your holidays.
> I am the candles in your forgotten
> candlestsicks. . . .
>
> Make me grow, my love, in soil as naked
> as it was created.
>
> (94)

Thus the mother who insists on mourning not only her sons who were "cut down" but the daughter who never saw the light of day is vindicated. The continuity between the European past and the Israeli present and future proves to be stronger than the discontinuity. This is partly because the birth of Israel, like all birth, is inseparable from bloodshed and suffering: "Can there / be spring without the danger?" (93). Thus the little sister who in the earlier poem is pitied because "she was not privileged to see / the light of the day" is now congratulated for having been saved from a terrible knowledge because she was "privileged not to know / a taste of return."(10) The irony here flows from the recognition, present throughout the poem in its many references to the three wars Israel had already fought in the desert, that the pariah people has become the pariah nation, and that the Jews in Israel, like their Diaspora ancestors, are destined to be persecuted and to live, if at all, under constant threat of destruction.

Far from returning from darkness to "the light of day," the clarity and elevation of the Commandments, the Jewish people's return to Sinai to recover the Covenant involves a plunge into more darkness and ambiguity. When, in the Eighth Gate of *Canopy*, there is a disagreement between two visitors to Saint Catherine's Monastery about the wisdom of making the traditional early morning ascent of Mount Sinai, the one who refuses to climb says:

> There's nothing
> there. Nothing. Except what
> cannot be reached
> in the light.
>
> (54)

The reason why God and his Covenant are said to reside only in darkness and mystery is that the Jewish people, having achieved its difficult return to the promised land, now finds itself "mixed up in an unfortunate / ambiguity" (58). Having carried the letters of the Covenant back to their source for validation and reconsecration, the Jewish people finds itself caught in a conflict between the Covenant and the historical necessity to survive within history, whose overriding commandment is an inversion of the Sinai injunction, saying to the Jews of a beleaguered Israel: "You may attack your brother / (shalt murder / shalt murder)" (63). The "unfortunate ambiguity" is in fact a horrible paradox whereby the price of Jewish survival may be the surrender of the very reason why Jewish survival was ever thought important.

The reaffirmation of the Covenant in the Sinai, like its abrogation in Lublin or Vilna, is sealed in blood. This wedding, like the abortive one in *My Little Sister*, requires death as the bride-price:

> in sandstone still

red from the drop of the covenant
my voice is wrapped in a package of vows
on a land in its time of bleeding:

I will pay for a marriage contract with my best
my chosen from the land.

(73)

This very recognition of the dreadful continuity between Israeli experience and that of the Jews during the Holocaust compels the survivor to search in the sands of the desert for that buried life which is in truth his own and without which he cannot guarantee his own survival.

. . . I will dig with fingers
down to the flesh the blood
until I hear their voice a voice
tearing the desert   coming back
split in long burrows
in the dry waste

that was not destroyed. That won't be destroyed
again

(27)

In the poem entitled "From Another Homeland," an Israeli soldier fallen in battle in the Sinai makes his last act before death the carving of his mother's name in the sand, with a gold tooth that is the sign of her murder and mutilation. His destruction transplants his destroyed mother from Europe to the promised land, where they share the common Jewish fate.

Canopy in the Desert yearns toward, but does not fully realize, the consummation of the marriage between past and present, Vilna and Sinai, the People Israel and the land of Israel. The section (82) in which the canopy missing from the wedding in *My Little Sister* is set up in the desert is entitled "A Canopy Fades." The glass is shattered to commemorate the destruction of the temple—the original *khurbn*—but the discordant element of burning memorial candles is introduced because, as the groom says, "my love is not at my side." The hope that the little sister expressed in Section 94 to be replanted "in soil as naked / as it was created" has not yet been fulfilled, but the poet himself, in his effort toward reconstruction, pledges in the last numbered section of *Canopy in the Desert* (96) to take "you, my little sister, . . . on my back. To carry you beyond / my naked plot of soil." She will at least be rescued for the imagination, a realm that exists beyond the plot of soil. In the coda with which he ends the poem, Kovner expresses both despair and determination. The eye of his mind beholds a dozen scenes that show forth, mysteriously, both "abyss within abyss" and "hidden canopies within canopies," fire-destruction and fire-consummation. If there is, after all, *no voice divine / no king to find,"* the poet wonders: "should I persist"? Within the order of nature he discerns a refuge, a plan, a map for all creatures, but "none for me." What remains to him is "only the curse," the inescapable fate that was assigned to him when it was assigned to the 600,000 slaves who 3,300 years earlier made the exodus from bondage into the promised land—and the new bondage of the Covenant. In the Second Gate of the poem, he had sought to evade this fate:

> Before
> I began my image was carved
> in the bedrock. There must be
> a way to get out
> to break through! To make a shortcut.
>
> (9)

But in the Eighth Gate, he had embraced, in preference to the alternative represented by the Christian monastery, the subjection of the Covenant that is the precondition of Jewish survival: "—will not die! / Will live enslaved" (56).

This subjection is again embraced in "A Returned Gate," when the poet praises "Those who love / and don't want to escape." (93) Although not a religious writer like Moshe Flinker or Nelly Sachs, Kovner too is possessed of a mystical sense of the linkage between Holocaust and rebirth, a mystical sense of Jewish existence itself. That this sense can exist in Jewish writers of the most rationalist cast of mind is proved by the work of the Jewish historian, Simon Dubnow, who insisted that:

> Jewry at all times . . . was preeminently a spiritual nation, and a spiritual nation it continues to be in our own days,

too. . . . Jewry, being a spiritual entity, cannot suffer annihilation: the body, the mould, may be destroyed, the spirit is
immortal. Bereft of country and dispersed as it is, the Jewish
nation lives, and will go on living, because a creative principle
permeates it, a principle that is the root of its being and an
indigenous product of its history.[25]

Kovner, sharing his view, believes that the return to Sinai
must be spiritual as well as physical. It therefore entails not
only the desire to embrace the homeland but the courage to
reject what Cynthia Ozick has called "the Diaspora of
freedom," which tempts—the more thoroughly to obliterate—those who seek to escape the burden of Jewish fate.[26]
As the poem draws to an end, the curse and the enslavement
of Jewish history are accepted as inseparable from the
return to the land from what seemed the nethermost abyss
of the Holocaust, and as the price of Jewish survival.

In *The Seventh Day* (1967), a book of conversations with
soldiers about the then recently concluded Six-Day War,
Kovner observed how Israel-born soldiers, who had thought
nothing more foreign to themselves than the fate of
European Jewry, kept associating themselves with it in
the time of crisis. He came to the conclusion that the Six-
Day War had been a turning point in history just because it
demonstrated to Israelis that their own fate was continuous
with that of the Jews of Europe, that they too must live with
the paradox of chosenness, must commit themselves to life
in defiance of the omnipresence of death. "In the Diaspora,"
he wrote, "fathers didn't bring up their sons to commit
suicide, or to despair. No one brought up his sons to
abandon Judaism. They taught them that it was their
destiny to be persecuted; but, at the same time, they
educated them to life."[27] Kovner, participant in the two
most important (and wildly improbable) events of modern,
perhaps of all, Jewish history, seeks to join the Holocaust
and the return to the homeland by a prodigious feat of poetic
imagination, which steps into the void left by the divine
silence to affirm that the Jewish people shall not die, but
live: "I speak to / myself I speak and speak I'll
return / I'll return here   alive."

Portions of this chapter first appeared under the title "Abba Kovner: Poet of Holocaust and Rebirth" in the October 1977 issue of *Midstream: A Monthly Jewish Review*.

The epigraph is reprinted by permission of Schocken Books Inc. from *The Messianic Idea in Judaism*, by Gerson G. Scholem. Copyright © 1971 by Schocken Books Inc.

1. "The Holocaust and the Struggle of the *Yishuv* as Factors in the Establishment of the State of Israel," in *Holocaust and Rebirth* (Jerusalem: Yad Vashem, 1974), p. 140.

2. Ibid., pp. 70-71.

3. *Major Trends in Jewish Mysticism* (New York: Schocken, 1973), p. 350.

4. Ibid.

5. *Young Moshe's Diary: The Spiritual Torment of a Jewish Boy in Nazi Europe*, ed., with introductions, by Shaul Esh and G. Wigoder (Jerusalem: Yad Vashem, 1971).

6. See Shemaryahu Talmon, "The Biblical Concept of Jerusalem," in *Jerusalem*, ed. Msgr. J. M. Oesterreicher and Anne Sinai (New York: John Day, 1974), p. 198.

7. See "Rescue," by Yehuda Bauer, et al., in *Holocaust* (Jerusalem: Keter, 1974), p. 124.

8. Sidra Ezrahi, "Holocaust Literature in European Languages," *Encyclopedia Judaica* 1973 Year Book, p. 116.

9. Norma Rosen has argued that the desire to make "good art" out of the Holocaust is in a way sacrilegious because it implies that the time for "transcendence" of the horror has already arrived. See her essay, "The Holocaust and the American-Jewish Novelist," *Midstream* 20 (October 1974): 57.

10. Hannah Arendt, *Eichmann in Jerusalem*, rev. ed. (New York: Viking Press, 1965), p. 153.

11. Irving Howe, "Auschwitz and High Mandarin," in *The Critical Point* (New York: Delta, 1975), p. 183.

12. Abba Kovner, Introduction to "A First Attempt to Tell" (Typescript of unpublished memoir), pp. 1-2.

13. Abba Kovner, "The Mission of the Survivors" (typescript of a speech of 17 July 1945, in the Moreshet Archives at Givat Haviva, trans. Moshe Luvish), p.2.

14. Ibid., p. 13.

15. "A First Attempt to Tell," p.2.

16. MS of a speech prepared as an address to the PEN Club in New York in February 1975, trans. H. M. Daleski, but never delivered.

17. Interview in *New York Times*, 6 March 1975.

18. Reprinted from Shirley Kaufman's introduction (p.xvii) to *A Canopy in the Desert*, by Abba Kovner, translated from the Hebrew by Shirley Kaufman with Ruth Adler and Nurit Orchan, by permission of the University of Pittsburgh Press. © 1973 by Shirley Kaufman. All

quotations from Kovner's poetry come from this volume, which contains Shirley Kaufman's translation of *My Little Sister, A Canopy in the Desert*, and other poems.

19. Ibid., p. xv.

20. Quoted in Frank Talmage, "Christianity and the Jewish People," *Commentary* 59 (February 1975): 59.

21. "A First Attempt to Tell," p. 32.

22. Quoted in *New York Times* article of 4 March 1975 on the Holocaust Conference of the Institute of Contemporary Jewry held in New York.

23. See Joseph Dan, "Will the Jewish People Exist in the 21st Century,"*Forum* 23 (Spring 1975): 61-67.

24. "Threnody for a Movement" (typescript of an unpublished essay), p. 45.

25. Quoted in Lucy Dawidowicz, *The Golden Tradition* (Boston: Beacon Press, 1968), p. 233.

26. Cynthia Ozick, "America: Toward Yavneh," *Judaism* 19 (Summer 1970): 265.

27. *The Seventh Day: Soldiers' Talk About the Six-Day War* (Harmondsworth, Middlesex, England: Penguin Books, 1971), p. 230.

Jewish history is dull, uninteresting, It has no glory or action, no heroes and conquerors, no rulers and masters of their fate, just a collection of wounded, hunted, groaning, and wailing wretches, always begging for mercy. You can see for yourselves that it can't be interesting. The least you can say is it's uninteresting. I would simply forbid teaching our children Jewish history. Why the devil teach them about their ancestors' shame? I would just say to them: "Boys, from the day we were driven out from our land we've been a people without a history. Class dismissed, Go out and play football."—"The Sermon," by Haim Hazaz

chapter 3

Between Diaspora and Zion:
Israeli Holocaust Fiction

Nowhere does the Holocaust inspire more sympathetic interest and remembrance and also more shame and revulsion than in Israel. The majority of the survivors live in Israel; the major centers of Holocaust research are in Israel; most of the world's museums devoted to remembering the victims and their destroyed cultured are in Israel. Israel is surely the only country in the world in which a national television audience will have its attention riveted to a "This Is Your Life" program that re-creates the life of a survivor of Auschwitz and introduces, among the hero's old friends, a woman who recounts the slow killing of her child in one of Dr. Mengele's experiments.[1] It is the only country in the world that annually honors, in formal ceremonies throughout the country, the six million Jews murdered by the Nazis with siren blasts, flags lowered to half-staff, and the prime minister delivering a formal address on the historical and moral relation between the Holocaust and the people and State of Israel.

Yet there is another side to the picture. The Day of Remembrance is called not only Yom Hashoah (Holocaust Day) but also Yom Hagevurah (Heroism Day), as if the action of a small handful of ghetto fighters were needed to counterbalance the passivity with which the vast majority of the victims went to their deaths. According to the Israeli writer Matti Megged, most sabras have thought of the European Jews contemptuously, as having gone like "sheep to the slaughter."[2] The formal title of the ceremony that takes place at Yad Vashem, as if aware of the omnipresence of this slur in Israel, is "Martyrs and Heroes Remembrance Day," implying that the millions who were not heroes can be made acceptable only if they are thought of as martyrs. Yet martyrdom traditionally implies a choice of death rather than abasement of oneself or desecration of God, whereas the victims of Hitler had no choice at all; conversion to Christianity or even, if that were possible, to Nazism would not have saved them. The speech of the prime minister on this day generally insists that the State of Israel has changed both the Jewish character and the external conditions that made the Holocaust possible, so that today Jews have both the internal fortitude and the external means with which to defend themselves against danger from the outside.[3]

This mixture of contradictory Israeli attitudes toward the Holocaust is an extreme version of the general Israeli ambivalence about the relation between Israel's present and the Jewish past in the Diaspora, in Exile. Nowhere are these contradictory attitudes and the emotions that underlie them more brilliantly illuminated than in Haim Hazaz's short story "The Sermon" (1942), from which the epigraph to this chapter comes. The story does not touch explicitly on the Holocaust. Rather, it conveys, through a lengthy speech given by a man named Yudka to his fellow kibbutz members, the whole problematic relation of Israelis to Jewish history. But since the Holocaust represented the culmination and also the end of Jewish history in Europe, it is safe to assume that the mixed attitudes of revulsion and affection that pre-Holocaust Jewish history inspired in Israelis like Yudka would be drawn out into their most extreme form by the Holocaust itself.

Although cast in the form of a dramatic monologue in the style of a Browning in prose, the story directs attention not to the presentation of character but to the exploration of "issues." On the surface, Yudka appears to have nothing positive to say, nothing to praise either in the Jewish past in Diaspora or the present in Israel. Much of his speech is an embittered complaint about the past, and yet when, in the final pages, he comes to speak of the Zionist present, he is resentful at the way in which it has cut itself off from the (deplorable) Jewish past.

In the first part of his speech, this generally silent man pours out a long-pent-up revulsion from Jewish history, to which he declares his "opposition." Strictly speaking, he maintains, Jews have no history at all because they have always been mere instruments of the Gentiles, who were the great movers and shakers of the world. Jewish history, so-called, is an unending tale of misery and woe, of passive suffering; it has no heroes, and endlessly chronicles the consequences of powerlessness. It then has the gall to take pride in just how much suffering the Jews have undergone and perversely to make a kind of ersatz heroism out of despair, as if it were somehow a virtue to have suffered. " 'See what great torments I withstand! See what untold shame and humiliation I suffer! Who can compare with me?' " Some Jews, he says, even have come to the conclusion that persecution itself keeps the Jewish people alive, and that without it they could not exist.[4] Such Jews, Jews with the Diaspora mentality, believe that "a Jew without suffering is an abnormal creature, hardly a Jew at all, half a *goy*. . . . " For Yudka the Jewish attachment to suffering is a badge of final degradation, self-degradation, because in truth "everything is rotten around suffering. . . . History, life itself, all actions, customs, the group, the individual, literature, culture, folk songs . . . everything!"

The Jewish attachment to suffering, the Jews' belief that there is even a kind of greatness and heroism in their suffering that raises them in stature above those who act within history, is, according to Yudka, the foundation stone of the Exile. So debased are the generality of Jews that they have inverted their own theology and fallen in love with Exile, which is to them sacred, "more *Jewish* than Jerusalem." If martyrdom is the base of the pyramid of Exile, then the belief in the Messiah is its peak, the crowning, fantastic myth that for two thousand years has given the Jews their justification for doing nothing to forward their redemption. "If not for this myth it would all have been different. For then, they would finally have had to go right back to Palestine, or . . . pass on out of the world." As it was, the messianic myth convinced them that they were prohibited to "force the end" and must remain in Exile until Heaven chose to redeem them. If any further proof than the myth itself were needed that the Jews do not really want to be saved and to return to the land of their fathers, it would be the folk tradition grafted onto the myth that says that a great catastrophe must immediately precede the redemption. What could better show forth the underlying fear of redemption, of returning to the land of Israel?

All of these tortured complaints against his people and their traditions would seem to make Yudka a spokesman for Zionist self-affirmation at the expense of Diaspora Jewry, self-fascinated by its very degradation. But here Yudka veers off in the opposite direction. Maybe Diaspora Jewry is right to be afraid. "What if it's true that Judaism can manage to survive somehow in Exile, but here, in the Land of Israel, it's doubtful? . . . What if this country is fated to take the place of religion, if it's a grave danger to the survival of the people, if it replaces an enduring center with a transient center . . . ?" If Judaism before survived for all the wrong reasons, perhaps now that all those external pressures and the suffering they brought and the kind of character they formed are removed, the Jewish people will cease to exist. Yudka now, to the considerable surprise of his fellow-kibbutzniks, launches into an attack on Zionism as the real uprooting of the Jewish people. If Zionism has at its base a revulsion from the experiences and values of the Diaspora, which has encompassed Jews for two thousand years, is not Zionism itself anti-Jewish? "To my mind, if I am right, Zionism and Judaism are not at all the same, but two things quite different from each other, and maybe even two things directly opposite to each other! At any rate, far from the same. When a man can no longer be a Jew, he becomes a Zionist."

Ironically, when Yudka charges that the land of Israel already is no longer Jewish, he is complaining precisely about the removal of all those aspects of Diaspora Judaism he had declared reprehensible during the first part of his speech. But the irony, we must remember, lies not only in Yudka or in the Palestinian Jews whom he represents but in the paradox that is Israel itself, all the more so in the aftermath of the Holocaust. Zionism had its roots deep in

Jewish tradition, yet predicated its success on a repudiation of the unworthy culture of the ghetto and shtetl that it held, in any case, to be doomed by the acrid dissolvents of Western culture. It sought to weaken the idea that the return to the land of Israel had to wait upon some great catastrophe that would bring the end of days, but it succeeded in establishing a state only after (though not because)[5] the Jewish people suffered the greatest catastrophe it had ever known and not merely the culture but most of the inhabitants of the ghetto and shtetl were destroyed. Somewhere between Yudka's extreme revulsion from Diaspora culture and his extreme insistence that a Zionism which rejects this culture is no longer Jewish the whole range of attitudes we shall meet in Israeli Holocaust fiction is encompassed.

Yehuda Amichai's novel of 1963, *Not of This Time, Not of This Place*, is not only the first major example of Israeli Holocaust fiction but, to judge by what has followed it, seems to contain within itself almost the whole potentiality of the genre. There are few important themes of Israeli Holocaust novels subsequent to Amichai's that are not adumbrated in this book: the desire of the German-born but Israeli-bred hero to recover his past and to avenge the murder of his family and friends; the frustration of revenge due to the Jewish incapacity for normal hatred; sabra (native-born Israeli) shame for, and disgust with, Jewish survivors of the Nazis; the distraction from historical mission into personal relations, especially sexual ones; the conflict between the longing to forget, and the compulsion to remember, the past; the paradoxical relation between the German death-factories producing Jewish corpses and the peacetime factories producing the German "economic miracle"; the nature and extent of German guilt. Amichai made available all these themes for those who have followed him: Bartov, Gouri, Ben-Amotz, Kaniuk. Most important of all perhaps, Amichai initiated the practice of concentrating attention on the moral questions that arise in the aftermath of the Holocaust while tacitly assuming that imaginative re-creation or simulation of the victims' unique experience is beyond the reach of art. "Ruth had seen many horrors before she died. Those who died like her removed many of the horrors from the world; they had seen these horrors and taken them along into their great oblivion, the scenes of carnage and the images of their murderers."

Not of This Time, Not of This Place tells the story of Joel, an Israeli archeologist of German birth, who, as the novel opens, finds himself in a state of spiritual dryness and vacillation. He is faced with the necessity to decide whether to spend his vacation at home in Jerusalem pursuing love (and forgetfulness), or in Germany seeking to recover his buried life and to take revenge against those who buried it. This seemingly trivial decision is in fact symbolic of the two paths open to the Israeli who would know the truth about his moral and spiritual relation to the Holocaust. Amichai approaches the question through a technical device that symbolizes and tries to represent the two choices available. He splits his hero into a narrator, who returns to Germany in search of his childhood and of revenge against those who mutilated it, and a third-person incarnation, also Joel, who stays behind in Jerusalem and falls in love with an American doctor, a Christian. This technical device is clever and enables Amichai to render more successfully than most of the Israelis who have followed him the Israeli reality, which in Bartov and Ben-Amotz, for example, comes, and very feebly, through flashbacks coursing through the minds of characters who are in Italy and Germany.

But the device has its drawbacks as well as its advantages. Having multiplied his hero, Amichai cannot resist the temptation to multiply other things as well, and to imply symbolic parallels at every turn. Joel's wife is named Ruth, and so was the childhood sweetheart whose story he seeks in Germany; he himself insists on renaming yet a third character Ruth.[6] In Jerusalem, we meet an Israeli concentration camp survivor who partially conceals his blue numbers with a mermaid tattoo, the concealment expressing his wish "to forget the past," its partiality expressing his wish "to remember the past." In his home town of Weinburg, Germany, Joel assaults a supposed Nazi whose tattoo turns out to be this very same mermaid. Melvin, the husband of the Jerusalem Joel's American mistress Patricia, was the commander of the American unit that destroyed Weinburg during the war. The Joel who goes back to Weinburg now meets Melvin in his new role as director of a film about the Holocaust. To the Weinburg Joel, Melvin seems the potent man of destruction, he himself the impotent, vacillating Hamlet-figure; to the Jerusalem Joel, seducer of Melvin's wife, Melvin appears in quite another guise. This merciless proliferation of symbolic linkages, intended to demonstrate what George Eliot once called the interconnectedness of all human fates, sometimes comes close to obliterating the main lines of the novel (which are complicated enough). One reason why this novel can stand as a kind of paradigm for all Israeli Holocaust novels is that it is overly busy.

There is a wry humor as well as significance in the fact that Amichai's protagonist is an archaeologist by profession. It is a well-known fact that archaeology is virtually the national pastime of Israel. This would seem to imply a national recognition that the fullness of present life is a function of its continuity with the past. But the past that Israeli archaeologists dig up is the past of ancient Israel, a civilization buried for thousands of years, rather than the past of their own parents and grandparents, whose dust lies in quite a different place. The deep-seated resistance to knowing this immediate past is epitomized early in the novel by a girl named Einat. She does not recognize the numbers half-concealed on Yosel's arm by the mermaid tattoo. "Born among the orange groves of Sharon," she is contemptuous of girls with "Jewish" names like Leah or Rachel or Ruth: " 'They remained in the Diaspora.' " Einat is proud of herself and much beloved of tourists because " 'she doesn't look Jewish at all.' " Einat represents Israeli rejection of the yoke of Jewish identity, the burden of the Jewish past that is not to be found through Palestinian archaeology or the Negev excavations she wants Joel to show her. "She was fed up with the talk about the Jews of

Europe—all this literature about the *ḥeder* and synagogue and Feierberg and Mendele that she had been made to study as a child. She was almost an antisemite, she said, and had her reasons, for she was employed afternoons in an office of former concentration-camp inmates." She too will reappear, with another name, in Germany.

The Joel who returns to Germany, like the Israeli archaeologist he is, searches for his roots, but in a different time and a different place from ancient Israel. His return to Germany is a return to his childhood. He wants to find out in all its terrible particularity how his childhood love Ruth, an amputee, was arrested, deported, and burned. He also learns, through investigation, how many of his other classmates, now "attached to my heart with terrible hooks," had been killed. But soon he feels that it would be a sacrilege to turn this trip into just one more archaelogical expedition. "Archaeology consists only of digging and restoring. A destroyed city is uncovered and soot is found on the bricks and stones, and one says that this city has been conquered; this city has been burned; slaughter was done in this city. But there is neither compassion nor desire to avenge. I, too, had reached this point, as if the purpose of my coming here was merely to reconstruct Ruth's last years." Catharsis cannot come through knowledge but requires action as well, for memories, unless they issue in action, become an acid that consumes the rememberer.

Joel's inability to carry out vengeance arises not, as in other novels dealing with this subject, from the alleged difficulty of distinguishing guilty from innocent Germans. On the contrary, he assumes that everybody in Weinburg except the American tourists could have been involved in burning Jews. The much-praised politeness of the Germans does nothing to blur the recognition that "if my father hadn't taken us out of the city in the early thirties, these courteous people would have sent us to the crematoria." When Joel questions a railroad official about his role in the transports of Jews, the official cracks under the questioning, "like the evil king in *Hamlet*." Both literally and figuratively, the German economic "miracle" is built on the ruins of the Jewish world. A supermarket is being built on the site of the Weinburg Jewish school and synagogue, in whose ruins this vacationing archaeologist finds the sermons of Ruth's rabbi father. A film of the Holocaust, complete with deportation scenes and mass shootings staged at gravesides, provides the ultimate example of industry and art living off the dead, and thriving in the process.

What paralyzes Joel and causes procrastination and inaction is not uncertainty but incapacity, the incapacity to hate. A sympathetic nun who says of the Germans, " 'All are guilty,' " asks him, " 'Have you learned to hate?' " " 'Not yet,' " he replies. Does he too, despite his Israeli experience of combat, suffer from the inherited Jewish disability? He goes into a hotel and notices people eating from big platters of venison, rabbit, and other hunters' delicacies. "Me, I eat only sheep led to slaughter, submissive cattle bellowing, stupid chickens. . . . " This has been his nourishment; he cannot be other than he is. He cannot exact the vengeance that he had hoped would enable him "to return to Jerusalem strengthened and unraveled like a complex riddle that had been solved."

The ultimate meaning of Joel's experience in Weinburg may rest in his encounters with another German-born Israeli (or ex-Israeli) named Leonora. She is the Weinburg version of Einat, the antisemitic sabra. She too is the beloved of tourists, and in fact models for posters that urge people to "Visit Romantic Germany." Also like Einat, she does not "look Jewish," and in fact was saved, at age six, by a German officer because of her "Nordic" features. She competes in the Weinburg skating tournament in the category of "stateless participants" who come in the wake of the standard-bearers of the different countries. She will not return to Israel: " 'I have nothing there. I like it here.' " For her devotion, she is rewarded with a role in the aforementioned movie: she makes love to a Gestapo commander while beyond the wall a Jew is shown being tortured. This is the fate of the spiritual counterpart of Einat, the "non-Jewish" Israeli who believes herself to have been born not from the Jewish people but from the sand of the desert. The Israeli who cuts herself off from the European Jewish past does not thereby join the past of ancient Israel, but the world of the Gentiles, which in a very imperfect universe may well mean the world of the Nazis.

The Joel who stays in Jerusalem immerses himself in his love affair with Patricia. He seeks to escape the burden of the Holocaust past, and even the burdens of consciousness itself, through sexual passion. The love affair, as Robert Alter has pointed out,[7] is intended to cover over ugly reality in the same way that the tattooed mermaid covers the blue numbers on the arm of the concentration camp survivor. Yet the detail with which Amichai traces the development of this romance seems excessive, and in a curious way analogous to the insufficiently intense concentration of the hero himself on the task of revenge, which does often get in the way of personal relations.

But the Joel who stays in Jerusalem, pursuing pleasure and averting his gaze from his own past and that of his people, is destroyed. Within a few hours of that moment in his affair with Patricia where "they attained perfection in their love," this Joel goes off to do some work in the Archaeology Building of the now largely abandoned campus of the Hebrew University on Mt. Scopus, which between 1948, when Jordanian forces overran East Jerusalem, and 1967 was in occupied territory and was accessible only to a few Israelis with permission from the UN. As he is wandering through the overgrown botanical garden, he looks out at the Dead Sea and feels at peace with himself and with the world. "Just then a mighty explosion rocked the mountain and a cloud of dust and smoke rose. . . . When they reached Joel, he was already dead." For the Joel who takes refuge from the specters of Hitler's war against the Jews, for any Israeli who does so, there is also no peace and no immersion in sheer presentness. Joel has been killed by stumbling over " 'an old mine . . . from another war apparently . . . not of this time. . . . ' "

The Joel who goes back to Jewry's European experience to reconstruct the last years of his childhood sweetheart's life discovers that digging up the past can be enlightening but also dangerous. Nevertheless, it is the Joel who stays in Jerusalem rather than confronting his and his people's past who is destroyed. Jerusalem, itself, moreover, is inherited by the Joel who has left it, who has delved into the past because that is the only way of living fully and honestly in the present. He has left, but left only in order to return, for "he who does not go forth cannot return."

But if the Jerusalem Joel's death by a mine left from Israel's War of Independence is a symbol of separation between himself and his alter ego, it may also be viewed as a symbol of the paradoxical union between the age-old Jewish experience in Diaspora and the Israeli experience in the homeland. Amichai's own sense of the relation between the Jews of Israel and their European past is expressed in his poem entitled "Jews in the Land of Israel," which begins with a reflection, of a sort very common in modern Israeli literature, on the signification of the names of Israeli citizens:

> We forget where we came from. Our Jewish
> Names from the exile reveal us,
> Bring up the memory of flower and fruit, medieval cities,
> Metals, knights that became stone, roses mostly,
> Spices whose smells dispersed, precious stones, much red,
> Trades gone from the world.
> (The hands, gone too).

The poet then stumbles over, and is momentarily halted by, a recognition that in some sense the Jews are strangers in their homeland, to which they have brought as baggage mainly their suffering:

> What are we doing here on our return with this pain.
> The Longings dried up with the swampland,
> The desert flowers for us and our children are lovely.

But here too, as Israelis have long since discovered, Jews live, just as they did in Europe, in the most precarious state, without ease, without happiness, without peace. The poet therefore comes to rest in the conviction that Jews have taken root in their homeland precisely because their centuries-long experience of suffering in the Diaspora is being continued in the land of Israel, and is an unsettling confirmation of the Covenant itself, whose original marks were the blood and pain of circumcision:

> Spilt blood isn't roots of trees,
> But it's the closest to them
> That man has.

The Brigade, by Hanoch Bartov (1965), is a novel that tries, albeit without sufficient concentration and single-mindedness, to penetrate to the heart of Israel's continuing crisis of national identity by studying the response of Palestinian Jews to the just-completed slaughter of their Diaspora brethren when they enter Europe as part of the army of occupation upon the victory of the Allies in June 1945. Here, as in Amichai's novel, we are concerned with the moral and metaphysical relations between the Israeli (strictly speaking, the Palestinian) Jew and the Jewish victims and German perpetrators of the Holocaust. But here the Israeli is epitomized not by the archaeologist but by the soldier, who has been defending his homeland by force of arms while his fellow Jews in Europe have been (or so it seems) the passive victims of genocide.

The spiritual background of this novel may be provided by two stories emanating from the Warsaw Ghetto, one little known, the other virtually an Israeli sacred memory. The first, recorded in Emmanuel Ringelblum's *Notes from the Warsaw Ghetto* and also in Chaim Kaplan's *Warsaw Diary*, is an account of an eight-year-old Jewish girl in a refugee center who screamed with a mad frenzy: " 'I want to steal, I want to rob, I want to eat, I want to be a German.' "[8] In extremity, the anecdote implies, the victim can survive only by emulating his torturer; the atmosphere of barbarism infects even the primary victims of the barbarians. The second story is the account of the uprising of the Jews of the Warsaw Ghetto, an uprising unprecedented in modern Jewish history; for after two millennia of submission to their fate, the Jews, on 19 April 1943, were using force against their enemies.

The Warsaw uprising was, to be sure, very belated. In

September 1942, shortly after the children of Janusz Korczak's orphanage were taken away, 310,000 Jews were deported from the ghetto to the death camps. In mid-October, Ringelblum asked himself in bitter reproach: "Why didn't we resist when they began to resettle 300,000 Jews from Warsaw? Why did we allow ourselves to be led like sheep to the slaughter? Why did everything come so easy to the enemy? Why didn't the hangmen suffer a single casualty? Why could 50 S.S. men (some people say even fewer), with the help of a division of some 200 Ukrainian guards and an equal number of Letts, carry the operation out so smoothly?" In November, he wrote in a similar vein: "The Jews . . . calculate now that going to the slaughter peaceably has not diminished the misfortune, but increased it. Whomever you talk to, you hear the same cry: The resettlement should never have been permitted. We should have run out into the street, have set fire to everything in sight, have torn down the walls, and escaped to the Other Side. The Germans would have taken their revenge. It would have cost tens of thousands of lives, but not 300,000. Now we are ashamed of ourselves, disgraced in our own eyes, and in the eyes of the world, where our docility earned us nothing."[9]

Yet even after the recognition became widespread that Jewish powerlessness, rather than mollifying the enemy, encouraged him, many opposed physical resistance as antithetical to the Jewish character, a desecration. We recall Alexander Donat's friend in the ghetto who argued: " 'For two thousand years we have served mankind with the word, with the Book. Are we now to try to convince mankind that we are warriors?' " By the time people chose to resist, eighty-five percent of the ghetto Jews were already dead. What made the uprising unique, according to Donat, was that it was undertaken without any hope of victory whatever. Its purpose was not so much to save lives as to return the Jews to history, to make of them something other than victims. "Although we were all doomed to a terrible death, we were gripped by a strange ecstasy. . . . I felt we were going to die but I felt a part of the stream of Jewish history."[10] That the Warsaw resistance was an epoch-making event for Jewish history became clear not at that time nor at that place, but five years later in Palestine. In 1948, the kibbutz named after the leader of the Warsaw ghetto uprising, Mordecai Anielewicz, held out—against all expectation and probability—for five days against an invading Egyptian army, and as a result the recently born state was saved. As Emil Fackenheim has pointed out, "The battle for Yad Mordecai had begun in the streets of Warsaw."[11] The Warsaw Ghetto uprising, teaching the lesson that in the long run nothing undertaken from a sense of justice is practically useless, became to the Jews of Palestine the crucial event of the Holocaust years, out-weighing the horror and "shame" of the fate of the great majority of the victims, who did not resist.

The Palestinian Jews who form the brigade of Bartov's novel have been sent to Europe officially for the purpose of rescuing the survivors and expediting their movement from the displaced persons camps to Palestine. But many of them in fact give priority to revenge over rescue. One character says that from the time his family fled Europe he dreamt only of returning through the battle lines and turning the tables on the Germans. Another, named Giladi, says that the Jewish Brigade has come " 'not for Roosevelt's freedoms or the British Empire or Stalin . We're here to take revenge. One wild Jewish vengeance. Just once to be like the Tartars. Like the Ukranians. Like the Germans.' " Even the chaplain of the brigade insists that the dead cannot be remembered nor their honor redeemed except through vengeance, " 'for he that avengeth blood hath remembered them; he hath not forgotten the cry of the humble.' "

But the brigade's leader, Tamari, keeps insisting that revenge distracts the brigade from its true mission, which is rescue. The ten commandments for a Hebrew soldier on German soil piously proclaim that the very act of coming into Germany as part of an army of occupation, with the Jewish flag and emblem as military insignia, constitutes vengeance; and the ninth commandment particularly enjoins the soldiers to " 'remember your mission: The rescue of Jews, immigration to a free homeland.' " Every act of revenge, Tamari warns, will interfere with their central purpose of bringing the survivors to Palestine, where they can become a part of the only future left to Jews as Jews.

The idea of a collective act of revenge against the German people is not merely the fantasy of the novelist, nor was it in actuality the impulse of a mad sadist or two. Yehuda Bauer, in his study of the Brichah movement, the underground organization that worked to bring 300,000 Jewish survivors of the Holocaust, through illegal immigration, from Europe to Palestine, has described in detail the conflict between those whose sole commitment was to flight and those committed both to flight and revenge. The faction led by Abba Kovner was revolted by the way in which the remnants, the inheritors, of the destroyed Jewish community were now investing all their energies in the establishment of committees, the shuffling of papers, the tedious paraphernalia of organized community life. Kovner and his group of partisans had for some time considered suicide, believing that once the war was over they could best show their solidarity with the victims, their respect for those tragic experiences, by joining the dead. Only the prospects of revenge and flight—in that order—could validate existence after the destruction:

> Life seemed justified only if some attempt was made to take revenge on the German people in such a way as to leave a lasting impression on its history and show that Jewish blood would not be spilled in vain. There was no point in simply killing a few, or even a few hundred, known Nazis. In the darkness of the despair of men and women who had seen their people—practically all their people—brutally massacred, the only meaning of revenge, and therefore of life, could be the mass destruction of Germans in the same way that the Germans had murdered Jews. The Germans had given rise to Nazism. Millions of Germans must have known, millions therefore should suffer. This could only be done by using poison.[12]

This poet's vision of death and revenge (not unlike the catastrophic fire dreamed into being by the poet Mordi in Haim Gouri's *The Chocolate Deal*) had considerable support within the Brichah movement (although it could not be spoken of openly) but it failed to win the majority, who moved away from Kovner and his followers toward more "practical" objects.

In *The Brigade*, the continuing debate between rescue and revenge hinges less on the desire of the would-be avengers to find a *raison d'etre* than on their need to separate themselves from the Jews who have been victims. Their hatred for the Germans is real, and they have a strong and immediate sense, again rather like Mordi's in *The Chocolate Deal*, of Germany as Sodom and Gomorrah, a country of " 'butchers and their henchmen, . . . the people who applauded them, . . . who welcomed the slaughter and grew fat on the spoil. . . . ' " But it is the Germans' victims by whom they feel themselves to have been tainted, the centuries-long Jewish " 'nightmare of helplessness' " from which they desire to awake. These would-be avengers have come back to Europe to destroy Germans, but before they can reach the battle lines, the Germans have surrendered. Yet what they fear is that it is less this accident of timing than their own Jewish character that frustrates the desire for revenge. They measure their success in separating themselves from the pacific and passive ethos of European Jewry by their ability to retaliate the injuries inflicted upon the very people from whom they wish to distinguish themselves.

By a strange paradox, the Jews of Palestine, who did far more than any other segment of world Jewry to save the remnants of European Jewry, are the most eager to separate themselves from European Jewry's life-principle. Elisha Kruk, the novel's narrator-hero, meets one of his relatives among the survivors and is astonished to find that this man managed to survive by working in the crematorium of a death-camp. "I was filled with revulsion at the thought of being connected with him." Covered with shame at the thought that he is related to such a creature, Elisha flees him as quickly as possible. Later, he confesses, of his relation to the survivors in general, that " 'I want to love their burnt faces, but I can't. I walk among them and I don't recognize a one. They're all strangers to me.' " If these people are Jews, can he be one? If these people are Jews, does he want to be one?

To Jews who believe they have reentered history because they belong to the first Jewish community in two thousand years to control its own fate, the shattered Jews of the European Diaspora must seem strangers. The Jews of Europe, especially of Eastern Europe, which contained the great reservoir of Jewish population before the Holocaust, had indeed been, as the speaker in Hazaz's story says, a collection of wounded, hunted, groaning wretches. But according to their ideal conception of themselves, they had managed to thrive, not merely in spite, but in a way because, of their difficulties, suffering, dependence. This ideal conception expressed itself, according to Irving Howe, in the great themes of Yiddish literature: *"the virtue of powerlessness, the power of helplessness, the company of the dispossessed, the sanctity of the insulted and the injured. . . . "*[13] "Normality" and self-sufficiency were for the majority of these Jews fantastical notions, notions suitable to, for example, Zionists, who could contemptuously be dismissed (in happier days than ours) as "those people [who] wish to be happy."[14]

Growing up in the beleaguered *yishuv*, Elisha had sought to leap backward over Diaspora Jewry to his biblical ancestors, and had on one occasion voiced his disgust with the Jewish tradition and literature of martyrdom, entreating: " 'Let's be just a little like we are in the Old Testament for once. . . . A little "eye for an eye," amen. A little of "the sins of the fathers on the children," amen. A little innocent blood under our fingernails so that for once we can have something to be sorry for, to really be ashamed of.' " Nevertheless, Elisha declines every opportunity that presents itself for revenge against the Germans. He and his friend Brodsky take a room in the elegant home of the family of an S.S. man but are unable to wreak vengeance on the defenseless women. When some of the brigade do attempt a rape, Elisha actually saves the women from his comrades by gunpoint. "I couldn't do it, couldn't stand to see a girl raped. Couldn't take it—my delicate Jewish soul." Elisha finds that he is saddled with the traditional Jewish disabilities, tied more closely to his immediate ancestors in Europe than to the heroes of the Bible: "We were soft weaklings, warped Diaspora Jews."

Elisha's reaction, and presumably Bartov's, to this

discovery of the continuity between Israeli and Jewish identity is a complicated one. There is no attempt to hide the sense of frustration at being unable to take revenge, or to soften the awareness that this failure to take vengeance will plague him like an incubus for the rest of his days. Neither does Elisha follow his Eastern European ancestors in interpreting impotence wholly as a virtue and an occasion for self-congratulation; it is even called a sickness at one point. But Elisha recognizes that chosenness involves distinction, and that no distinction can be more important than that between Jew and German. Jewish identity offers no way out, but only a choice between two curses, the curse of history and that of God. If the Jews can take revenge only by thinking and acting like the Nazis, " 'that would be more than ironic,' " says one character, " 'it would be history's curse.' " Instead, the Israeli must live with the paradox of chosenness: "Now I knew: such were we, condemned to walk the earth with the image of God stamped on our foreheads like the mark of Cain. . . . Like a camel's hump, beneath which I and all of us would have to walk forever as beneath the coat of arms of a knight: 'How can we beat them if we become like them?' " The Israeli is still a Jew, and the Jew is forbidden to become a German. The voyage of the Jewish Brigade to Europe was after all a test not of the ability to take revenge but to resist temptation: "Thank God I did not destroy myself in Germany, thank God that was beyond me. I am what I am."

The main problem with this formulation is that the Israeli's recognition of his indelible Jewish character grows less out of his experience of actual European Jewish survivors of the Holocaust than out of a revulsion from the act of vengeance against helpless Germans. The survivors have already departed from the novel when the hero comes to recognition of his ultimate identity with them. Nevertheless, Gouri has succeeded in making this encounter with the Holocaust an instrument for understanding the difficulties inherent in the Israeli's self-definition as a Jew. For it is not just the members of the Jewish brigade but all the Jews of the State of Israel who can find no resting place between the two extremes: the Diaspora worship of the purity of powerlessness and the prophet's injunction to uproot Amalek "utterly."

Compared with the other examples of Israeli Holocaust fiction, Haim Gouri's *The Chocolate Deal* (1965) is a novel of almost ascetic severity. Gouri does not indulge in explanations, or atmospheres, or descriptions, or even coherence. The world of circumstantial reality has only the barest existence in this book, which is so bleak and abstract as to make it nearly unrecognizable as a novel. It is the one Israeli work of Holocaust fiction that carries to its logical and perhaps absurd extreme the view that a literary work that seeks to embody a world from which coherence, order, and logic have fled should itself be incoherent, disordered, and illogical. If one's subject is supreme disorder, Gouri assumes, that subject should not be contained within an orderly framework. The frustration experienced by the writer who seeks to encompass the Holocaust within an imaginative mould should be felt by his readers as well— and there can be few readers of *The Chocolate Deal* who have not felt frustrated by the elusiveness of the story, dialogue, and ultimate meaning of this remarkable book. The tentativeness with which the setting, characters, and story are set forth is such that any description of the novel must be hedged about with "apparently," for there is here little that is certain, tangible, definite. The temptation is strong to dismiss Gouri's book with Matthew Arnold's sensible dictum: "One gains nothing on the darkness by being . . . as incoherent as the darkness itself." Nevertheless, the temptation should be resisted.

The story is set in the ruins—"the motionless remains"— of a city that we are invited (though not required) to call Germany after the war. We begin with a reunion between two Jewish survivors, Rubi Krauss and Mordi Neuberg. According to one of the several disembodied voices of the narrative (none of which may be safely identified as the novelist's), Mordi has been hopelessly defeated and diminished by his suffering and the loss of his family and his people. For him the decision to survive is itself problematic. The process of recovery, he thinks, involves reaching the "level of the pampered who allow themselves refusal or preference." Out of pity for himself, he has momentarily pushed aside the terrible questions pressing on him and made the existential decision: " 'I choose, therefore I am Mordi.' " His friend Rubi is eager to look for relatives, especially a lawyer named Salomon. But Mordi, knowing that everyone (and, he assumes, everything) is dead, tries to discourage him from the attempt. Meanwhile, they take shelter in an abandoned warehouse in the courtyard of the Convent of the Merciful Sisters. Shelter is necessary because events of biblical enormity are taking place: "Outside the flood begins."

"Before the flood," we learn, Mordi had gone "west," that is, had left the Jewish world to pursue Western European culture, and had written a doctoral thesis on troubadour poetry. His professor had helped him to find refuge in a monastery, and left him with the prophetic warning, which also justifies the temporal scheme of the novel, that " 'just as there are earthquakes, so there are, among men, timequakes.' " This time is out of joint, and nothing can ever set it right, least of all the efforts of poets and artists. "Who," asks a voice, "can talk about paintings now? Who has a head for paintings?" The book's official representative of time and memory, of the lingering possibility of coherently linking the present with the pre-Holocaust past, is one Schechter, "the uncrowned King," a watchmaker who owns no watch. But it is Mordi, the representative of art, who speaks against meaning and against hope. This former poet even warns Rubi against saddling himself with so negative a spirit, one who might turn him into "a total wanderer in a world of chaos, a world where even the song of a bird will seem sin's accomplice to you. . . . "

Yet at the outset of the book Mordi himself is willing to consider the possibility of a new beginning. Thus, in the one passage in the novel in which Gouri allows himself to participate in so plebeian an impulse of Israeli Holocaust writing as the desire to redeem disaster in Europe through rebirth in Palestine, Mordi asks:

> What's certain? Maybe we'll go from here to another land, we'll go and try it out. Meanwhile we can look for an address. It's not easy, I know. Many houses are shut and covered with soot, and others are too blown open. But in the meantime we have to move and think and change. We'll go and adjust ourselves accordingly. Perhaps we'll succeed, and then we'll be so different and far away we can make a new start in a new place. We'll get other clothes. Get other names.

This is the first and the last time in the novel that Mordi expresses anything that resembles a desire to join again the world that had so recently spat him out.

The crucial piece of action in the novel occurs near the beginning of the book, even though its pivotal character is revealed only much later. A horrific fire breaks out in an apartment house "of many stories, magnificent, crowded." The catastrophic magnitude and fury of the blaze make us aware that this is a story not merely of the geographical entity called Germany but of a Germany that had become, what the narrator here calls it, "Sodom and Gomorrah." By those two words, Gouri wishes to bring before our mind's eye, with literal accuracy, the two neighboring cities of the Bible, which were destroyed by fire from Heaven because all the people in them had become equally guilty. Contemplating this scene of "Primordial Chaos," Rubi suddenly grabs a wet blanket and a ladder and, risking his life, saves a "blond-haired little girl" from the top floor of the burning building. Rubi's motives for the heroic act are not clear. He had wanted to do something so that he could get out of the position where people were always taking care of *him*. He wanted to assert that he was alive, and intended to go on living.

Yet his heroic action causes his friend Mordi deep pain. This apparently beautiful and generous act, according to Mordi, " 'finally leaves behind a darkness sevenfold.' " The rescue is really a betrayal, in which you " 'atone, in one moment, for the long crime against the many.' " Mordi saw this seemingly heroic act as Rubi's taking it upon himself to forgive criminals for crimes he had no right to forgive, since he was far from being the only, or the most, injured party. By rescuing the girl, Rubi had betrayed " 'all those in whose behalf nobody climbed up to the seventh floor.' " This is the case not only because the little girl turns out to be the daughter of Dr. Hoffman, "a successful skin doctor" (i.e., perpetrator of scientific mass murder) but because Germany *is* Sodom and Gomorrah, and its guilty population deserves punishment by fire from above. To save Hoffman's daughter is to leave all the other little girls crying through eternity. For what sin had they committed that they did not merit to be rescued by a Rubi Krauss? The rescued girl's father turns out to be a mass murderer, as well as the inheritor of Uncle Salomon's apartment and belongings, because *any* traffic with this world, which has been created in their image by Germans, is traffic with murder.

Mordi's vehement objection to Rubi's heroic action is an aesthetic as well as a moral one, and is made partly in the language of a poet. He calls the rescue the climax of a " 'false play'," the ruination of a true poem, albeit a poem conceived by a diseased imagination, warped by vengeful-ness: "Ah, who," asks the narrator about the fire, "created, in his cockeyed dream, a vision so absurd, so gorgeous? For what purpose? What frenzied poet turned his sick imagina-tion or blind desire for revenge into fact?" Since for Mordi the only satisfactory relation that can exist with the post-Holocaust world is one of vengeance, the ruination by Rubi of the vision of vengeance seems to deprive Mordi of all desire to live. "The claim that I have an obligation to fight in order not to become one of the defeated has only a weak hold on me. I'm too smart and too tired to marshal the energies needed for going on." He can no longer think about "the wonderful countries of immigration" or about changing his name to suit a new life, for he would only be a burden to Rubi. He has no future.

Mordi wishes his death to be seen as a spiritually inconclusive exhaustion, rather than a passionate protest against an unjust, indifferent god. "Protests," he says, "are addressed to someone. Don't imagine any bold movement against the powers above. . . . All that's going on here is nothing more than a silent diminution." We are, he says, living "in days when there is no King and every man does what is right in his own eyes. . . . "

Rubi, for his part, must decide whether he wishes to tie his fate to Mordi and be loyal to the brotherhood of invalids that has for so long included him, or to break free of these impediments and rejoin the world. He goes to bed with a woman he meets in the streets. After the act, he learns that she is none other than Gerti, who had worked as the maid of Salomon, but is now the secretary to Dr. Hoffman. Every connection with the world leads back to the Gestapo. Gerti is the perfect representative of a society in which "scarcely any are troubled by the problem of crime and punishment, with mousy thoughts of regret, so as to permit their neighbors time to get used to the new situation, allowing that it's hard to ask for more than that and what's done is done."

Between Gerti's body and what it proffers—recovery through sexual immersion, which is tainted with Nazi criminality—Mordi stands as an obstacle. "Let's go die together," thinks Rubi about Gerti. "A shared sorrow is half a sorrow. . . . I'll go to her. I'll leap over his torso. . . . " The self-forgetfulness that he seeks in Gerti's body must contend with the spirit of Mordi, "the dead guardian of my life," with the "cadaver stench exuding from his long thoughts." When he leaves Gerti's bed, Rubi discovers that Mordi has expressed his loyalty to the murdered in for him the only authentic way—by dying himself, apparently by suicide.

The remainder of the book traces Rubi's attempts to escape from the fraternity of victims, and his eventual discovery that, as Mordi had insisted, there is no way of escape but by dealing with the criminals. Rubi believes that Mordi died because he "look[ed] too much into things. . . . " Yet without him Rubi feels deprived of his ground of being, emptied, afflicted by "a weird lightness in myself." He too looks into things, but is cautious about keeping his glance an inch above morbidity. In one of the novel's many passages that in its elliptical compression seems closer to poetry than to fiction, the mixture of hope and desolation in a Holocaust survivor is movingly expressed:

> Many things vanished. The weak beatings of the heart remained. The sources. Luckily the sun kept its orbit, magnificently unconcerned. Therefore a few certainties endured, like the winds of heaven: East. West. North. South. Day and night. The seasons of the year. There was, in this, a sort of splendid abundance of mockery. What was left for him to do with the seasons of the year, or the winds of heaven? But the passing of time prompts the feeling of going from here to there.

The question of whether the time measures progress or the going has any meaning must not be asked.

Eventually Rubi is forced to admit that Mordi was right about the futility of seeking Uncle Salomon, who is but one of "many many disappearances." But Rubi still takes refuge in supernatural explanations. "The number of those no longer heard from or seen became so large that he imagines they were summoned heavenward." Unfortunately, the eyes offer no support to the imagination; and so he resorts to "the illogical explanation that some giant, merciful sorcerer turned all the missing ones into stone so they wouldn't be marred by the fisticuffs of those unlike themselves." Gouri's toying with these metaphysical conceits is not, as it may seem, an indulgence in blasphemy but a suggestion that religious "explanations" of the Holocaust as a glorious resurrection are themselves blasphemous.

The ultimate confirmation of Mordi's allegation that merely to remain alive is to betray the victims and embrace the murderers is the "chocolate deal" of the title. In order to ease the food shortage, the American occupation authorities have diverted to the market considerable amounts of surplus military chocolate. This is the opportunity for Rubi to satisfy his desire for riches, if only he can find someone who will help him first to lower the price of the chocolate so that he can buy it cheaply, then to raise the price so that he can sell it at a profit. From the ghost of a murdered friend named Moshko he receives the advice to exploit the desire for peace and quiet of the innumerable people in this "bloody city" who are prepared to pay a good price for these elusive commodities. To do this, Moshko says, Rubi will need "the opinion of a doctor and the hired pen of a famous man." Although the word is never used, Gouri here appears to offer, if not quite an allegory, at least a parabolic representation of the moral taint that must attach to those who accept reparations from the German government. Rubi confronts Dr. Hoffman with his crimes— " 'By the way, how many young girls never reached the canopy on account of you?' "—and invites him to escape responsibility for them by issuing a false medical opinion to the effect that the chocolate has a pacifying, tranquilizing quality, presumably the last thing a German public wants. Dr. Hoffman complies and is rewarded amply with the chance to go far away, and take a new name, "southwestern, hot and gay."

If the "chocolate deal" does indeed refer to German willingness to pay and Jewish readiness to accept "reparations," then Rubi's deal with Hoffman would be an extension of his earlier guilt in offering forgiveness on behalf of those who are no longer alive to express their opinion in the case. It is a commonplace that "reparations" did not cover all the surviving victims of German brutality; rather, as Raul Hilberg points out, it comprised "in the main only refugees from Germany and the nonrepatriable displaced persons who had passed through camps on German soil." Jewish survivors from northern Europe, from the East, from the Balkans, even from Austria, were excluded. But the more serious omission, from a moral point of view, was the failure of the Jews who chose to deal with the Germans to step forward as the heirs in law of the destroyed European community. Instead they asked the perpetrators of the crime "to pay for the incompleteness of their job" by compensating the few who survived, thereby purchasing silence and safety.[15]

It is typical of the novel's willed indefiniteness and tentativeness that the consummation of the chocolate deal should be put off to the future and that the last brief chapter should be written wholly in the future tense. Apparently, just as Mordi had foretold, Rubi will be deeply tainted merely by staying alive, and how much more so by freeing Dr. Hoffman instead of killing him, and by repaying the treacherous Gerti for opening the door of the business world to him with minks and diamonds. But he will also try to reforge the link that his own actions have broken by returning to the old cemetery and setting up a tombstone on Mordi's grave. In our final imagined glimpse of Rubi's future, he is at Mordi's graveside, still wearing the signs of mourning, and summoned by Mr. Shechter, the watch-maker, the uncrowned king, the man who represents the faint possibility of overcoming the disunity between past and present caused by the timequake that was the Holocaust.

Of the Israeli novels about the Holocaust treated in this chapter, none is less recognizable as the work of an Israeli than *The Chocolate Deal*. No one reading this book is likely to guess that its author is an Israeli, much less that he is an active nationalist and one of the original signatories (in August 1967) of the Manifesto of the Land of Israel Movement, which insists on the historic and religious right of the Jewish People to the Land of Israel.[16] Rubi is said to have asked Mordi to "go far away" with him, and Mordi to have insisted on staying behind, in the vast European graveyard. But there is no indication that this faraway place is more likely to be Jerusalem than London or New York. The concern with the moral implications of reparations is indeed an Israeli preoccupation, but it is here presented so abstractly and also individually that it can hardly be labeled as Israel's peculiar problem rather than that of German Jewish survivors. Finally, in its resistance to the possibility that there might be some middle course between killing the Dr. Hoffmans and making common cause with them, the novel—until its final conciliatory scene in the cemetery—comes close to saying that any form of life after the Holocaust (including, if only by implication, life in Israel) is a betrayal of the victims of the Holocaust.

Dahn Ben Amotz's *To Remember, to Forget* (1968) is a first-person narrative of inordinate length told by a young Israeli architect named Uri Lam who was born in Germany and lost his parents and a brother and sister to the Nazis. In 1959, he returns to Germany, allegedly after much soul-searching, to claim reparations. His doubts about whether he has the moral right to accept reparations for the suffering of his parents and thus to give absolution on their behalf—doubts that will recur frequently throughout the period of his "adventures" in Frankfurt—have been temporarily squelched by his desire to buy an old Arab house on Jerusalem's border and a new car. His underlying aim in returning to Germany and his past is to close the matter of the Holocaust once and for all, to forget all that had happened to his family, to forget the abstract question of retributive justice. Although it is not readily apparent in what way his rather feeble remembrance of the Holocaust interferes with either the activities of his life or his peace of mind, Ben Amotz asks us to believe that Uri suffers considerable distress when he is forced to remember what he would rather forget.

The sharp presentation of mutually exclusive moral alternatives—execute justice upon the criminal, or become his collaborator—that characterized Gouri's novel appears in this book only as something to be frowned upon as the outlook of morally obtuse Israelis when they learn of Uri's fate in Frankfurt: namely, that he has married Barbara Stahl, a German girl, daughter of a manufacturer of optical equipment, whose first orders, in 1942, were from the German War Department for binoculars, telescopes, and periscopes. In one of Uri's endless "imaginings" of the immediate future, he hears his friends in Israel say: "Uri married a German girl and is living in Frankfurt. Impossible. It's true. He lost his whole family in Germany, went there to collect reparations, and married a German girl. How's that for an outrage! He marries the daughter of his family's murderers, is awarded reparations, and uses this to raise a family." The style in which the narrator imagines this reaction indicates his contempt for it. He is reenforced in this view by Barbara, who is a paragon of all the modern virtues—sexually experienced, the thinking man's liberal in her "opinions," and a reader of Buber, who for Uri is a long face and a long beard he once saw in Israel. She assures him that he is justified in pursuing and accepting reparations because they are not meant as atonement for German crimes but only as a partial compensation to victims to help them survive.

The contrast between the severity of Gouri and the self-indulgence of Ben Amotz is well illustrated by an episode in which Uri (like Rubi in *The Chocolate Deal*) visits a house formerly belonging to Jews (Uri's parents, in fact), but now occupied by Germans. Here too Ben Amotz tries to show his sophistication by blurring the sharpness of moral distinction between victim and criminal. Have not Arabs been displaced as well as Jews? Is not Uri himself planning to use his reparation money to buy a house formerly belonging to an Arab who fled during the War of Independence? Besides, the new German occupants of the house of Uri's parents are themselves refugees who have had to scrimp and save to buy and rebuild this wreck. No Dr. Hoffmans, they.

This desire to blur the distinction between German and Jew, especially between German and Israeli, characterizes the book. It expresses itself through what might be called the rhetoric of "complexity" and the banality of sophomoric questions based on tenuous analogies. Is the anonymous German caller (who turns out to be an Israeli prankster) who objects to Barbara marrying a Jew any worse than the caller Uri imagines in Jerusalem who will object to his marrying a German when he and Barbara move there? At another point, Uri is asked by Martin Schiller, a German whose homosexuality is intended to conciliate our sympathy with him because it separates him from the "normal," virile Germans, what he would have done in 1933 if he had been eighteen and German? Ben Amotz is as a rule content to rest in the heavy portentousness of these questions, as if it had never occurred to him that between the actuality of what the Germans did and the potentiality

of what other people *might* have done, there remains a
yawning chasm.

In dealing with postwar Germany, the novelist shows a
similar inclination to ask "big" questions for which he has
not formulated, either imaginatively or morally, any clear
answers. "Normal" Germany is castigated as the collective
inheritor of the Nazi regime by Martin Schiller, the
homosexual son of an army officer who arranged the
transport of Jews to death camps. Martin flaunts his
homosexuality in order to humiliate his father and outrage
the whole society of normal, respectable Germans.
"Millions of normal people. Talk to them and you won't
believe there's another Germany. The merchants, officials,
the lower middle class. Good citizens who did as they were
told, who neither knew nor wanted to know what was
happening behind the fences, right under their noses—they
are the normal ones. The scar-faced students, the new rich
gaping at Germany's industrial wonders, the Nazis in
government offices who speak of democracy as if they
invented it, the aristocracy sated with culture, switching
from the production of arms, soap, and poison gases to the
production of washing machines, cosmetics, optical equipment, and insecticides.' " He argues that all those who were
involved in the final solution—and by his calculation that
would involve millions—should be castrated, " 'their
memory and genes erased forever.' " Martin Schiller (whose
very name seems to suggest that he, and not the mutant
generation preceding him, represents the true Germany) is
so oppressed by the sense of guilt that he does not allow
himself to dislike particular Jews " 'even if they are
uncongenial.' " Schiller is a constant irritant to Uri,
because he insists relentlessly on justice and forces the hero
to remember what he wants to forget, even as his own
miserable life exemplifies the fate of those who demand
remembrance and justice. The "other Germany," the
Germany willing to reject entirely the Nazi heritage, moral
and material, is, according to Martin, the Germany of " 'the
un-normal.' " These righteous characters are " 'beatniks,
pot smokers, priests of opium and hashish, homosexuals,

deviates.' " This group of Germans not only questions the need for a strong, united Germany, but the need for " 'any nation to exist—and not Germany alone, but any nation that toys with anthems, boundaries, and flags.' "

Although Ben Amotz does not intend us entirely to adopt Martin's views of the new Germany (which are contradicted by Uri's own experiences of Barbara and of her father, for example), it is remarkable that, writing in 1968, he does not see their implications for Uri's own nation—Israel—which does toy with anthems and flags, and has more than a passing interest in "boundaries." Whereas in 1959, the date of the novel's action, the view that Nazism, a distinctly internationalist movement,[17] was only an extremely aggravated case of the disease of nationalism, might have been dismissed as a typical liberal cliche, by 1968 it had been made by young Germans of the "New Left" into the underpinning of "anti-Israelism." Barbara, as well as Martin, is a liberal universalist, and it is hard to escape the feeling that if she had not married Uri and moved to Jersulem in 1959 she might have been arranging charity balls in Frankfurt for the PLO after the 1967 war. Elie Wiesel, in an open letter to young Germans of the New Left written in 1968, said: "By taking a stand against the Jewish people today, you become guilty of what was done to Jews yesterday. By agreeing to deliver to death the survivors of yesterday's massacres, you become, today, the executioner's accomplice and ally."[18] The lack of any awareness of this relationship between "anti-Establishment" and anti-Israeli Germans is a distinct failing in a book that assumes that Israeli self-understanding depends upon an accurate knowledge of the current relation between Germans and Jews. The book is filled with allusions to the resurgence of Nazism in Germany in the form of veterans' organizations, right-wing fringe parties, and so on, but gives no hint of the fact that the latest form of antisemitism is growing among the unwashed revolutionaries.

In the same open letter, Wiesel wrote that "for a German today there is no possible salvation outside his relationship with Jews. Your path will never lead to man unless it leads to us first."[19] But in Ben Amotz's novel, the character who tries to apply this conviction is revealed to be a masochist. Her name is Erna, and she belongs to a Christian organization that does practical work in Israel to atone for German crimes. When Uri, after the first quarrel with his wife (one of the many marriage-manual exempla of the book), seeks revenge by taking Erna to bed, he discovers her to be a woman who can gain pleasure from sex only if she is beaten in the process. The incident suggests (though not to Uri) that young Germans who show an overdeveloped sense of responsibility for their ancestors' guilt are at bottom literally sick with masochism.

Barbara, with her rational outlook, commonsensical attitude toward reparations, and willingness to treat Jews as individuals instead of covering them with the blanket of liberal condescension, is offered as the ideal German of the postwar generation. It is she who forces Uri the Israeli to come to terms not so much with her German identity as with his Jewish one. Uri thinks of himself as an Israeli rather than a Jew, and his views on religion, are characteristic of that half-educated intelligentsia that Israel, in its progress toward "normalization," now shares with other democratic countries. He has been in a synagogue only twice in his life, and parades his illiteracy in Judaism as a sign, rather like his taste in clothing and women, of sophistication and high culture. On the two occasions in the novel when he consciously seeks to identify with the Jewish victims of the Holocaust, he describes his emotions in explicitly Christian language. In his honeymoon visit to Dachau—yes!—with Barbara, he "yearned to feel the crown of thorns, to reach my hand into the fog and touch their frozen fingers. I searched for a sign, the faintest sign of stigmata." When he goes to a masquerade ball as a Chassidic Jew, he fancies himself traversing the stations of his "Via Dolorosa." "Why am I dragging myself around like a crucified Christ? You'd think I was really Jewish."

What disturbs Barbara, however, is not Uri's lack of Jewish religion (for she is properly agnostic herself) but his willingness to be identified, in the eyes of others, as an

Israeli rather than a Jew. Many of Barbara's friends find it hard to believe " 'that Jews and Israelis are one people. They're so different, in behavior, in personality, in outward appearance. Take Lam, for example, who'd guess he's a Jew?' " Whereas Barbara cringes at these compliments and repudiates the distinction, Uri takes pleasure in the fact (which is one of the elements of the novel's unreality) that his own self-definition is recognized by the Gentiles as well. " 'I'm no Jew,' " he upbraids her, " 'I'm an Israeli—and the two are not synonymous.' "

The belief of many Israelis, especially the avowedly secular ones, that the form of life they have created in Israel has almost no connection with past Jewish life in the Diaspora is brought under scrutiny in the last segment of *To Remember, to Forget*. Israeli sociologists have often explored Israeli attitudes toward "Jewishness" by asking young Israelis whether, if they were to live abroad (not necessarily in Germany, of course) they would wish to be born Jews. Professor Simon Herman, who has thoroughly investigated the relationship between Jewish and Israeli identity, reports that when he posed this question to a substantial number of Israeli students, only a minority (thirty-seven percent) of the secular students answered affirmatively, thirty-four percent said it would make no difference to them, and fully twenty-nine percent said they would prefer not to be born Jews if they lived outside of Israel.[20] Uri Lam belongs to this twenty-nine percent, until Barbara goads him into an act of self-discovery.

Stung by her criticism of him, Uri decides to attend the social event of the season in Frankfurt, a masked ball, as a Chassidic Jew. "I, Uri Lam, would be a Jew for one night. I will finally know what it means to be a Jew." Predictably, the reaction to him is hostile, indeed antisemitic. The hostility forces him to play the adopted role more fully than he had anticipated, so that he must forsake his secular Israeli identity even to the point of refraining from the smoked pork. Irritation with his antics grows until he is attacked by two ushers who rip off his beard and his yellow patch and are about to eject him bodily from the ball when he is rescued by Martin Schiller, dressed in the black uniform of an S.S. officer. Distressed by the amusement the other masqueraders seem to get from this odd turn of events, Schiller quickly reverts to the true relationship of Nazi to Jew and himself beats Uri from the hall.

This is the culminating scene of the novel, and it turns out to be something of a blank cartridge, making a big noise but not hitting its target. The conflicting intentions of the book reveal themselves in the confused symbolism of the costumes. Schiller wears the costume of his ancestral opposite, the S.S. officer, Uri the costume not of his ancestral opposite but of his fraternal, if distant, relation: the Chassid. Uri's relation to a Chassid is not the same as Martin's relation to an S.S. hoodlum, but Ben Amotz manages the scene in such a way that the distinction is lost on everyone, apparently including the author. " 'For a minute,' " says Uri to Schiller, " 'I thought you were a real Nazi.' " " 'And I thought you were a real Jew' he said." Having gone to the ball in order to "know what it means to be a Jew," Uri soon decides that in fact he "came to remind the amnesia victims of their past." The desire to discover his own identity, to find what continuity, if any, there is between the Jew and the Israeli, gives way to the desire, already carried out countless times in the book, to "test" the Germans, to provide for them a moral gymnasium in which they can be challenged " 'to remember that it can all happen again—today, tomorrow, here or anywhere.' " The desire to teach the Germans a lesson, even if it is the wrong lesson, even if they are incapable of learning a lesson, overcomes the compulsion to learn the truth about himself.

To Remember, to Forget lacks both the technical re- sources and the intellectual stamina to resolve any of the questions it raises. Its incessant use of the device of flashback (as well as what might be called "flashforward" to imagined eventualities) is as much a cliché as are many of its characters and situations: the "Ugly Israeli" abroad, the German-Jewish refugee returning to his "native land" so as to help prevent another such catastrophe, the endless banalities of the developing romance between Uri and

Barbara. Ben Amotz's refusal to commit himself is evident through the last page of the novel, which returns us to Israel, where the child of German Barbara and Israeli-Jewish Uri is born on the day Eichmann is arrested: "Signifying what? I don't know. The end of one chapter and the beginning of another? . . . Perhaps." Strictly speaking, this indecisive posturing is only that of the protagonist, since we never hear directly from the author himself. But there are too many instances in the novel when we cannot decide whether the inadequacy of the language to the experience the author wishes to convey is a reflection on the protagonist-narrator or on Dahn Ben Amotz. In the absence of some implied standard of judgment distinct from Uri's, it requires an excessively charitable reader to dissociate the author wholly from his creation. Ben Amotz seems to have carried his reader into the wilderness that is the relation between Germans and Jews, Jews and Israelis, and then to have abandoned him there.

Yoram Kaniuk's *Adam Resurrected* (1971) is imaginatively the richest, and linguistically the most inventive and energetic, of the examples of Israeli Holocaust fiction we have examined. Both spiritually and geographically, it is set more firmly in Israel than any of the others (including Amichai's) and is the only one of the novels that makes the relation between Israel and the Holocaust its overriding concern, permeating every relationship between characters, every aspect of the action. This is the more remarkable in that the action comprises many levels of experience, various modes of being, from the animal to the human, from the natural to the supernatural. In its insistent combination of moral urgency with a comic spirit, and of fantasy with realism, *Adam Resurrected* is reminiscent of Swift and Kafka. Highly ironical yet intensely serious, aggressively cynical toward, and yet curiously respectful of, belief of any kind, the novel pours scorn and mockery on conventional notions of sanity and health in the aftermath of an apocalyptic event like the Holocaust, but finally acknowledges, with Schiller, that " 'not everyone who laughs at his chains is free of them.' " This is especially the case with Kaniuk's treatment of religion. He is skeptical of it yet recognizes it as an organic element of human experience that can be discarded only at the cost of greatly diminished life. The novel's openness to metaphysical speculation and religious emotion vastly enriches Kaniuk's exploration of a subject that cannot easily be contained within the banal and pedestrian categories of monism and naturalism.

Kaniuk has created a fable by means of which he can test the hypothesis that Israel exists not only to rescue the survivors of the Holocaust but to heal them, in soul as in body. Most of the book's action takes place in the desert town of Arad, Israel, at the Institution for Rehabilitation and Therapy, which ministers primarily to European refugees from the Holocaust who have been unable to recover from the horrors of their experience. This mental hospital was founded in 1960 by an American millionaire from Cleveland named Mrs. Seizling under the influence of a survivor named Schwester, who, when they met in Tel Aviv, convinced her that the main task of the new state was to bring the Messiah. According to this woman, a passionate mystic, God has spoken only with psychotics, a commodity with which no land is so richly endowed as Israel. Her theory of the Holocaust is that the Jews were punished for betraying their God by being turned into "smoke and ashes." Israel, which gave refuge to the fools and heroes among the Jewish people—"the clever Jews immigrated to America or died in Europe"—has become a land of mystified and humiliated survivors who fill the night with their shrieks. Although from one point of view it may seem a misfortune that the Holocaust survivors "have turned this country into the largest insane asylum on earth," it is also an opportunity, for only through these lunatics will the nation achieve reunion with God. The Institute will have the dual function, therefore, of healing those whose bodies have been rescued, but whose souls " 'are still in the furnaces,' " and of initiating conversations with God.

The chief candidate for messiahship is the consummate

lunatic and resident genius among the Institute's patients, Adam Stein. Adam had been a circus clown of great renown and wealth in prewar Germany whose dubious good fortune it had been to be recognized by the commandant of the death camp to which he was transported as the agent, years earlier, of his own salvation. For S.S. Commandant Klein of Auchhausen had, as a young man, been on the verge of suicide when he was saved from himself by Adam's clowning. Now that he occupied the God-like position of death-camp commandant, Klein elected to show his gratitude by offering Adam a "contract" whereby he could save his life by becoming (literally) Klein's dog and the camp clown. In the latter capacity, he would entertain (and thus deceive) the Jewish victims, including his own wife and daughters, as they were being led to the gas chambers. (Klein very much wanted his victims to die in peace, for "there was something unaesthetic, unclean, about the shrieks of the dying who want to go on living.") Thus was Adam saved by his peculiar gift, but also victimized by it, for henceforth he could only protect himself from the shame and guilt of his crime by blotting out the memory of Gretchen and Lotta, who had gone to their death trustingly and peacefully, thanks to the reassurance conveyed by Germany's greatest clown, their husband and father.

Although his extrasensory powers and gifts of prestidigitation make Adam Schwester's primary candidate for the Messiah, his own experiences and resultant convictions make him the worst. Having once been a dog, he can no longer be a Jew. Deranged he may be, but the Jewish derangement is not for him. By his experiences, he is "estranged from the Messianic vision, from the Jewish madness, from the incomprehensibility woven during more than a thousand years into a compendium of pining and expectation that finally brought about the creation in the East of a nation of Blue Numbers." Not only the messianic impulse but the impulse toward national rebirth is alien to Adam's mind when the war ends. "Palestine," he thinks, "is nothing but a joke. Refugees, escapees, bits and pieces of humanity, chaff tossed in the wind, they cannot establish a homeland for themselves and are not worthy, perhaps, of having one." Klein has fulfilled his promise of financial compensation and escape for his dog-clown, and Adam has also received a half-million dollars for his circus, which had functioned in his absence all through the war. He returns to Berlin, invests in Germany's economic miracle (which is treated with the withering scorn characteristic of Israeli Holocaust writing on this subject), and becomes a millionaire. His composure, deathlike yet luxurious, is shattered only by the news that his daughter Ruth, whom he had thought dead, is still alive in Israel. For the first time, he thinks about his relation to Germany, both in his formative years and now. Was he not, like the camps, a product of German culture? What was the camp itself but the apotheosis of that culture? "Grimm fairy tales and Luther's essays and the inner thoughts of every proper German were fulfilled in Auchhausen." True, he was treated regally in postwar Berlin after returning from the furnaces Berliners had built for him. But, as the great clown who had freely chosen to live again among his persecutors, what was he other than the Germans' "insurance policy against Hell, in case there was anything more terrible than the things they had created with their own hands?"

Adam returns to Israel in 1958, only to find that Ruth has died in childbirth shortly before his arrival. Her husband, bitter against Adam for what he had done in the camp, takes the clown to the cemetery and dares him to make his daughter laugh now. In the attempt, Adam reverts to his dog-character of the war years and is institutionalized. The director of the Institute for Rehabilitation and Therapy in Arad is Dr. Nathan Gross, whose folly is the "ardent liberalism" that insists on believing in the possibility of curing and rescuing victims of the Holocaust without recognizing that the Holocaust was not just a historic but an apocalyptic event, which has created a new world in which everything must be learned through suffering or with the help of those who suffered. Dr. Gross thinks that forgetting the atrocity is the beginning of recovery for his patients, but the patients think otherwise and persistently return to the Holocaust inferno. This Jerusalem-born disciple of Freud is sympathetically presented, however, because although he has spent his entire life searching for sanity, his experience with the survivors has unsettled his faith in the superiority of sanity.

If the citizens of Israel want health and sanity in their society, if they want a decisive break with that miserable past which culminated in the Holocaust, they should never have promulgated the Law of Return. Building a homeland out of committed idealists is one thing; building it out of shattered survivors is another. " 'You accepted us,' " Adam chides, " 'with open arms, like a fool. That was a fatal error, the Law of Return will beget the end, we shall cause the soil to rot, pollute the atmosphere. We shall remember. We shall be like frontlets between your eyes.' " Yet in the central action of the novel, we see Adam as the agent not of pollution but of health, for it is he who presides over the recovery of an Israeli boy whose schizophrenia is Adam's own: he has become a dog, and lives on all fours just as Adam had done in the camp and often still does. Dr. Gross, less rigid in his naturalism than his fellow doctors, who have completely given up hope for returning the dog-child to his human self, allows Adam to take charge of the child. The true physician reluctantly admits that those who have never been sick cannot understand, much less bestow, health; only the sick can. " 'We,' " says Dr. Gross to his angry Israeli medical colleagues, " 'are ants on the surface of the Earth trying to understand the pains of Mars men.' " Men like Adam have come not from another continent but from another planet. Bereft of his own daughter, and reminded by the boy's howling of the wails of children in the death camps whose mothers had already disappeared and who were awaiting their own death, Adam finds a reason to live in helping the child to recover. By presiding over the evolution of a dog into a child, a process usually requiring millions of years, Adam has in effect become a sort of God, though hardly the one for whom Schwester had hoped. His miracle takes the form not of a messianic revelation but of a healing process in which two sick people cure each other.

If the way in which Adam Stein cures, and is cured by, the dog-child who is reborn as David, king of Israel, represents the zenith of fulfillment in the novel, then Adam's failure to realize the messianic expectations of Schwester is the nadir of disappointment and desolation. The question of exactly how the God of Israel was related to the Holocaust is the pervasive quandary of the novel, announced in the opening epigraph from Josephus that asks, of an earlier Jewish disaster, why God was absent, "so totally absent, during the Great Destruction." Schwester's reply to this question is that God's logic and man's are not the same, and that even the Holocaust reenforces the continuity of the cosmic dramatic struggle between God and His people, who chose each other and remain mutually responsible. Ranged against this childless woman, however, are the voices of inmates whose children have been killed or hideously disfigured in the Holocaust and who are in Mrs. Seizling's institute precisely because they cannot live with the knowledge that the God of Israel can sanctify His chosen people only by burning and mutilating them, and making Satan the instrument of His purpose. Thus Arthur Fine has become a compulsive arsonist who burns not only buildings but people (including his own child) because he wishes to imitate the actions of the divine father who sanctifies His children by burning them. "I wanted to sanctify her," he says of a woman he fell in love with in Israel, "but she didn't understand and fled, not knowing how much I loved her. If she had known, she would have sung in the fire " Another inmate named Wolfovitz, whose Thersites voice reverberates through the novel, writes a letter to God (for to whom but the Master of the Universe should he address his complaints?) in which the Nazis are called "your messengers . . . your boys." Adam, in whose brain congregate all the terrible stories and derangements of the other inmates, fluctuates between despair over the absence and feebleness of the Jewish God, who is a bully in His neighborhood but "scared stiff" among the other nations, and resentment of the horrible implications of His omnipresence and omnipotence. The difference between the

Germans and the Jews, says Adam, is the difference between "the nation that thought God chose them and consequently chose God who abandoned them, and a nation that thought God would not choose them and consequently attempted to escape from God but God chose them as a scourge against the believers."

Eventually, despite his contempt for the Schwester woman and her messianic schemes, Adam allows himself to be caught up by them and by the expectant eagerness of Wolfovitz and Arthur Fine, which he would like in some way to satisfy. Adam therefore organizes an escape from the Institute into the desert that surrounds it. In the course of the expedition, Adam becomes convinced that he is, after all, the prophet and messenger long sought by Schwester, and that he is truly leading them toward God. The conviction is all the more irresistible because he wants to believe, always has believed, just the opposite: namely, that no God will speak to him and that he then will have to reveal the terrible truth of His absence to them. In fact, a God does speak to Adam, but he chooses to reveal nothing of Him to the "nation" of inmates that has come to seek Him, for the voice he hears is none other than that of Commandant Klein. The Germans' oft-repeated claim that if there were another world, they would rule it as totally as they did this one,[21] is confirmed. " 'I'm waiting,' " Klein tells his former dog and clown Adam, " 'and I'll always be waiting for you at the end of the road.' " Invited to kill his Commandant-God, Adam declines, because without this mocking and hateful God, there would be no one to talk to: " 'In these synthetic, beheaded days, that is the only dialogue that makes sense.' " In a kind of reenactment of his role as deceiver and purveyor of false security in the camp, Adam tells the "nation" of his followers that there was nothing in the desert, consequently nothing to look forward to. " 'You've built a house for nothing. Waited for nothing. He won't come.' "

Adam conceals his vision of God because he does not believe the others could go on living if they shared it with him. He also wants the Institute to resign its religious mission—no salvation for the Jews in that direction!—and content itself with its healing function, however ineptly performed it may be. Adam's encounter with God in the form of an S.S. commandant convinces him that " 'Jewish history is over, or maybe it's just beginning.' " When he first met the dog-child, he knew "neither what to give, nor what to say, nor how to rescue." For he himself was then "seeking a savior." Having now carried that quest to its terrible but, given the Holocaust, logical conclusion, Adam is at last able to rescue the child and thereby himself. This is the best bargain the Jews can now strike with history: not joy but peace, not greatness but sanity, not God but man. This is a vast diminution. "Life is so sad without God!" exclaims Adam. "Still, man is left. I am here, and I have a child. . . ."Once Adam has recovered, he becomes blank and dull in a way, and his lover, the chief nurse of the Institute, loses all interest in Adam Stein, whose old self had to die before he could be reborn. "Sanity is sad. Nothing happens. I live today in a lovely, good valley, The heights are gone forever. There are no more frightful deserts, and I no longer leap into the fire, I'm afraid I'll get burned." Besides, the God who offers sanctification only through burning has been unmasked for what He truly is.

The bizarre quality of many of the incidents and characters in *Adam Resurrected* serves to underscore Kaniuk's understanding both of the Holocaust and of Israel, the two events of modern Jewish history that compete in incredibility. The metamorphosis of human beings, erect and tall, into four-legged animals is an old literary metaphor that was given a new force once the Germans arranged to exterminate the Jews as if they were bedbugs, with poison gas. Even the specific metaphor here employed by Kaniuk was a literal reality in one camp in Rumania, in which arriving Jews were told: "You have come in on two feet, and if you do not end your lives here, you will be allowed to leave on four feet only." (In this camp the Jews were fed on a diet which resulted in paralysis, so that when the trial of war criminals opened in Bucharest after the war, many of the Jewish witnesses "were indeed able to walk on all fours only.")[22] The Arad Institute, at once a house for the treatment of those disfigured by the Holocaust and a gateway into the messianic era, is symbolic of Israel itself. Thus, when Mrs. Seizling endowed it, she stipulated that its architecture be aggressively ugly so that it would be the appropriate symbol of a nation "hastening to set up house for a transient generation in a place where you must strike root upside down, a location to which old people were coming in order to be born anew in the womb of their ancient mother whose loins were clogged with holy dust." Even the skeptical Adam must confess his grudging admiration for those who have discovered that their sanctuary was also their homeland, and contained not only their future but also their remote past. "They have guts, their blue numbers can be rubbed off. At night they may weep, but in the daytime they stomp across any limitation, across the wasteland, taming everything, omitting any fun, any beauty, any charm."

Adam's way is different. He cannot keep his waking and sleeping life, his work and his suffering, his past and his present, in separate compartments. Arrested by his own conscience as much as by those who confine him in the Institute, he can work his way back to health only through his past suffering, shame, and guilt. In the process, he becomes Kaniuk's symbol for Israel's right moral relation to its Diaspora inheritance. Israel can serve as a healer to the survivors, but only if it recognizes that in the depths of their experience, the very experience that has made them ill, they may themselves have found a capacity to heal others. Israel cannot recover the Messiah from the wreckage of the Holocaust, because He was never there. The novel endorses the sentiment of those sages of the third and fourth centuries alleged by the Talmud to have said of the long-awaited Messiah: "May he come, but I do not want to see him." When Adam does see him, and declares to this Commandant-God that Jewish history is either over with or just beginning, he appears to express his creator's conviction that Israelis will be either the last Jews on earth or the beginning of a new nation.

The Holocaust exploded many assumptions about Western civilization and many theories about the nature and future of Jewish existence. It offered grim confirmation of only one ideology: Zionism. Zionism had from its beginnings maintained that in the post-Enlightenment era Judaism in the Diaspora was doomed. The Enlightenment attack on all religion had brought down the old barriers: to assimilation and to barbarism. Once the Enlightenment had destroyed the Christian structures of the old Europe, Jews could assimilate into the larger society without going through the trauma of conversion. But when secular antisemitism arose, it could not be confined within the old limits of religious Jew-hatred, which had condoned the humiliation of Jews but proscribed their murder. The Zionists would have been wholly justified in saying, to non-Zionist Jews, after the Holocaust: "We told you so."

The finality of the destruction wrought by the Holocaust, both in literal actuality and in the minds of the Jewish survivors, cannot be too much stressed. One of the most striking depictions of it may be found in a collective journal written by a group of young survivors of Buchenwald, who formed an agricultural commune on German soil just after the war with the aim of training themselves for a new life in Palestine. They could have lived fairly comfortably in the D.P. camps on charity, but chose instead to found "Kibbutz Buchenwald" because of their conviction that for Jews the European experience was conclusively at an end. They were warned by authorities that "all Jews who did not wish to go back to their homelands would be listed as stateless. . . . " But they soon learned of the fate of those who did return to their "homelands." One of their group had returned to Poland, only to encounter a murderous Jew-hatred. "The majority of the Polish people, Moshe declared, have only one idea: to eliminate the Jews." But the other members of Kibbutz Buchenwald no longer needed the prod of Jew-hatred to turn them toward Palestine. During the suffering in the German camps, "all that kept us interested in life was the hope that we could tear ourselves out of Europe at the earliest possible moment, and go to Palestine to live and work in the interests of our people."[23]

In view of all this, it is remarkable that the body of Israeli Holocaust fiction that we have been examining should see in the Holocaust a summons to critical self-examination rather than an occasion for self-congratulation. If, as has often been alleged by its enemies, Zionism has a propensity for polemic and propaganda, it is certainly in abeyance in these novels, which if anything show an overly refined sensitivity to anything resembling Zionist self-satisfaction. Yet who offered help to the survivors of the death camps more than the Zionists? More important, what offered hope to these survivors but the promise of Zion, the last remaining possibility for the continuation of the historic Jewish civilization that had just been destroyed in Europe?

If, in treating the Holocaust, Israeli novelists have preferred the path of national self-criticism to that of national self-satisfaction, this is less a tribute to their modesty than to their caution. They all know that the Jewish people has passed through a crisis unprecedented in its history; they are by no means certain that the crisis is over, or that the second half of the twentieth century will deal more gently with the Jews than the first half did; they feel too close to the terrible event to be sure that anything of permanent value has survived the storm or been built in its wake. Gershom Scholem speaks for them all when he says: "It is not surprising that there are as yet no signs of a reaction, of one kind or another, to the profound shock of the Holocaust. Such a reaction, when it comes, could be either deadly or productive. We hope it will be productive; that is why we are living here, in this Land."[24]

The epigraph for this chapter, from "The Sermon," by Haim Hazaz, and the quotations in the pages that follow are copyright 1956 by *Partisan Review*. Reprinted by permission.

1. The survivor honored was Gabriel Dagan; the woman was Ruth Elias. See Phillip Gillon, "An Unusual Hero," *Jerusalem Post*, 27 June 1975.

2. Ibid.

3. See the report of the speech by the then prime minister, Yitzhak Rabin, in *Jerusalem Post*, 8 April 1975, p. 1.

4. The French sociologist, Georges Friedmann (in *The End of the*

Jewish People?, 1965), following the lead of Jean-Paul Sartre, has argued that Jewish self-consciousness in the Diaspora is merely a function of antisemitism. Of this theory, it is perhaps sufficient to quote Hannah Arendt's remark that "even a cursory knowledge of Jewish history, whose central concern since the Babylonian exile has always been the survival of the people against the overwhelming odds of dispersion, should . . . dispel this latest myth" (*Antisemitism*, Part One of *The Origins of Totalitarianism* [New York: Harcourt, Brace & World, 1951], p. xi). The theory that antisemitism sustains Jewish existence also overlooks the little anomaly posed by the fact that antisemitism led to the destruction of European Jewry.

5. Hillel Halkin, that most astute observer of relations between Israel and the Diaspora, makes this point clearly: "It is commonly asserted, even in sympathetic accounts of Zionism, that the movement to establish a Jewish state succeeded in the end only because of the catastrophic intervention of the Holocaust. If anything, the truth is the opposite. The Jewish communities annihilated by the Nazis were the most 'Zionised' of any in the world long before the rise of Hitler to power, and they could have done more for the Zionist cause as live immigrants to Palestine than they ever were able to do as dead martyrs used to prick the conscience of the world" (*Letters to an American Jewish Friend: A Zionist's Polemic* [Philadelphia: Jewish Publication Society, 1977], p. 39).

6. A similar kind of symbolic multiplication, including twinning and a whole gallery of women named Ruth, is used by Yoram Kaniuk in *Adam Resurrected* (1971).

7. Robert Alter, *After the Tradition: Essays on Modern Jewish Writing* (New York: E. P. Dutton, 1969), p. 169.

8. *Notes from the Warsaw Ghetto: The Journal of Emmanuel Ringelblum*, ed. J. Sloan (New York: Schocken Books, 1974), p. 39.

9. Ibid., pp. 310, 326.

10. Alexander Donat, *The Holocaust Kingdom: A Memoir* (New York, Chicago, and San Francisco: Holt, Rinehart & Winston, 1965), pp. 103, 142.

11. Emil L. Fackenheim, "The Jewish People Return to History," in *Zionism: The Attack in the United Nations and the Future of the Jewish People* (Miami Beach, Fla.: Council of Jewish Federations and Welfare Funds, 1975), p. 8.

12. Yehuda Bauer, *Flight and Rescue: Brichah* (New York: Random House, 1970), p. 26. See also Michael Elkins, *Forged in Fury* (New York: Ballantine Books, 1971).

13. Irving Howe and Eliezer Greenberg, eds., *A Treasury of Yiddish Stories* (New York: Viking Press, 1953), p. 38.

14. This is reported to have been the reply of Hermann Cohen, the German-Jewish philosopher, when asked why he, a committed Jew, was not a Zionist (Jacob Katz, "Zionism and Jewish Identity," *Commentary* 63 [May 1977]: 52).

15. Raul Hilberg, *The Destruction of the European Jews* (Chicago: Quadrangle Books, 1961), pp. 750, 739.

16.   Rael Jean Isaac, *Israel Divided: Ideological Politics in the Jewish State* (Baltimore and London: Johns Hopkins University Press, 1976), p. 165.

17.   Hannah Arendt points out that "not only the Nazis, but fifty years of antisemitic history, stand as evidence against the identification of antisemitism with nationalism. The first antisemitic parties . . . were also among the first that banded together, internationally" (*Antisemitism*, p. 4).

18.   Elie Wiesel, *One Generation After* (New York: Avon Books, 1972), p. 208.

19.   Ibid., p. 207.

20.   Simon Herman, *Israelis and Jews: The Continuity of an Identity* (Philadelphia: Jewish Publication Society, 1971), p. 53.

21.   Holocaust diaries and memoirs often refer to the Nazis' peculiar love of beating Jews into unconsciousness and near death, and then telling the stupefied and dazed victims when they awoke: "Well, you see, we rule in the next world too."

22.   Raul Hilberg, *The Destruction of the European Jews*, p. 496.

23.   *The Root and the Bough*, ed. Leo W. Schwarz (New York and Toronto: Rinehart, 1949), p. 324.

24.   Gershom Scholem, "Reflections on the Possibility of Jewish Mysticism in Our Time," *Ariel* 26 (Spring 1970): 46.

Half of his people had been tortured and murdered, and the other half were giving parties.—Isaac Bashevis Singer, *Enemies*

chapter 4

The Holocaust in American Jewish
Fiction: A Slow Awakening

During World War II, American policy toward rescuing Jews from Europe could have been the occasion of a tragic conflict of loyalties for the American Jewish community. Yehuda Bauer has succinctly described that policy as follows: "Every humanitarian consideration was dropped, and the slogan 'rescue through victory' became the statement of official policy. This policy did not take into account that few Jews would remain to be rescued after victory."[1] The conflict never occurred: the Jews of Europe were left to be murdered, and their brethren in the United States, who barely thought of allowing their Jewish loyalties to "interfere" with the war effort, remained largely undisturbed by tragedy or divided loyalties.

If one large segment of American Jews, descended either actually or spiritually from the German Reform movement, had always believed that they were Americans of the Jewish persuasion rather than members of the Jewish people, another large and vocal group, those descended from Eastern Europe and imbued with the ethos of Jewish radicalism and socialism, believed themselves to be, not Americans of course, but internationalists first, and Jews second (if Jews at all). Irving Howe has pointed out the way in which Eastern European Jewish socialists, from the beginning of their life in America, "yearned to bleach away their past and become men without, or above, a country." They stubbornly denied that there could be any problems peculiar to Jews as a people and worth addressing as such. To admit this possibility was for them particularism, provincialism, nationalism. "Rebelling against the parochialism of traditional Jewish life," says Howe, "the Jewish radicals improvised a parochialism of their own— but with this difference: they called it 'universalism.' "[2] By the time of the Holocaust, socialism no longer held so compelling a sway over American Jews as it once did. Yet their loyalty to, and enthusiasm for, President Roosevelt derived largely from a belief that, even though he retained the capitalist structure of American society, he had done much to realize their old socialist program through piecemeal reform. At the very time, therefore, that Franklin Roosevelt was, by doing nothing to admit Jewish refugees to the United States, sending hundreds of thousands of Jews to their death, American Jews were his most fervent, uncritical, and reliable bloc of supporters. Even when the war was over and the full extent of Roosevelt's shameful guilt became known, the long-standing conviction of the American Jewish community that the best way to ameliorate the condition of Jews was to ameliorate American society at large was unshaken.

Not long after the war, a generation of American Jewish writers* arose who purported to satirize every aspect of American Jewish life. Every American Jewish malady, still more any American malady that could with any plausibility be labeled Jewish—suffocating maternal affection, suburban vulgarity, materialism, kitchen religion—was mercilessly pilloried. But the fact that the most powerful, or at any rate, least powerless, Jewish community in the world had abnegated responsibility for its helpless brethren during their hour of utmost need did not, apart from a few isolated instances, provoke moral satire. Another malady from which the Jewish satirists studiously withheld their irony was the Jewish infatuation with leftist political movements, a delusion that gives every indication of being the most damaging to Jewish existence, the most permanent in its destructiveness, since the seventeenth-century delusion with Sabbatai Zevi.

These two great avoidances were connected with each

---

*I include in this group not only American Jewish writers who accept the label calmly but also those, like Philip Roth, who protest that "I am not a Jewish writer; I am a writer who is a Jew." I do not include American Yiddish writers or someone like Wiesel, who writes in French. American Jewish poets who have dealt seriously with the Holocaust include Irving Feldman, Anthony Hecht, Charles Reznikoff, and Shirley Kaufman.

other in more than an accidental way. It is not the fashion of any satirist to select as his primary subject precisely those moral evasions of which he has himself been guilty or those false idols after which he has himself been lusting. It is a hero and not a clod who declares for himself and his author Norman Mailer that " 'the massacres and pogroms, the gas chambers, the lime kilns—all of it touched no one, all of it was lost.' " The imagination of American Jewish writers was not effectively touched by the Holocaust either during its occurrence or for two decades afterward (this despite the fact that detailed information about the massacres was available to those who could read newspapers from December 1942). One of Saul Bellow's characters in his 1944 novel *Dangling Man* provides the exception that tests the rule. Awaiting induction into the army, the hero Joseph dreams that he is in a low chamber surrounded by rows of murdered people, one of whom he has been charged with identifying and reclaiming. His charnel-house guide reads from an identity tag a place name which reminds Joseph that "in Bucharest . . . those slain by the Iron Guard were slung from hooks in a slaughterhouse. I have seen the pictures." In horror, he jumps back "in the clear," and claims that "I was not personally acquainted with the deceased. I had merely been asked, as an outsider." He wonders why he and his friends have so easily accustomed themselves to the slaughter in Europe and why they have so little pity for the victims. But his answer does not venture beyond the most charitable of explanations: "I do not like to think what we are governed by. I do not like to think about it. It is not easy work, and it is not safe. Its *kindest* revelation is that our senses and our imaginations are somehow incompetent."

The causative link that, in my view, exists between the absence of the Holocaust and the absence of satire of the American Jew's love of leftist humanitarianism from American Jewish fiction is also hinted at in this literally exceptional novel. The eventual induction of Bellow's hero into the army not only takes him away from the dreamworld of American freedom back to the European world of limited choice and unlimited bloodshed; it also forces him to give up his scholarly work on the Enlightenment. In fact, however, his fascination with this subject had already begun to wane, for reasons that are evident in his explanation of why he quit the Communist party: " 'You see, I thought those people were different. I haven't forgotten that I believed they were devoted to the service of some grand flapdoodle, the Race, *le genre humain*. Oh, yes, they were! By the time I got out, I realized that any hospital nurse did more with one bedpan for *le genre humain* than they did with their entire organization. It's odd to think that there was a time when to hear that would have filled me with horror.' "

The Enlightenment and the French Revolution granted Jews equal rights simply because they belonged to *le genre humain*. Despite the Enlightenment's unconcealed hatred of Judaism (and often of Jews), no group believed more fervently than the Jews that the Christian Trinity had been supplanted as a motive force in the European mind by the new Trinity of Liberty, Equality, and Fraternity. The revolutionists would grant everything to the Jews as individuals, but nothing to them as a people or a distinct group. Jews impressed by the new dispensation came to believe that they must relinquish their national character in order to assimilate with "humanity." They were not noticeably disturbed by the fact that in practice their assimilation was not with all humanity but with the particular people among whom they lived. Thus, while the People Israel was rapidly improving itself out of existence, the other peoples—the French, the Poles, the Germans— were asserting their national rights more boldly than ever.

But no conviction has ever been more resistant to negative evidence than the belief of the Jewish leftist in the promises held out to him by declarations of human rights. The leftist-supported pogroms in Russia in the 1880s; the espousal by every left-wing party in nineteenth-century France of antisemitism; the Dreyfus Affair; the refusal of the German Socialists to condemn antisemitism during the 1930s; the destruction of European Jewry amidst worldwide indifference: such an accumulation of horrors might have been thought finally destructive of the delusory belief in emancipation, equality, assimilation, and enlightenment. A non-Jewish observer like François Mauriac, when he witnessed trainloads of Jewish children standing at Austerlitz station in Paris awaiting deportation to the death camps, knew that "the dream which Western man conceived in the eighteenth century, whose dawn he thought he saw in 1789, and which . . . had grown stronger with the progress of enlightenment and the discoveries of science—this dream vanished finally . . . before those trainloads of little children."[3] But the faith of the Jewish universalist has proved more immune to the evidence of mere experience than that of the French Catholic; and everything we know of Jewish life in the United States shows that this faith has survived the Holocaust itself. Here a majority of Jews do not merely look upon the varied offspring of Enlightenment universalism as conducive to Jewish existence but actually believe Judaism itself to be coextensive with them.

The persistence of the universalist-humanist delusion among American Jews even in the wake of the Holocaust is nowhere represented with more symbolic force than in Bernard Malamud's story "The Lady of the Lake" (1958), one of but two stories in his work dealing directly with the Holocaust.[4] The protagonist comes into a small inheritance and decides to go abroad "seeking romance." In the States, where "a man's past was . . . expendable," he was Henry Levin, but once in Europe Levin takes to calling himself Henry Freeman, thus symbolically severing his Jewish ties. When he meets an attractive Italian girl named Isabella he identifies himself as an American but denies his Jewish identity. He wonders, since "he absolutely did not look Jewish," why she should ask the question of him, but quickly dismisses it as a quirk. "With ancient history why bother?" One of her attractions, to be sure, is precisely a face that carries "the mark of history," that is, of "civilized" Italian history. But at the crucial moment, when he comes to propose marriage to Isabella, she reveals her breasts, on whose "softened tender flesh" he recognizes the tattooed blue numbers of the concentration-camp inmate that show her Jewish identity. " 'I can't marry you. We are Jews. My past is meaningful to me. I treasure what I suffered for.' " Levin-Freeman suddenly discovers the emptiness of his freedom and, having deprived himself by his deception of what he most desired, can only stammer, " 'Listen, I-I am—.' " But before he can supply the missing label, Isabella disappears into the night. In the aftermath of the Holocaust, it is not enough for the American Jew simply to be an American, or even simply "to be." To embrace the fullness of life that Isabella here represents, he must embrace the particularity of his Jewish identity, an identity that is forevermore inseparable from the experience of the Holocaust.

Levin-Freeman is symbolic not only of the American Jew who has evaded his moral responsibility and impoverished his life by cutting himself off from the Jewish past. He may also be taken as a symbol of the American Jewish writer who, in embracing what Cynthia Ozick has called the "Diaspora of freedom," has doomed himself to the obscurity of a perpetual involvement "with shadow, with futility, with vanity, frivolity, and waste."[5] He has denied the novelist's responsibility to engage and extend his readers' imaginative sympathy, and he has impoverished his own art by separating his Jewish characters from their history, which could have provided him with that norm of behavior without which satire becomes sterile.

Thus the "silence" of most American Jewish writers on the Holocaust was not (as has sometimes been urged in their defence) an awed acknowledgement of the unspeakable and unimaginable character of the evil that occurred, or the implicit admission that what is absolutely unprecedented in human affairs cannot be imitated in a literary action. American Jewish writers have hardly been struck dumb in the face of various evils that (however mistakenly) they consider on a par with Auschwitz and Treblinka. Carlyle once spoke of the unique eloquence of "the SILENCE of deep Eternities, of Worlds from beyond the morning-stars."

But the long silence of American Jewish literature on the Holocaust was eloquent only of its own failure to shake off the incubus-like ideological superstitions of modern Jewry and grasp its proper subject—even though to do so would have been to admit that Jewish suffering had been not merely an indiscriminate part of man's inhumanity to man but unique, and that the human rights granted to Jews as "freemen" and individuals had been an invitation to self-destruction. As Norma Rosen recently wrote, "The Holocaust is the central occurrence of the Twentieth century. It is the central human occurrence. It cannot therefore be more so for Jews and Jewish writers. But it ought, at least, to be that."[6]

Among the best-known American Jewish writers, with the exception (again) of Saul Bellow, this silence even today has not been broken. But if we now turn from speculation about why we have not had, in America, a substantial literature of the Holocaust to evaluation of what we do have, we will notice a gradual awakening in our literary culture that seems to have been spurred by the Eichmann trial and the Six-Day War. Since the sixties, a number of American Jewish writers, including some of the most gifted, have sought to rediscover for us in the Holocaust our own buried life.

We still frequently notice, in this literature, the deep-seated reluctance to conceive of specifically Jewish suffering, as well as a compulsive desire for discovering analogies between Jewish suffering and that of whatever oppressed and allegedly oppressed group (not excluding the Arabs) is at the time of writing the special beneficiary of liberal-left benevolence. The most hideous example of this tendency is probably Richard Elman's pseudo-documentary novel *The 28th Day of Elul* (1967). The novel's hero is a survivor who writes from Israel to the lawyer of a deceased American uncle to prove that he is truly a Jew and therefore deserving of his uncle's legacy. By way of explaining to the lawyer what Hitler's victims endured, the best he can do is say "they were treated like niggers." The worst he can think to say of the German murderers themselves is that they are like Americans, who are "just as guilty" because they dropped bombs on Hamburg and Dresden—or like (to this point does egalitarian nihilism invariably lead us) Israeli army officers. The German organizers of mass killing were, according to the moral and historical perspective of this writer who is all knowingness and no knowledge, just like bourgeois functionaries everywhere. " 'We even have them in Israel . . . with patches over their eyes.' " This book, whose narrator-hero says he is no more a conscious member of the Jewish religion than of the "human race," bears out in a truly remarkable way Cynthia Ozick's further observation that "whoever thinks it necessary to declare the Jews members of 'mankind' is not quite sure of the very proposition he finds it necessary to declare; and, like Shakespeare, he can end by confusing the victim with the victimizer."[7]

Even in works infinitely superior to Elman's in literary tact and moral imagination, we often encounter the desire to make the Jew into "an archetype of the eternal oppressed."[8] This may begin with the understandable intention to relate the Holocaust to what is readily available in the experience of the author and his imagined audience. But it can end by transfusing the blood of Jewish culture and Jewish experience into the *caput mortuum* of universalist ethical demonstrations.

In Edward Wallant's *The Pawnbroker* (1962), the hero is Sol Nazerman, who lost his wife and children during the Holocaust and himself suffered mutilation through medical experimentation. Formerly a professor in Poland, in his American incarnation he is a pawnbroker whose shop exists to subserve the interests of a Mafia gangster. He believes that all life has been gassed and burned in those crematoriums where he had himself been forced to work. His hopes amputated long ago, his greatest wish now is to be free of human relationships beyond the formal ones required by his home life with the shallow, assimilated "American" family of his sister, and by his business transactions with the derelicts who frequent his shop. To satisfy his biological needs, he occasionally sleeps with a survivor named Tessie Rubin. The act is a form of necrophilia, a consummation not of tenderness or love but of the desperation and anguish of people who have lost the will to live. He resents the attempted intrusion upon his privacy and unfeelingness by a well-intentioned social worker, Miss Birchfield. His true life is among the dead, and comes to him in dreams of his murdered family and people. Wallant conveys very powerfully the spiritual distance that separates Nazerman from his mindless relatives, his hostile black and Puerto Rican customers, and the woman who loves him yet wishes the blue numbers on his arm and the memories they represent would disappear altogether. " 'There is,' " he tells Miss Birchfield, " 'a world so different in scale that its emotions bear no resemblance to yours; it has emotions so different in degree that they have become a different *species!*' "

Finally, however, Wallant proves as unwilling to accept this wall of separation and distinction as the naïvely well-intentioned social worker, who hopes to "cure" Sol of his "bitterness" and make him a *"human being"* again. Sol has refused emotional relationship not only with her but also with his black Puerto Rican assistant, Jesus Ortiz, who emulates Sol in what he takes to be the peculiarly Jewish magical power of pawnbrokerism. When Jesus asks about those same blue numbers, " 'Hey, what kind of tattoo you call that?' " Sol replies, " 'It's a secret society I belong to. . . . You could never belong. You have to be able to walk on the water.' " Jesus has some vague sense of, and curiosity about, the suffering that is evident in Sol's face and manner: " 'Niggers,' " he complains, " 'suffer like animals. They ain't caught on. Oh, yeah, Jews suffer. But they do it big, they shake up the worl' with their sufferin'.' " But Jesus is entirely ignorant of the specific sources of that suffering, the Holocaust not being one of those irritants to the feelings of minorities for the alleviation of which the American educational system offers its famed "sensitivity" training. Sol has no desire to enlighten Jesus, and neither does Wallant himself. Indeed, it is characteristic of American Jewish writing, drawn compulsively to the relationship between blacks and Jews, invariably to assume that although Jews are under the most compelling of obligations to fathom black suffering, blacks are under no obligation whatever to fathom Jewish suffering, much less to have heard about it. (It is truly a wonderful example of liberal condescension which assumes that blacks may be complete human beings without achieving imaginative sympathy with their neighbors, whereas their neighbors are absolutely required to identify with the plight of blacks if they are to live lives that are both moral and fully integrated.)

It is only when Sol can be made to suffer for Jesus that Sol's icy encasement will melt away, that his rehabilitation will be possible, and that his own suffering will be subsumed within the general suffering of humanity. The curative process begins when he discovers that his Mafia employer also runs the house of prostitution where one of his black customers works. He remembers the sexual enslavement of his wife by the Gestapo, and, even though he has always taught Jesus that belief in money is the only absolute in this world, he now refuses to be paid with money from the whorehouse and is brutally beaten for his new finickiness. The barriers to memory are now down, and Sol's nightmare visions begin to penetrate his waking life and crack his unfeeling armor.

Heavy symbolic operations now come into play, all of them intended to validate Jewish suffering by linking it, through Christian Symbolism, with the plight of dark-skinned Americans. Jesus, who has been conspiring with a gang of black hoodlums to rob the shop of his employer, goes into a church before joining his comrades. Looking at a statue of Jesus Christ, he is struck by the vague recognition that this savior of his was not only a white man and therefore incapable of knowing what blacks must endure, but also a Jew and therefore linked with the pawnbroker. "And He was a Jew, too, like the Pawnbroker; there's a laugh for you. He tried to imagine the Pawnbroker in a position like that, nailed up on a cross. . . . He began to chuckle, harshly. Wouldn't everybody be shocked to see Sol

Nazerman up there, his arm with the blue numbers stretched out to the transfixed hand?" At last illumination has come to Jesus Ortiz on this little matter of the blue numbers; it is in truth a property of crucified humanity. Sol Nazerman, whom Ortiz knows to be a possible, albeit not intended, casualty of the armed robbery, becomes fixed in his mind's eye as Jesus Christ crucified. The old literary-psychological device of the "double" asserts the interdependent existence of the Puerto Rican and the Jewish Jesus, whose surname, it now dawns on us, bears a strong resemblance to "Nazarene." In the robbery, it is Jesus Ortiz who literally "dies for" Sol Nazerman by stepping in the line of a bullet. With his death, Sol's long-dead emotions burst into life.

The symbolism may at first seem imprecise, working to conceal rather than reveal meaning. But in truth the symbolism of the doubling has its own logic, however unappealing. Jesus Ortiz has been sacrificed on behalf of Sol Nazerman, in that his death serves to bring Sol back to life. But Sol too has been sacrificed, not so much for Ortiz as for the suffering humanity he represents, not so much in his body as in the uniqueness of his memories and of the Jewish people's suffering. In his final dream, Sol walks over the desolate grounds of the death camp, "monument to a forgotten race." He meets an S.S. officer who turns out to be the Mafia gangster, and informs Sol, " 'Your dead are not buried here.' " The tears that signify Sol's return to life are at first mysterious to him, "until he realized he was crying for loss of one irreplaceable Negro who had been his assistant and who had tried to kill him but who had ended by saving him." The dilution of the Jewish literary imagination brings even a fine writer like Wallant to the point where the Jews are asked not merely to give up their lives for the benefit of downtrodden minorities but their deaths as well.

Touching Evil (1969), by Norma Rosen, is a novel whose reach far exceeds its grasp. It tries to imagine how Americans, specifically non-Jewish American women, who have been touched by the evil of the Holocaust might try to think and feel and imagine their way into the lives of those who had been tortured and killed. The two crucial dates of the story are 1944, when the older of the two women central to the story, having been shown photographs of the death camps at the very moment when she is being seduced, vows she " 'will never marry or have children,' " and 1961, when the younger woman, Hattie, dutifully follows the Eichmann trial on television during her pregnancy. She too has misgivings about propagating the species because, in her view, the Germans have poisoned the very process of generation. But her burgeoning into motherhood is vital to her spiritual existence because it is the path by which she enters into the lives of those whose blood will otherwise be covered by the earth. She suspends her personal rhythms of existence and identifies herself with those "far-gone pregnant women in their forced march; the woman giving birth in the typhus-lice-infested straw; the woman who was shot but did not die, and who dug her way from under a mountain of corpses that spouted blood. . . . "

Unfortunately, Norma Rosen has not pursued this striking central idea with sufficient concentration. She too allows herself to be diverted by the temptations of analogy, of heavy symbolism, and feminist topicality. In fact, the book concludes with the older woman "looking for Jesus," who, precisely like Wallant's character of the same name, is a Puerto Rican misled by his evil friends into criminal actions, and aspiring to take him in as Hattie has taken in the pregnant Jewish woman of the Holocaust during the process of childbirth. Even the crucial scenes in which the hysterical Hattie compares the labor room of a New York hospital to a concentration camp are so enveloped in feminist rhetoric that many a reader (especially today) will forget that their point (as the author herself has felt obliged to explain)[9] is to finalize the identification between Hattie and the women whose stories she has heard in the Eichmann trial, not to present women as the oppressed race.

Daring, even brilliant, as is the central idea of *Touching Evil*, it would have been far more daring if Rosen had made the heroine who seeks to identify with the Jewish victims of Hitler through the shared burden of motherhood a Jew herself. For in no respect has the refusal of most American Jewish writers to allow their awareness of Jewish history and of the Holocaust to impinge on their depiction of American Jewish life shown itself so glaringly as in their relentless attack upon "the Jewish mother." This well-known monster of American fiction, who suffocates her offspring with egoism parading as affection, was created not merely in willful ignorance of what Singer calls "the generations-old dolor of the Jewish mother . . . who bled and suffered so that murderers should have victims of their knives," but with a stolid, almost stupid refusal to consider that the paralyzing dilemmas faced by hundreds of thousands of Jewish mothers in Hitler's Europe might just possibly have touched the consciousness and affected the behavior of at least a few of their American counterparts.

Just how great was the failure of awareness, how monstrous the thoughtlessness, of the Jewish writers who invented this caricature should be evident to anyone who reads *Anya* (1974), by Susan F. Schaeffer. The extraordinary achievement of this novel, probably the best American literary work on the Holocaust, cannot be conveyed by a description of just one of its themes; but nowhere is its special power to convey the enormity of Jewish suffering during the destruction process more evident than in its depiction of the agony of Jewish mothers. Susan Schaeffer has given to all those nameless and unremembered women who were forced to choose between life and a mother's loyalty to her child, or—more horrible yet—between the relatively "easy" death of the gas chamber and that death in the burning pit which she would share with her child if she did not abandon him, "a monument and a memorial."

Anya is a historical novel in the form of a memoir written by Anya Savikin some years after she is brought to New York from the D.P. camps. It is truly historical—and uniquely dignified—in that the author refuses to distance herself from the woman who tells the story through irony or the wisdom of hindsight. Rather, she tries to view the events of the Holocaust cataclysm as they would have appeared to an ordinarily intelligent person caught up in them. In fact, not only Susan Schaeffer, but the fifty-two-year-old woman who tells her own story, in 1973, resists the temptation to separate herself from the young woman who endures the war years. We are made to feel how an eighteen-year-old assimilated Jewish girl spending her summers at elegant resorts and reading *Mein Kampf* in a hammock might very well dismiss it, as Anya does, as "a fairy tale." The novel takes us over much of the familiar Holocaust terrain— prewar pogroms in Poland, the invasion and bombardment of Warsaw, selections, killing by shooting and killing by gas; yet invariably the writer makes us feel that we are experiencing these things afresh, seeing them with new eyes. She tells, with a wealth of detail that is part of the novel's meaning, of the life of her wealthy, assimilated family in Poland before the war, of the arrest, torture, and murder of her father, sister, brothers, husband, and, finally, mother; of her own suffering in the camps, and of her miraculous escapes and survival, made possible by her determination to save her daughter.

The novel is as much about memory as about the Holocaust. Anya tells us that her great wish had always been to be taken over by "the continuity of life": to marry, to bear children, to accumulate the physical record of family memory in pictures and furniture and jewelry; then, at the last, to die a normal death. Perhaps no writer since Thomas Hardy (as poet) has expressed so well as Schaeffer the paradoxical way in which material possessions form the texture of a life, and make us human. When she and her family are brought to the killing center at Ponary, Anya feels that their lives depend most of all on her ability to retain through memory the world—only ten blocks away in their apartment in Vilna—from which they are now separated by what seem "huge deep cliffs filled with violent water." "I started to picture the stove. It seemed very important that I remember every detail, as if all our lives depended on it." That in some sense they *do* depend on it is recognized by the Germans as well. Thus, when Anya visits a ravaged Warsaw much later in the story, a Polish cart-driver tells her how the Germans killed not only people, but the trees and the furniture. " 'Kill all the furniture?' I echoed helplessly. 'You know, couches, chairs, credenzas, kill them. There should be nothing left for anyone to come back to.' " When you are living in what Anya's mother taught her to call "biblical times," the boundaries between what is living and what is dead are obliterated. For Anya, at the end of the war, the dead are more real than the living, and memory serves not to retain that which still exists but to recover that which is no more. It is a dangerous but indispensable faculty: "Then I opened the box: There was Momma's big diamond ring, and Poppa's diamond ring, and her pin, my diploma, my index from medical school, the pictures of Stajoe and me near the rock at Druzgeniekie. . . . But something had escaped from the box like a dangerous gas. It was time, old time. I had to take care not to breathe it in." That massive infusion of the details of everyday life that has characterized the realistic novel since Thackeray finds in this novel its true justification. By conveying so richly the fullness of an individual life, Schaeffer, without more than glancing at the dimensions of the Holocaust, makes us see how far beyond imagining is the loss of six million lives, each of them a treasure house of association and memory.

When she has lost almost everything and everyone, Anya must be taught by her mother how and why to survive. The elder Mrs. Savikin, a splendid character who both un-derstands and embodies the naturalness of custom, insists that even in the Vilna ghetto her daughter must comb and wash and put on lipstick if she wants to retain the human image and survive. When the ghetto is being liquidated, the order goes out that all women with children are to be killed. "Some of the women heard it and ran away from their children. 'How could they do it?' I asked Momma. 'Everything for life,' she answered dully; 'everything to live.' " Then Anya and *her* mother are sent in opposite directions at the segregation point, the younger to live, for a while, the older to die at once. Anya tries to stay with her mother, but to no avail; and the last words of the mother whom she will never see again are: " 'You will live! You have someone for whom to live!' " This is her way of reminding Anya of what she has already taught her by example: that the continuity of life for which she had hoped now resides in the daughter Ninka, who has been hidden with a Christian family. The little girl has become the repository of all those destroyed lives. " 'She is the photograph album,' I thought, seeing myself turn the pages with Momushka."

The last segment of the novel takes place in the United States, where Anya has settled with her second husband, a survivor of Auschwitz. When the war ended, she had decided at once: " 'I am going to Palestine, or America.' " But her choice was made for her by the Communists, NKVD parading as Zionists, who arrested her and so blocked her way to Palestine. America threatens, actually and symbolically, the desecration of her experience and the spoliation of her memories. Having escaped the European inferno, she must now be plagued by the predators on the streets of New York. On Yom Kippur, the family's apartment is burglarized and the treasured family photos stolen: "It was a tragedy for me, a real tragedy. I had so little of them left." Worse still, she is disappointed in the daughter, the recipient of all her love who now turns out to be herself unloving. But the memories are by now fixed in her mind, independently of the photos. Her dismay over her daughter is lessened when she recalls two women living in California who had saved themselves by hiding when Gestapo officers held up their children and asked the mothers to step forward. She cannot understand mothers who could abandon their children, but she does not condemn them, for "there were no normal lives during the war, no ethical lives." Nevertheless, when she says that even now, in the safe haven of the United States, "I cannot even leave my living child alone for one second," Susan Schaeffer does not invite us to sneer but to see and understand.

It is in the United States that Anya reflects (virtually for the last time) on the meaning of all that has happened, to her and to the Jewish people. Although her Jewish illiteracy ran deep, she had begun to feel her way toward a belief in God from the time when, as a girl in medical school, she had been saved by an accident of fate from a horrible pogrom perpetrated against Jewish girls by the other medical students. She sat in perplexity with her mother after the event, thinking " 'What for, the chosen people, what for? Chosen for what? For this, to be endlessly persecuted, just because we are Jewish?' And it was then I began to believe. Even the endless persecution was a form of being chosen." Why, she now asks, was she saved when all the rest of her family went under? "Always I felt this hand over me. Always, I was the lucky one." But her world was obliterated, "destroyed, erased, as if it were less than a spelling lesson on the blackboard," and now the Jews are reduced to the humiliation of accepting reparation money, as if one could offer compensation for a whole world, "nothing less than the globe my father's hand rested on."

If her own survival remains a mystery to her, the Holocaust itself remains a greater one. Was the Holocaust perhaps a punishment for intermarriage? "Sometimes I think it is a payment for our new country, for Israel." Anya can never come to any definite conclusions. Her reflections are presented not for their profundity but for their conformity to her experience, with which they keep pace. She has no interest whatever in finding out what "other, wiser people" think it all meant, for "Who can know what it meant? I don't believe anyone can. So I satisfy myself with simple answers that suit the weather of the day." Anya's impulse to understand her experience comes to rest not with what Bellow's Mr. Sammler contemptuously refers to as "explanations" but with her sitting down to put her feelings on paper. In the last page of the book, she re-creates and recovers her destroyed family in a dream, in a new house, which will not vanish, and which in fact comprises the novel that stands before us, a triumph over time.

American Jewish Holocaust writing concentrates most of its attention on the problems of individuals, whether they are survivors, like Anya or like Bellow's Artur Sammler, or American Jews who belatedly react to what they had watched from a distance, or perhaps not watched at all. For the most part, its characters are not participants in a process of rebirth and recovery that involves them with the Jewish people as a whole or even with the Jews of their own country. When the hero of Bellow's *Mr. Sammler's Planet* (1970), upon hearing news of the outbreak of the war in 1967, hastens to secure a journalistic assignment that will take him to Israel, he is fleeing what suddenly strikes him as the historical irrelevance of Jewish America. The contrast here with the literature of Israel may seem unsurprising. Yet it requires some explanation if we take at all seriously the claims made by American Jewry, usually implicitly but sometimes explicitly, that the American Jewish community, by far the largest in the world in numbers since the destruction of European Jewry, is a continuator and an inheritor of that ravaged civilization as much as Israel is, and has if not an equal then at least a unique role to play in the Jewish future. Only two American Jewish writers have tried to grapple with this question, and to imagine a communal response to the Holocaust that is creative and that does not consist of the answer: Israel. The alternative answers can also be identified by place-names: Yavneh and Bene Brak.

In 1969 and 1970, Cynthia Ozick published, within a period of a few months, a short story and an essay that defined two American Jewish responses to the Holocaust and the relation between them. The story, a small masterpiece, was entitled "Envy; or, Yiddish in America."[10] In it she ironically but affectionately re-created the ambience of American Yiddish writers, for whom continuation of Yiddish, the language of the majority of the victims of the Holocaust, constitutes the most meaningful form of Jewish survival. "A little while ago," writes one of the story's characters, "there were twelve million people . . . who lived inside this tongue, and now what is left? A language that never had a territory except Jewish mouths, and half the Jewish mouths on earth already stopped up with German worms. The rest jabber Russian, English, Spanish, God knows what. . . . In Israel they give the language of Solomon to machinists. Rejoice—in Solomon's time what else did the mechanics speak? Yet whoever forgets Yiddish courts amnesia of history." The story conveys its author's profound dissatisfaction with what one of the characters archly refers to as "so-called Amer.-Jewish writers." It conveys too the sense that Yiddish and Hebrew have now, because of the Holocaust and the establishment of the State of Israel, exchanged their traditional roles within Jewish life, with Yiddish, now the language of martyrdom, acquiring a sacred status, and Hebrew, used (often badly) by bus-drivers and peddlers of unkosher meat in Tel Aviv, becoming the language of the folk and the street. Yet this very transformation and elevation of Yiddish into the language of a coterie, who seek meaning and salvation through continuing to write in it, would itself seem the final confirmation that Yiddish language and literature, which for centuries actually did perform many of the functions of a homeland for people who had none, can no longer do so. The elegiac note in this mainly comic story can be deeply moving: " 'In Talmud if you save a single life it's as if you saved the world. And if you save a language? Worlds maybe. Galaxies. The whole universe.' " But how can a language itself in need of salvation save others?

Cynthia Ozick sought an answer to this question in her lecture/essay of 1970 entitled "America: Toward Yavneh."[11] Yavneh traditionally and literally, of course, refers to the place in which, in the year 70, following the fall of Jerusalem to the Romans, the sage Yohanan ben Zakkai established an academy that became the spiritual center of Judaism after the nation ceased to be an independent political entity. Yavneh continued to flourish as a religious center: in it the canon of the Bible was formulated and the Mishnah was begun. Thus Judaism could be said to have survived and, in one sense, flourished even after the Jewish Commonwealth was no more.

By applying, however tentatively, the term *Yavneh* to

America, Ozick does not, like some subsequent exploiters of this metaphor, intend to congratulate American Jewry on a moral or intellectual character superior to that of Israeli Jews. On the contrary, she makes clear that American Jews for the most part remain in their corner of the Exile because they love to be flattered for having those very traits that are so easily (and often fraudulently) claimed by people without power or responsibility, their devotion to "Mankind" (rather than to Jews), their pacific character, their wide-spreading, indiscriminate philanthropy. "In America . . . the fleshpots are spiritual. The reason we do not Ingather is not because of our material comforts, but because of our spiritual self-centeredness." Indeed, her whole thrust up to this point in her essay is that when the Jews went into Exile their capacity for literature seemed to abandon them, especially when they chose to address, as most American Jewish writers still do address, the principle of "Mankind" rather than the culture and problems of their own people. Nevertheless, she finally expresses the hope that just as Spain was for a time in the Middle Ages a sort of Jerusalem Displaced, so can America be.

" 'Yavneh,' " she says, "is an impressionistic term, a metaphor suggesting renewal. The original Academy at Yavneh was founded after the destruction of the Temple; the new one in prospect coincides with the restoration of Zion." She expresses the hope that the Yavneh of America can share responsibility for Jewish destiny with the Jews of Israel. In a kind of division of labor scheme for the reconstruction of a shattered people, she envisions Jerusalem as the healer of wounds, the bringer of health, the safekeeper, and Yavneh America as "the Aggadists, the makers-of-literature." Although most of her essay has demonstrated, rather conclusively, that Diaspora culture has been largely a disaster, and that "there are no major works of Jewish imaginative genius written in any Gentile language, sprung out of any Gentile culture," she now makes a declaration of faith in the ability of American Jewry to preserve itself by making a new culture. This culture will itself be partly the result of the restoration of Israel, partly the result of the Holocaust, and yet it will have its own character, its own principle of life.

The main instrument of this reconstruction will be a creative union between Yiddish and English that Ozick labels New Yiddish, and that she hopes will become, just as "old" Yiddish was, "the language of multitudes of Jews, spoken to Jews by Jews, written by Jews for Jews." If doubters ask who is to invent such a language, her answer is that it has already been invented, that her essay itself is written in it, that Norma Rosen's *Touching Evil* and Saul Bellow's *Mr. Sammler's Planet* are novelistic examples of it. Just as a dialect of Middle High German was once changed into Yiddish by being made the instrument of Jewish peoplehood, Jewish necessities, so too can English be transformed into New Yiddish by Jewish writers who have found their proper subject—the Holocaust and Jewish fate—and can transmute the characteristic rhythms and intonations of Yiddish into English.[12]

Although few readers have failed to be impressed by Cynthia Ozick's brilliance of mind and style, many come away from the essay feeling that she is something like the magician who puts eggs into a hat and brings forth—eggs.[13] Her procedure is similar to that of the Gothic revivalists of the nineteenth century who thought to recreate the civilization of the Middle Ages by imitating its architecture, even as they maintained that all architecture was inevitably an index of the ethical values of the civilization that produced it. But if criticism cannot create a new culture, perhaps it can, as Matthew Arnold believed, create a new literature. Cynthia Ozick's call for American Jewish culture to assume, alongside Israeli Jewish culture, responsibility for the reconstruction of Jewish life, has already stirred a response among younger writers, most notably in Arthur A. Cohen's *In the Days of Simon Stern* (1973). This novel, garrulous, pedantic, and badly structured, is nevertheless rich in idea and imaginative power, and unique among the works of American fiction we have surveyed in two respects. It views the Holocaust from the perspective of Jewish religion, and it attempts to imagine, in America, a collective rather than individual response to the destruction of European Jewry.

The novel's narrator is blind Nathan Gaza, a survivor of Auschwitz whose name calls up that of the prophet of Sabbatai Zevi, the false messiah of the seventeenth century who appealed to the desperate hopes of masses of Jews in the aftermath of unprecedented massacre. Nathan tells his story in English, but deplores its inadequacy as a language of prophecy and says he uses it only because Simon Stern, who thought English second only to Hebrew, demanded it. Nathan tells the story of Simon Stern, whose parents were informed, before his birth in 1899, that their son would be the Messiah, but that his emergence would be contingent on their own death. Simon does not learn of his identity until much later, in fact, just after he learns from the modern Elijah, Chaim Weizmann, in his Madison Square Garden speech of 1943, that two million Jews have already been killed. No sooner does Weizmann say that " 'we are being destroyed by a conspiracy of silence' " than Simon is stricken with impotence, forever incapable of physical love because his creative destiny must be fulfilled in other realms. He now receives the letter that his father had written him in 1899 telling him that he is the Messiah. The linkage between the death of his parents by fire in the previous year and the death of two million Jews quickens his sense of mission. "Why is it always so," asked Simon's father in his revelatory letter, "that good should come out of evil?" Up to this time in his life, Simon's messianic energies have gone into the accumulation of sixty million dollars' worth of real estate. But the simultaneous revelation of his messianic destiny and of the destruction of the Jews of Europe raises the question of whether what the Book of Daniel calls "the time of beating wings" is at hand. Nathan, true to his prophetic role, reflects: *"The world, it is said, will be saved either when it has become so transparently magnificent that the Messiah appears as a reward or when it aches so from misery that the Messiah comes like a medicine. But there's a third way. The Messiah comes into our midst when men are speechless."*

Although Simon and his friends do place advertisements in the *New York Times* informing the nation of the details and magnitude of the slaughter and urging the Allies to bomb the death camps, they do not undertake political action. Simon dreams of confronting Roosevelt over his callous refusal to ransom the Jews and take them in, but his dream is not translated into action. Simon gives five million dollars to endow a Society for the Rescue and Resurrection of the Jews, whose actions during the war are fictional confirmation of the accusation (made by Hilberg and others) that in the midst of the slaughter American Jews thought, when they thought at all, not of political action to effect rescue but of postwar salvage operations. Simon's society has as its primary purpose the preparation of centers and domiciles for the restoration to the remnant— for, as the Bible says, there always *is* a remnant—of their souls as well as their bodies.

Cohen himself is more interested in pursuing the idea of a separate destiny for post-Holocaust American Jewry than in a political critique of the American Jewish community during the war. Whereas in *Anya* the heroine ends up in America purely by accident, here the decision to go to America rather than to Eretz Israel is a conscious one, forced by Simon Stern. Simon actually goes to the D.P. camps to select the choice survivors and urge them to go to New York with him rather than to Palestine. " 'Some will want to go and cannot. Others will not want to go and I will persuade you to come.' " As if to emphasize the competitive character of the choice, Cohen shows Simon's speech to the survivors precipitating a battle between the two factions. "There was a momentary silence as the assembly considered his invitation and then a cry went up: 'To America. To America.' And others replied, 'To the Land. To the Land. *Eretz Yisrael.*' Fists hit against the air and arms struck out against others."

Eventually the refugees are brought to New York, and the process of rehabilitation begins. Simon Stern envisions, not exactly a Yavneh, but "a small Bene Brak as in the days after the destruction of the ancient temple," a Bene Brak in New York City that will bear witness that " 'despite all, everything, Jews will endure.' " The original Bene Brak, like the original Yavneh, became important only in the first century of this era, when, following the destruction in Jerusalem, a group of sages moved there and made it into a famous seat of learning, where Rabbi Akiva established his great academy. The very idea that a Bene Brak could arise in New York City after the Holocaust constitutes an audacious challenge to modern Israel's role as the rightful inheritor of the destroyed Jewish civilization of Europe.

The task of giving a semblance of civility to a community of survivors of bestiality is engaged with energy. Simon is proclaimed Messiah at a meeting of the Society, and the "endurers" begin to rebuild a Temple replica as well as to regain the pride, courage, and tenacity of the Jews who built the original. But from this high point all is decline and dissolution: we have had no more than what Nathan calls "a fulfilled moment." The same may be said of the novel itself, for the idea of building a restored Jewish civilization in New York City is even more quixotic than that of building it on a new literary language. Cohen is prepared for this objection, which is met by one of his characters, who says that really there is "no difference between Simon Stern and David Ben-Gurion. He drew none of the haughty distinctions between those who build castles in the sky and those who build castles in the sand." Once again, we meet the notion of a division of labor between the two inheritors of the Jewish remnant, Israel and Diaspora. But here the idea has an enormous arrogance absent from Cynthia Ozick's formulation. For in truth the speaker asserts not equality between the partners but the superior spirituality of the partner whose castles are built *only* in the air. True, the castles in the sky built in New York and those in sand built in Eretz Israel are both shaky and unstable, but "the former were the constructions of visionaries and the latter the constructions of unskilled engineers. The fact that the visionaries had kept the People alive for thousands of years was proof enough that the engineers would in time learn their trade." There could be no more stunning illustration than this of what Hillel Halkin has called the tendency of some American Jewish intellectuals to imagine the entire Jewish people "with its body in the East and its soul in the West."[14]

Despite its shortcomings, *In the Days of Simon Stern* asks important questions about the political and theological implications[15] of the Holocaust, questions either prohibited or tacitly avoided by most American Jewish writing. It forces us to look back at the conduct of American Jewry and of Jewry's favorite senators and president during the Holocaust and to ask whether, in Simon's words, "the murderers are . . . the ones who do not pay attention." It also explores, with more audacity than perhaps any work except Moshe Flinker's diary and Nelly Sachs's poetry the bearing of the Holocaust upon the ancient Jewish idea that messianic redemption will come through historical catastrophe. Above all, it suggests a new future for American Jewish writing by opening the question of how to reorganize Judaism in the Diaspora after the European Diaspora has been destroyed, and of how American Jewish culture can assume, alongside Israeli Jewish culture, responsibility for the reconstruction of Jewish life.

The Holocaust has, then, finally become a subject of American Jewish fiction, finally made itself felt as an event of Jewish history and significance. This ought to be a cause of satisfaction, even if it is a strange satisfaction that comes from assimilating to the imagination a catastrophe that befell us over three decades ago. But, alas, we have no time to enjoy even this qualified satisfaction, for the Jews do not seem able to extricate themselves from the storm center of modern history. If world events and American policy continue on their present course, American Jews may once again find themselves faced with a tragic choice between their identity as members of the Jewish people and their identity as American citizens. If our writers have at last begun to equip us for tragedy, they will at least have saved us from the worst calamity.

1. Yehuda Bauer et al., "Rescue," in *Holocaust* (Jerusalem: Keter, 1974), p. 124.

2. Irving Howe, *World of Our Fathers* (New York and London: Harcourt Brace Jovanovich, 1976), p. 291.

3. Introduction to Elie Wiesel, *Night* (New York: Avon Books, 1969), p. 7.

4. The other, "The German Refugee," tells of a Jewish survivor in New York, who kills himself after learning that his Gentile wife had converted to Judaism, been arrested despite her mother's proof of the daughter's origins to police, and then murdered in Poland.

5. "America: Toward Yavneh," *Judaism* 19 (Summer 1970): 267.

6. "The Holocaust and the American-Jewish Novelist," *Midstream* 20 (October 1974): 57.

7. "A Liberal's Auschwitz," in *The Pushcart Prize: Best of the Small Presses*, ed. Bill Henderson (Yonkers, N.Y.: Pushcart Book Press, 1975), p. 127.

8. Ibid.

9. "The Holocaust and the American-Jewish Novelist," p. 59. That the possibility of confusion on this point is not to be underestimated is demonstrated by the extraordinary phenomenon that involves the identification of Sylvia Plath as a Holocaust poet. Irving Howe, in his essay "The Plath Celebration," remarks on Sylvia Plath's habit of identifying her own difficulties with her father with the Jews' suffering at the hands of the Nazis, that "there is something monstrous, utterly disproportionate, when tangled emotions about one's father are deliberately compared with the historical fate of the European Jews; something sad, if the comparison is made spontaneously" (*The Critical Point* [New York: Delta, 1975], p. 166).

10. Originally published in *Commentary* 48 (November 1969): 33-53; reprinted in Cynthia Ozick, *The Pagan Rabbi and Other Stories* (New York: Alfred A. Knopf, 1971).

11. See above, note 5.

12. See, on this subject, Irving Howe's "Down and Out in New York and Chicago," in *The Critical Point*, p. 127.

13. That even the most famous practitioner of New Yiddish—Saul Bellow—does not seem to know he is using this new language is an embarrassment Cynthia Ozick deals with in her short essay, "Hanging the Ghetto Dog," *New York Times Book Review*, 21 March 1976.

14. Hillel Halkin, *Letters to an American Jewish Friend: A Zionist's Polemic* (Philadelphia: Jewish Publication Society, 1977), p. 83.

15. On this point, see Alvin Rosenfeld's important review in *Midstream* 19 (August/September 1973): 72-75.

With an effort which up till now has never been repeated I managed to reach the cultural level of an average European. In itself that might be nothing to speak of, but it is something insofar as it has helped me out of my cage and opened a special way out for me, the way of humanity.—The ape in Kafka's "A Report to an Academy"

chapter 5

The Destruction and Resurrection of the Jews
In the Fiction of Isaac Bashevis Singer

The best-known utterance about the Holocaust in the writings of Isaac Bashevis Singer is the concluding statement of the English version of *The Family Moskat*: "Death is the Messiah. That's the real truth." The setting is Warsaw at the time of the Nazi bombardment and invasion in 1939; the speaker is Hertz Yanovar (a Jew who has substituted psychic research for religion). The statement gains its tremendous force less from the events within the novel than from the reader's knowledge of what will befall the Jews after the novel ends, not only in Poland but everywhere in Europe. But it is also intended to pass adverse judgment upon the Jewish impatience for redemption, an impatience that expresses itself still to some extent in the religious longing of the traditional Jew but primarily in the developmental superstitions of the modern secular Jew. The novel shows how the Russian Revolution of 1905, which had accelerated the break-up of the Jewish world, had, paradoxically, quickened the messianic expectations both of the Chassidim who deplored this disintegration and of the *maskilim* (enlighteners) and leftists who welcomed it.

The Family Moskat is a study of the prospective victims of the Holocaust and of the reasons for their victimization. That Singer should, both in this novel and elsewhere, assume that the Holocaust is to be understood, insofar as it *can* be understood , primarily as an event in Jewish history, represents both an advantage and a shortcoming of his method. Singer never accepts the implications of the old joke told by liberals about the antisemite who claims that the Jews had caused World War I and gets the reply: Yes, the Jews and the bicyclists. Why the bicyclists? asks the antisemite. Why the Jews? asks the other. On the contrary, Singer sees the major catastrophes of Jewish history in the

Diaspora as so many announcements of the Holocaust, of which they are the prototypes. Nowhere in his fiction does Singer assume that the Jews were the accidental victims of the Holocaust, or that the disaster might just as well have befallen another people. When Reb Dan Katzenellenbogen ponders the relationship between the pacific ethos of the Jews and the orgiastic violence of the gentiles, and asks of the latter: "What were they seeking? What would be the outcome of their endless wars?" we know what the answer is: the destruction of the Jews. A Europe for which the prospect of murdering Jews had become, in the late nineteenth century, a primary principle of social unity, cannot be said to have stumbled accidentally upon the Jews as victims. But if Singer avoids the pitfalls of the approach which assumes the perfect innocence of the Jews and the accidental nature of their victimization, he may be said to go to the other extreme in that he tends to view the Nazis as only the latest in the long succession of those murderous outsiders who have obtruded themselves upon Jewish history again and again. "Yes," sighs the narrator of *Family Moskat*, "every generation had its Pharaohs and Hamans and Chmielnickis. Now it was Hitler."

In *The Slave*, a novel ostensibly dealing with the plight of Jews in seventeenth-century Poland in the aftermath of the fearful massacres perpetrated upon the body of the Jewish people by the Polish peasant-revolutionary Chmielnicki, Singer is clearly writing about the Holocaust. Virtually all the questions that Singer's explicit Holocaust literature characteristically asks are posed in this novel. " 'Why did this happen to us?' " one of the men asked. " 'Josefov was a home of Torah.' " " 'It was God's will,' " a second answered. " 'But why? What sins did the small children commit? They were buried alive.' " How, the novel's hero asks, can the mind grasp such a quantity of horrors? "There was a limit to what the human mind could accept. It was beyond the power of any man to contemplate all these atrocities and mourn them adequately." What was the role of God in all this? Could so much evil really be explained as a test of man's faith, of his free will? "Did the Creator require the assistance of Cossacks to reveal His nature?"

Could Chmielnicki really be a part of the godhead or was it perhaps true that this massacre of the Jews revealed the existence of a radical evil in the universe, a devil who had no celestial origins? *The Slave* also shows us Jews who are forced to dig their own graves before they are executed, berates the Jewish community for its shameful failure to offer forceful resistance to the murders, and preaches the sacred duty of remembering forever those who were slaughtered. "Through forgetfulness," Jacob says of himself, "he had also been guilty of murder." In its dwelling upon the physical obscenities of the mass murders, *The Slave* may even be said to deal more concretely with the Holocaust than those novels and stories that approach it frontally.

Our reaction to Singer's tendency to generalize the Holocaust in this way will depend in part on whether we view antisemitism as a phenomenon deeply embedded in Western culture or as a movement quite distinct from religious Jew hatred, a movement that grew up only in the nineteenth century. Since a novelist ordinarily writes about what he knows, which in Singer's case is the Jews and the Christians of Poland, we can hardly expect him to give us a portrayal of the German murderers of Polish Jewry. Yet we might reasonably expect that a writer who in treating the Holocaust recognizes the centrality of the question "Why the Jews?" should at least not preclude us from asking the question, although he cannot ask it himself, "Why the Germans?" That Singer should implicitly short-circuit this question is the more disturbing in view of the fact that he cannot finally convince us or himself that the Holocaust is no different in kind from the long series of disasters that have befallen the Jews since the seventeenth century. *The Slave* celebrates survival and recovery; the characters of *Enemies* who have survived the camps never recover and cannot return to life.

Singer is not only not discriminating in his treatment of the murderers of the Jews; he at times comes close to viewing them as merely a function of the Jews' failure to be true to themselves and to their best traditions. The difficult and painful question of the Jews' co-responsibility for the disaster that was to engulf them is raised often in *The Family Moskat*, both by Jews and gentiles. At a political discussion early in the book, one of those overheated conspiratorial gatherings of Jews that Singer loves to recall, a man named Lapidus upbraids his leftist friends with this classic utterance: " 'We dance at everybody's wedding but our own.' " Leftist Jews, ready, even eager, to spill their ink and their blood lavishly for the liberation of every other oppressed group, have called into question the very existence of the Jews as a people. The Bialodrevna rabbi, for his part, charges that the enlightened Jews are "lead[ing] their own children to the slaughterhouse," a remark that gains in impact from the later description, filled with Singer's vegetarian zeal, of the actual slaughterhouse that Asa Heshel and Hadassah visit. A Polish inspector adds his sinister voice to this chorus of accusers when he tells Hertz Yanovar, who has been arrested (mistakenly) on charges of Communist activity, that the massive Jewish involvement in Bolshevism exacerbates antisemitism and "puts the very existence of the Jewish race in danger."

If we suspect Singer of stacking the evidence against his left-leaning Jewish characters, we should remember that his accusation of self-destructive zealousness can be amply confirmed by external sources, and particularly by the testimony of two of the most astute Jewish leaders of the early part of this century. Chaim Weizmann said that hundreds of thousands of young Jews in early twentieth-century Russia were convinced revolutionaries "offering themselves for sacrifice as though seized by a fever." Yitzchok Leibush Peretz wrote of the 1905 Revolution, which roused the hopes of so many leftist Jews, that the pogroms that accompanied it demonstrated a painful truth that the Jews would ignore at their peril: "In the hands of the Jew, the reddest of all flags has been placed forcibly and he has been told: 'Go, go on and on, with all liberators, with all fighters for a better tomorrow, with all destroyers of Sodoms. But never may you rest with them. The earth will burn under your feet. Pay everywhere the bloodiest costs of

the process of liberation, but be unnamed in all emancipation proclamations, . . . You are the weakest and the least
of the nations and you will be the last for redemption."[1]

Although it has been frequently and correctly observed,
sometimes by Singer himself,[2] that his literary roots lie
outside the Yiddish tradition, although within the Jewish
tradition, there is one important respect in which he is a
continuator of Abramovitch, Sholom Aleichem, and Peretz.
Like them, he looks upon the Jews, with a rare exception
here and there (usually, in Singer, a Zionist exception), as
political imbeciles, incapable of recognizing not just
political actualities, but the most fundamental political and
human necessity—that of self-preservation. It is therefore
hardly surprising that the verdict of his fiction should go
clearly against those Jews who undermined first their right
to exist as a people and then, inevitably, their right to exist
at all by embracing the Socialist distinction between the
Jews as a people—a particularly reactionary and obscuran-
tist people— and individual Jews who enlisted in the party
of humanity. The running argument in Singer's novels of
modern life, over whether the hatred of Jews is increased by
those Jews who retain their Yiddish and their caftan and
their sidelocks or by those who assimilate themselves to the
host culture by speaking Polish and shortening their
jackets and their hair and their memory, was settled by
history itself, for the plan to eliminate Jews from the face of
the earth originated in a country where Jews aped the
manners and the culture and often the religion of their
prospective murderers. (To be sure, the German grand-
children, or at least great-grandchildren, of those Jews who
had repudiated their faith would not have been among the
murdered of Auschwitz; but they might have been among
the murderers. " 'If we don't want to become like the
Nazis,' " says Herman Broder in *Enemies*, " 'we must be
Jews.' ")

But this application of the wisdom of hindsight (which,
we should add, is better than the stupidity of hindsight)
is not the core of Singer's analysis of the Jews' core-
sponsibility for the terrible fate that befell them. The hero

of *Enemies*, looking back upon the destruction of his people, believes that the Holocaust will have had one (and only one) salutary effect if it has discredited the delusion of progress: "Phrases like a 'better world' and a 'brighter tomorrow' seemed to him a blasphemy on the ashes of the tormented." It was precisely the belief in progress, whether defined by Darwin or by Marx, that implicated Jewish *maskilim* and Jewish socialists in the deluge that eventually overwhelmed them and their brethren. First, it was this belief that sanctioned the elimination of biologically inferior species and socially backward classes; second, it intensified secular messianism and so prepared the arrival of the latest in the long line of false messiahs who have been a curse upon the history of the Jews.

In her brilliant essay on *The Manor*,[3] Mary Ellmann has shown how pervasive is the influence of Darwinian evolutionism on that novel's "emancipated" characters. According to her, Singer's critique of Darwinism dwells upon its tendency to blur distinctions between man and animal, Jew and gentile, piety and impiety. My own view is that the main thrust of Singer's attack is directed against the evolutionist belief in perpetual and progressive motion because, as historians have often argued, it is analogous to the Marxist belief in the infallibility of the historical process:

> The conversation turned to religion. Zipkin said straight out that he was an atheist. . . . Man, as Darwin had proved, was descended from the apes. He was just another animal: *homo sapiens*. Zipkin began discussing the doctrines of Marx, Lassalle, and Lavrov. The Polish Jew, he said, had once had a real place in society. Before the liberation of the serfs, he had acted as an intermediary between the landowners and the peasantry. He had outlived his role and become little more than a parasite. He wasn't productive, didn't speak the language of the country in which he lived, and sent his children to cheders. How long was the Jew going to wash himself in ritual baths and walk around in tzizis?

Darwin's Nature and Marx's History, hypostatized, speak with one voice on the Jewish people: *they* are the chief impediment to the removal of inferior races and backward classes that biology and history demand. When Ezriel Babad asks Zipkin whether all the Jews, including their own parents, must be destroyed because they are not peasants, his sister screams: " 'Leave our parents and the Jews out of it. . . . A parasite is a parasite, even if he's your father.' "

In *The Estate*, which continues the story of *The Manor*, the most articulate exponent of the view that both history and nature use mankind merely as raw material for the fulfillment of their high purposes is Zadok, the wayward son of the Chassid Jochanan. Zadok believes the moral laws of the Jews are confuted by the laws of biology that sanction, and indeed require, the Malthusian struggle for existence and catastrophic wars. " ' It's the same to nature who kills whom. For thousands of years bulls have been slaughtered and nature has kept quiet. . . . Why should a human life be so dear to Nature?' "

Zadok's reference to the slaughter of bulls as a model for the slaughter of men serves to remind us that Singer's vegetarianism, which he has called his only dogma,[4] however embarrassing it may be to some of his admirers, is crucial to his understanding of the Holocaust. For Herman Broder, "what the Nazis had done to the Jews, man was doing to animals." Singer believes that acceptance in any form whatever of the theory that might makes right must eventually victimize the Jews. Hence, in the dreams of Yoineh Meir, the slaughterer who in the story of that name forsakes his calling because he comes to believe that injustice to dumb beasts retards messianic redemption, "cows assumed human shape, with beards and side locks, and skullcaps over their horns." Singer's saints, like Jochanan, whose son will welcome the killing of bulls and of men, are not only troubled by the slaughter of animals but express tenderness over flies and bugs, as if they could feel that it was to be but a short step from the metaphorical depiction of Jews as parasites to their literal extermination as bugs.

But Darwinist-Marxist historicism is for Singer something more than just a modern expression of the doctrine

that might makes right. It inspires in him a special revulsion because it joins to this doctrine the principle that
morality is a consideration not of the present but only of the
long run, and that the evil of the moment may be justified as
working the good of the developmental process. This
principle, too, is a modern version of what is for Singer an
ancient evil, which has spectacularly manifested itself in
Jewish history in the form of apocalyptic messianism.
Satan in Goray is Singer's most elaborate portrait of the
type of the false Messiah, or rather of the atmosphere from
which he is engendered. In this novel, and also in the story
of "The Destruction of Kreshev," Singer shows that in the
messianic frenzy that existed during the lifetime of
Sabbatai Zevi in the seventeenth century and even long
after his apostasy and death, many Jews, convinced of the
Talmudic precept that the Messiah will come when one
generation is either wholly innocent or wholly guilty,
plausibly decided that the way to hasten redemption and
the coming of the Messiah was to plunge deeper and deeper
into evil and degradation. This seemed a shorter, less
winding path, than that of plodding virtue. In "Destruction
of Kreshev" Shloimele, a secret follower of the false
Messiah, goes so far as to say: " 'I love fire! I love a
holocaust . . . I would like the whole world to burn and
Asmodeus to take over the rule.' " The moral of all such
stories of impatient attempts to hasten the coming of the
Messiah is enunciated by the old-fashioned narrator of the
last two chapters of *Satan in Goray* at the end of that book:
"LET NONE ATTEMPT TO FORCE THE LORD: TO END
OUR PAIN WITHIN THE WORLD: THE MESSIAH WILL
COME IN GOD'S OWN TIME. . . . "

When Singer moves to a modern setting, apocalyptic
messianism becomes historicist activism that expresses
itself through the by now familiar motto: "Worse is better."
Precisely by exacerbating the evils, anomalies, and hatred
within the existing social system, one is preparing the
liberation from some mysterious region of the impulse that
will remove anomaly, injustice, and hatred altogether.
Ironically, however, it is now the religious characters or

those who retain nostalgic sympathy for the Jewish religion who become the exponents of patience and the critics of messianic urgency. In the nineteenth century, the Jews who altogether repudiate their religious faith adopt a secular faith, whereas it is Ezriel Babad, vacillating between the enlightenment of Western Europe and the obscurantism of Chassidism, who passes judgment on his sister's belief in redemption, redemption through violent revolution: "She wanted to free the peasants and the proletariat. Like their father [the rabbi], she campaigned against the company of Satan. But what would come after victory? Not redemption, not saints who benefited from the splendor of the Divine glory, but lots of newspapers, magazines, theaters, cabarets. More railroads, more machines. . . . " Ezriel's own daughter, Zina, becomes a kind of schlemiel-revolutionary who masquerades as a pregnant woman and experiences the birth pangs not of the Messiah but of a revolutionary arms smuggler whose cartridges burst from under her dress in a trolley car. Appalled by the results of all these secular attempts to realize the millennium, Ezriel resolves that even his own pacific ideal of cultural pluralism "could not be brought about forcibly, nor could the Messiah be compelled to arrive." If Ezriel had survived to experience the Holocaust, he would, like his creator Singer, have viewed Hitler as a creation of Jewish as much as of German history. "The belief in false Messiahs," Singer has said, "is very old and very young. What was Stalin if not a false Messiah? And what was Hitler if not a false Messiah?"[5]

What Ezriel opposes to the future-oriented visions of the Darwinists and Marxists who wish to accelerate the movement of natural and social history is the wisdom of standing still or even moving in reverse that is embodied by the Chassidim. "When one gazes at the Talmudic scholars, one actually sees eternity. . . . How wonderfully they have isolated themselves amidst all this madness! They do not even know that they are at the end of the 'Magnificent' and bloody nineteenth century. In their Houses of Worship, it is always the beginning." For Ezriel, the stationariness of the

Chassidim, their entire indifference to the messianic hopes of the Darwinians and revolutionists, their contempt for the alleged decrees of Nature and History that declare them parasitical and obsolete and reactionary, represent a splendid affirmation of human freedom and afford a glimpse of eternity itself.

For survivors of the Holocaust, however, the Chassidim are no longer distinctly available as a living embodiment of resistance to historical inevitabilities, or supposed inevitabilities. The characters in *Enemies*, many of them, live with the fear that the Holocaust really did show that the nineteenth-century ideologues who claimed that the voices of Nature and History were the voices of God were right after all. " 'Slaughtering Jews,' " says Masha, " 'is part of nature. Jews must be slaughtered—that's what God wants.' " One can no longer see eternity in the Chassidim because they and eternity itself have been consumed by the Holocaust. " 'Everything has already happened,' Herman thought. 'The creation, the flood, Sodom, the giving of the Torah, the Hitler holocaust. Like the lean cows of Pharaoh's dream, the present had swallowed eternity, leaving no trace.' " *Enemies* does not (like Bellow's *Mr. Sammler's Planet*, for example) explore the possibility of recovery from the trauma for those Jews who have survived the Holocaust, but assumes that for the Jews generally the Holocaust was the end of the world. For Herman, the only future lies in the past, as it exists not in living anachronisms like the Chassidim but in what he calls "Jewish books." For Herman, and by implication thousands like him, there is no community or homeland to which to return. "These writings were home. On these pages dwelt his parents, his grandparents, all his ancestors."

But what of the homeland that did in fact arise after the death of European Jewry? To put the question another way, does Singer ever countenance a Jewish defiance of history that expresses itself as a living social reality rather than through nostalgia and literature? For many Jews, especially young people in the D.P. camps after the war, Zionism was precisely that spiritual impulse which alone could both overcome the degradation and defy the absurdity of the Holocaust. Singer's treatment of Zionism, although at a considerable remove from the center of his imaginative world, nevertheless conveys his sense of how far the Jews can resist the sentence of death that modern historical "laws" appear to have decreed for them by themselves taking action within history.

Singer's most ambitious Holocaust novel, *The Family Moskat*, is also his most Zionist one. The book offers a series of parallel scenes intended to demonstrate that neither believers nor skeptics are capable of fathoming the enormity of Jewish suffering. When, at the outbreak of World War I, the Jews are expelled from Tereshpol Minor, Rabbi Dan Katzenellenbogen, as he guides the exodus of his people, is assailed with the all-expressive "*Nu?*" by the town freethinker and apostle of Western enlightenment, Jeku-thiel the watchmaker:

> "*Nu*, rabbi?" he said.
> It was clear that what he meant was: Where is your Lord of the Universe now? Where are His miracles? Where is your faith in Torah and prayer?
> "*Nu*, Jekuthiel," the rabbi answered. What he was saying was: Where are your worldly remedies? Where is your trust in the gentiles? What have you accomplished by aping Esau?

To Jekuthiel it is inescapably clear that the Jewish God has been far less faithful to His people than they to Him; and to Rabbi Dan it is just as clear that if God cannot help the Jews, nothing can, for what salvation can come from imitating the ways of the oppressor? Both are right in what they deny, but unsupported in what they affirm. In either case, as Rabbi Dan says to himself: "The old riddle remained: the pure in heart suffered and the wicked flourished; the people chosen of God were still ground in the dust. . . . "

A similar parallelism aligns Rabbi Dan with his grandson Asa Heshel. Both labor during a lifetime over manuscripts grappling with the ultimate questions. The grandfather had produced three sackfuls of manuscripts, and "there had been a time when he had entertained the idea of publishing some of his commentaries." But a few days after the outbreak of World War I, "he crammed his manuscripts into the mouth of the stove and then watched them burn. 'The world will survive without them,' he remarked." Asa Heshel, a few days after the outbreak of World War II, repeats Jekuthiel's question, asking Barbara, " 'What do you think of God now, tell me.' " But he acknowledges the futility of his own hedonistic solution: "In the drawer of his desk lay an old version of 'The Laboratory of Happiness,' written in Switzerland. Asa Heshel unscrewed the door of the stove and thrust it inside."

If the mystery of Jewish suffering cannot be fathomed by the intellectual efforts of either the believers or the skeptics, perhaps the best response would be an existential one, in which action would cut through the knot that intellect has not been able to untie. "Get thee out of thy country" is an injunction with deep roots in Jewish consciousness, and one that sounds in the ears of several characters in *The Family Moskat*, including Asa Heshel himself, who after his first brush with antisemitism in Warsaw says to himself: " 'Yes, Abram is right. I've got to get out of Poland. If not to Palestine, then to some other country where there's no law against Jews going to college.' "

Since Abram Shapiro, who is something of a Chassid but more of a lecher, is the most prominent spokesman for Zionism among the novel's major characters, the book can hardly be said to be a Zionist tract. Nevertheless, Zionism is distinctly set apart from socialism, communism, and other left-wing movements that arouse the wrath of the orthodox, for the very good reason that only Zionism grasped the dimensions of modern antisemitism and understood its implications for the future of the Jewish people.

Abram rails against the Jewish intellectuals who gain their university credentials by loudly proclaiming that Jews are a religion, not a nation, and that the backward, dirty Jews from the east pollute the Western European atmosphere. He insists that the Exile alone has made of the Jews the " 'cripples, *schlemiels*, lunatics' " who inhabit Warsaw: " 'Just let us be a nation in our own land and we'll show what we can do. Ah, the geniuses'll tumble out of their mothers' bellies six at a time—like in Egypt.' " Abram's claims for Zionism are expressed with the hyperbole that characterizes all his utterances. Yet he sees with lucidity what is concealed, by vanity or self-interest or even good will, from the eyes of the modernizing, worldly assimilationists, who (like Adele Landau) seek to become indistinguishable from the gentiles: " 'And I suppose if we all put on Polish hats and twist our mustaches into points, then they'll love us,' Abram rejoined, and twisted at his own mustache. 'Let the young lady read the newspapers here. They squeal that the modern Jew is worse than the caftaned kind. Who do you think the Jew-haters are aiming for? The modern Jew, that's who.' " All the subsequent events of the novel will bear out what Abram says.

Apart from the Orthodox Jews, the most active opponents of Zionism in the novel are the socialist and communist revolutionaries, whose devotion to "humanity" slackens only when the Jews come into view. *The Family Moskat* is the first major work by Singer in which the intensity of his dislike of leftist political movements makes itself felt. There can be no doubt but that Singer views socialism and communism as antithetical, first to the interests of the Jews, then to the interests of society, and ultimately to those of humanity itself. It is significant that Singer endows an anti-leftist character named Lapidus with some of the memorable utterances of the novel even though he appears in but a single scene and has no role whatever in the action. Lapidus disturbs the smug humanitarianism of the circle of Jewish leftists gathered at Gina Genendel's by pointing out that they weep bitter tears over every Ivan, every Slav, every oppressed nation of the world, except the Jews. He recounts an experience he had in Siberia that epitomized the self-deceptive masquerade of Jews who seek a secular substitute for the religion they have deserted: " ' . . . I saw a bunch of Jews, with scrawny beards, black eyes—just like mine. At first I thought it was a *minyan* for prayers. But when I heard them babbling in Russian and spouting about the revolution—the S. R.'s, the S. D.'s, Plekhanov, Bogdanov, bombs, assassinations—I started to howl.' "

Lapidus lashes these Jews who, in strict accordance with

socialist doctrine, deny the existence of the Jews as a people. Some deep-seated impulse of treachery leads worldly Jews to deny only to the people from whom they have sprung those human rights that are indivisible from national rights. Bernard Lazare once wrote of emancipated French Jews: "It isn't enough for them to reject any solidarity with their foreign-born brethren; they have also to go charging them with all the evils which their own cowardice engenders. . . . Like all emancipated Jews everywhere, they have also of their own volition broken all ties of solidarity."[6] Lapidus, for his part, is, like Abram, a Zionist who sees no solution to the anomaly of Jewish existence in an increasingly antisemitic Europe except " 'a corner of the world for our own.' "

Lapidus and Abram insistently ask the socialists why Jews should relinquish their nationality in order to assimilate with "humanity." In fact, they argue, if assimilation were successful, it would merge the Jewish people not with all humanity but only with the Polish people (or the German or the Hungarian), so that the division and strife of nations would continue just as before, but the People Israel would disappear from the earth. The Holocaust was to prove that assimilation was impossible in any case. For it was just as Hosea had long before predicted of the faithless of Israel: "She shall run after her lovers, but she shall not overtake them" (Hosea 2:9).

For the mature characters in *The Family Moskat*, Zionism is, as Theodor Herzl once said, "a return to the Jewish people even before it is a return to the Jewish homeland." It is not accidental that Asa's first Zionist utterances in the novel come on the occasion of his return from Switzerland to Tereshpol Minor. Upon entering the synagogue, Asa is overcome by "a heavy odor that seemed . . . to be compounded of candle wax, fast days, and eternity. He stood silent. Here in the dimness everything he had experienced in alien places seemed to be without meaning. Time had flown like an illusion. This was his true home, this was where he belonged. Here was where he would come for refuge when everything else failed." This joy in homecoming seems to depend on religion, yet when

Asa tries to explain his feelings to his grandfather, what he says is that Jews are a people like every other people, and are now "demanding that the nations of the world return the Holy Land to them." The conjunction of the two passages is striking. Very soon there will be no Tereshpol Minor synagogue in which to seek refuge and home when all else fails—as it does—and the Zionist contention that the Jews of Europe are building on sand will be borne out.

It remains for the generation of Asa's children and their friends to translate the desire for a return to the Jewish people into "practical" Zionism. Young Shosha Berman marries an authentic Zionist pioneer named Simon Bendel, who clearly represents the most vital element of the youngest generation of Polish Jews in the novel. Singer's desire to single out Zionism from among the myriad political movements that contend with each other for the loyalties of Polish Jews disaffected from traditional religion is evident in his treatment of Simon and his beleaguered group of Hebrew-speaking agriculturists: "Everyone was against them—the orthodox Jews, the Socialist Bundists, the Communists. But they were not the kind to be frightened off. If the Messiah had not come riding on his ass by now, then it was time to take one's destiny into one's own hands."

It is precisely this desire of Zionism to preempt the tasks reserved for Messiah that provokes the wrath of the orthodox: " 'What's bothering you, rabbi? We are building a Jewish home.' " " 'Except the Lord build the house, they labor in vain that build it.' " This is not a debate, such as may be found in *Satan in Goray*, over the desirability of hastening the arrival of the Messiah by aggravating the evil situation of humanity so that deliverance will come to a generation steeped in degradation. Everybody, apart from the communists, recognizes that in a world dominated by Hitler, this would be a labor of supererogation. Rather, the Zionists take upon themselves the task reserved by religious tradition for the Messiah because they sense that modern antisemitism is not just another form of religious Jew-hatred but the instrument of a scheme to destroy the Jewish people forever.

The entire novel is animated by a tremendous pressure

toward some kind of apocalyptic resolution of the worsening condition of the Jews of Europe. Early in the book, before either of the World Wars has taken place, it seems to the orthodox that things cannot get worse than they are:

> Speakers were thundering that Jews should not wait for Messiah to come, but build the Jewish homeland with their own hands. . . . The truth was that the Jews were being persecuted more and more. Day by day it became harder to earn a living. What would be the end of it all? There was only one hope left— for Messiah to come, to come quickly while there were still a few pious Jews left.

During World War I it seems even more certain to the orthodox that the cup must at last be full. What can be the meaning of the endless suffering of the Jews but that redemption is at hand? " 'Enough! It is time! High time for the Messiah!' " Even the fabric of daily life is interwoven with messianic expectation, so that Adele's delivery pains provoke the remark "Everything is attended by suffering . . . birth . . . Messiah. . . . " With the approach of Hitler, even many of the pious go off to Palestine, complaining about their elders and their God: " 'The old generation knows only one thing: Messiah will come. God knows, he's taking his time.' "

The culminating event of the novel would seem to be precisely the occasion on which Singer, if he wished, could demonstrate the convergence of catastrophe with redemption, Holocaust with rebirth in the homeland. It is the last Passover to be celebrated by the Jews of Warsaw before they and their civilization are buried in universal darkness. The celebration looks backward to the great holiday occasions earlier in the novel, when the spiritually dispersed members of what had formerly been the community of Israel are briefly united with their people and with their best selves; and it also looks forward to the yawning emptiness of the Jewish future in Europe. So insistent is Singer on the irresistibility of Jewish fate that for this Passover celebration he goes to the trouble of recalling, from Palestine as well as America, those characters who have already emigrated, despite the fact that all the Jews still resident in Poland "were possessed of the same thought: to be helped to get out of Poland while there was still time."

   The Passover, described in great, loving detail by Singer, is the novel's most beautiful and most terrible occasion. Not only does it summon up and reenforce the memory of past holidays; it is a holiday on which the original redemption of the Jews from bondage and deliverance to their promised land is commemorated and the hope of their imminent salvation and return to the ancestral homeland is more immediate than at any other time of the year. In a voice broken with weeping, Pinnie Moskat recites: " 'And it is this same promise which has been the support of our ancestors and of us, for in every generation our enemies have arisen to annihilate us, but the Most Holy, blessed be He, has delivered us out of their hands. . . . ' " From the point of view of Jewish religion, Hitler is only the latest repetition of the Amaleks who have plagued the Jews throughout their existence. Yet many at the seder table wonder to themselves: "Would a miracle happen this time too? In a year from now would Jews be able again to sit down and observe the Passover? Or, God forbid, would the new Haman finish them off?"

   The Passover service traditionally concludes with the exclamation "Next Year in Jerusalem!" If Singer wished to see in the qualified triumph of Zionism a kind of redemption for which the Holocaust had been a horrible price, or in the State of Israel a realization of the messianic expectations of so many of his Holocaust victims, here exactly would be the point for him to reveal his conviction. But he does nothing of the kind. Instead, he pointedly omits any mention of "Next Year in Jerusalem!" in his description of the seder and concludes with Pinnie's question: " 'These unleavened cakes, why do we eat them?' " Even though the novel treats Zionism sympathetically, and in this very chapter we are told that Asa's son David is observing the holiday in Palestine with his fellow pioneers, Singer will not endorse historicist views of the Holocaust as the labor pains of national rebirth or religious views of it as the price of redemption. Rather, he wants above all to convey the sense that for the Jews of Europe the end was at hand, and in a more absolute sense than any that could have been conceived by either orthodox or nationalist Jews. When Abram the Zionist tries to console the gloomy Asa by

remarking that " 'the end of the world hasn't come yet,' "
Asa replies that " 'the end of our world *has* come.' " The
final scene of the English version of the novel[7] allows no
hint of apocalypse in this disaster, no glimpse of a
redemption beyond the catastrophe.

In the deepest sense, then, the Zionists of *The Family
Moskat* who flee to Palestine are as homeless, as desperate
for refuge, as Herman Broder of *Enemies* in the United
States. For Singer, the ultimate refuge is in the instruments
of Jewish spirituality. For him, "the two thousand years of
exile have not been a dark passage into nowhere but a grand
experiment in upholding a people only on spiritual values.
Even though we have attained the land we longed
for . . . this experiment is far from being concluded."[8] At
the end of *The Manor*, Calman Jacoby finds a refuge from
the acrid dissolvents of Polish Jewry not in the land but in
the spirit of his ancestors, as embodied in his shelves of
sacred books that reunite him with past generations. "The
Hebrew letters were steeped in holiness, in eternity. They
seemed to unite him with the patriarchs, with Joshua,
Gamaliel, Eliezer, and with Hillel the Ancient. . . . Among
these shelves of sacred books, Calman felt protected."
Calman understands, though he cannot conceptualize, the
truth that all those secularizing and reformist movements
within the Jewish community that sought to confer upon
the Jews emancipation and human rights had in fact
deprived them of their freedom and their humanity. To be
human was to stand where one's ancestors had stood,
rooted in the language and laws and customs that were a
permanent affront to evolutionism and progressivism.

For the survivors of the Holocaust, Jewish books become
not only the means of remaining human by returning
into the buried life of one's ancestors; they become the
instrument for the resurrection of the dead. As another
character, Herman Gombiner in the story called "The
Letter Writer," says: "The spirit cannot be burned, gassed,
hanged, shot. Six million souls must exist somewhere."
Gombiner, during an illness, goes in search of his lost
relatives, and his quest leads him, via Canal Street in New

York City, into an underworld charnel-house, where he meets a gravedigger tending the bones. " 'How,' "asks Herman, " 'can anyone live here?' " " 'Who would want such a livelihood?' " The answer, of course, is that this is where Singer has chosen to live.

We can see this very clearly in one of his supernatural tales called "The Last Demon." Of the many stories in which Singer uses a first-person narrator who bears marked resemblances to the author, none comes so close to representing the author's inner relationship to his own work as this one. The narrator of the tale tells of his plight as the last remaining demon, whose occupation is gone because man himself has become a demon: to proselytize for evil in these times would be carrying coals to Newcastle. Like Singer himself, the last demon has been deprived of his subject, the Jews of Eastern Europe. "I've seen it all," he says, "the destruction of Tishevitz, the destruction of Poland. There are no more Jews, no more demons. . . . The community was slaughtered, the holy books burned, the cemetery desecrated." Like Singer, the last demon attempts to speak as if history had *not* destroyed his subject and as if he could defy time: "I speak in the present tense as for me time stands still." Like Singer, the last demon knows, or thinks he knows, that there is no judge and no judgment, and that to the generation that has indeed succeeded in becoming wholly guilty the only Messiah that will come is death: "The generation is already guilty seven times over, but Messiah does not come. To whom should he come? Messiah did not come for the Jews, so the Jews went to Messiah." Like Singer, finally, the demon must sustain himself on dust and ashes and Yiddish books. "I found a Yiddish storybook between two broken barrels in the house which once belonged to Velvel the Barrelmaker. I sit there, the last of the demons. I eat dust. . . . The style of the book is . . . Sabbath pudding cooked in pig's fat: blasphemy rolled in piety. The moral of the book is: neither judge, nor judgment. But nevertheless the letters are Jewish. . . . I suck on the letters and feed myself. . . . Yes, as long as a single volume remains, I have something to sustain me."

The attempt to resurrect the shattered remnant of Jewish life in Israel, one of the most extraordinary instances of national rebirth in history, one of the outstanding examples of Jewish defiance of history, ultimately plays but a minor part in the great body of Singer's fiction. Rather, he chooses to make of literature itself the instrument for preserving the memory, and resurrecting the souls, of the dead. The literature upon which this massive responsibility devolves is no longer a sacred one, nor is it written in Hebrew, the traditional sacred tongue but also a language that, in Singer's view, is now "becoming more and more worldly."[9] Yet, through an ironic reversal of the traditional relationship between Hebrew and Yiddish, the language of the majority of the victims of the Holocaust becomes for Singer the *loshen khoydesh*, the holy tongue of the Jewish people. "The deader the language," Singer has said, "the more alive is the ghost. Ghosts love Yiddish, and, as far as I know, they all speak it. . . . I not only believe in ghosts but also in resurrection. I am sure that millions of Yiddish-speaking corpses will rise from their graves one day, and their first question will be: Is there any new book in Yiddish read? For them Yiddish will not be dead." And, we are implicitly invited to add, because of Yiddish they will not be dead. In his literary character, which is to say in his subject and language, Singer has made himself into a splendid anachronism whose flourishing existence defies the death-sentence imposed upon the Jewish people in the nineteenth century and nearly carried out in the twentieth.

1.   *Peretz*, trans. and ed. Sol Liptzin (New York: YIVO, 1947), p. 18.

2.   I. B. Singer and Irving Howe, "Yiddish Tradition vs. Jewish Tradition: A Dialogue," *Midstream* 19 (June/July 1973):34.

3.   Mary Ellmann, "The Piety of Things in *The Manor*," in *The Achievement of Isaac Bashevis Singer*, ed. Marcia Allentuck (Carbondale: Southern Illinois University Press, 1969).

4.   Marshall Breger and Bob Barnhart, "A Conversation with Isaac Bashevis Singer," in *Critical Views of Isaac Bashevis Singer*, ed. Irving Malin (New York: New York University Press, 1969), p. 42.

5.   David M. Andersen, "Isaac Bashevis Singer: Conversation in California," *Modern Fiction Studies* 16 (Winter 1970-71):430.

6. Bernard Lazare, *Job's Dungheap* (New York, 1948), p. 97.

7. Irving Saposnik, in a vigorous and intelligent (although, in my view, ultimately mistaken) article entitled "Translating *The Family Moskat*," *Yiddish* 1 (Fall 1973): 26–37, has compared the differing implications of the English and Yiddish endings of the novel. He attaches great importance to the fact that the closing pages of the original, Yiddish version depict a group of Zionists escaping from Warsaw.

8. "Yiddish, The Language of Exile," *Judaica Book News*, Spring/Summer 1976, p. 27.

9. Ibid.

The twentieth-century ruins of that world to which so many Jews gave their admiration and devotion between, say, 1789 and 1933 (the date of Hitler's coming to power), has grown sick of the ideals Israel asks it to respect. These ideals were knocked to the ground by Fascist Italy, by Russia, and by Germany. The Holocaust may even be seen as a deliberate lesson or project in philosophical redefinition: "You religious and enlightened people, you Christians, Jews, and Humanists, you believers in freedom, dignity, and enlightenment—you think that you know what a human being is. We will show you what he is, and what you are. Look at our camps and crematoria and see if you can bring your hearts to care about these millions." And it is obvious that the humanistic civilized moral imagination is inadequate. Confronted with such a "metaphysical" demonstration, it despairs and declines from despair into lethargy and sleep.—Saul Bellow, To Jerusalem and Back (1976)

chapter 6

Saul Bellow: A Jewish Farewell
To the Enlightenment

From the beginning of his career as a novelist, Saul Bellow has been impelled by a powerful sense of the inadequacy of Enlightenment principles and categories to encompass and interpret modern experience, particularly the experience of the Holocaust. His first novel, *Dangling Man* (1944), was set in 1942-43. Its hero, a young man named Joseph who is awaiting his induction into the U.S. Army, has been working on a series of biographical essays about the philosophers of the Enlightenment. He was "in the midst of one on Diderot" when he received his draft notice and "began to dangle." That his belief in the dispensation according to the gospel of the Rights of Man had already begun to wane is evident in his depiction of a Communist friend named Jimmy Burns who had dreamt of "becoming an American Robespierre" and in his account of his own disillusionment with the Communist party, the modern expositor of the universal rights of mankind. The Communists, he had believed, were devoted to "the Race, *le genre humain.*" But by the time he left the party, he "realized that any hospital nurse did more with one bedpan for *le genre humain* than they did with their entire organization." Joseph's study of the Enlightenment has not prepared him for the carnage that is taking place on the continent of Europe, to which he will soon be transported. "We do not flinch at seeing all these lives struck out; nor would those who were killed have suffered any more for us, if we, not they, had been the victims. I do not like to think what we are governed by. I do not like to think about it. It is not easy work, and it is not safe. Its kindest revelation is that our senses and our imaginations are somehow incompetent."

The hero of *Mr. Sammler's Planet* (1970) knows conclusively what young Joseph could only guess at—that the Holocaust had exploded forever the Enlightenment conception of man as naturally good, in rational control of his mental and physical universe, and potentially able to use that control to create a heavenly city on earth. Like Joseph, Artur Sammler had once been a child of the Enlightenment and had devoted himself to a scholarly work on one of the great expositors of Enlightenment principles, H. G. Wells, whom he had known very well during his years in Bloomsbury. Indeed, before the Holocaust, Wells had been the object of his life's work. Wells had based his utopian ideas for a renovated world on the application of scientific principles to the enlargement of human life: "the building of a planned, orderly, and beautiful world society." But Wells himself, basing all his hopes on the naturalism of Enlightenment epistemology, was not prepared to reckon with those subterranean forces that erupted in modern Europe. Thus Sammler, in his post-Holocaust incarnation, spends all his time in the Forty-second Street Library reading the mystical Meister Eckhardt when everybody supposes him to be working on his memoir of Wells. For he knows that "poor Wells, the natural teacher, the sex emancipator, the explainer, the humane blesser of mankind, could in the end only blast and curse everyone." Sammler does say, by way of extenuation, that Wells "wrote such things in his final sickness, horribly depressed by World War II."

Unless one recognizes the extent to which, in Bellow's mind, the Holocaust functions as a metaphysical refutation of Enlightenment assumptions, he will not easily find the center of this novel. Even so acute an observer of Bellow's work as Irving Howe has written of this book: "Lively-odd figures, brilliantly managed incidents—but what does it all come to? That, until the very last paragraph, is the question one keeps asking about *Mr. Sammler's Planet*."[1] Much of the book does seem intent on merely conveying to us the touch and tone of life in upper Manhattan, the way people and things look and sound, the kinds of ideas (or what the poverty of the English language compels us to call such) favored by the semi-educated New York intelligentsia, whose conversation is "often nothing but the repetition of liberal principles" couched in the terminology of the *New York Times.*

Bellow has, of course, throughout his career studied the desperate and highly cerebral forms that personal existence takes in large American cities like Chicago and New York. But his characters generally have a sense of the relation between their own life and that of the old world. Some of them suppose this world and its inhabitants to have been greater, more heroic, than the shrunken version of mankind that inhabits American cities. Others, however, like Einhorn in *The Adventures of Augie March* (1953), have a more accurate sense of the relation between Europe and America:

> There is some kind of advantage in the roughness of a place like Chicago, of not having any illusions either. Whereas in all the great capitals of the world there's some reason to think humanity is very different. All that ancient culture and those beautiful works of art right out in public, by Michelangelo and Christopher Wren, and those ceremonies, like trooping the color at the Horse Guards' parade or burying a great man in the Pantheon over in Paris. You see those marvelous things and you think that everything savage belongs to the past. So you think. And then you have another think, and you see that after they rescued women from the coal mines, or pulled down the Bastille and got rid of Star Chambers and *lettres de cachet,* ran out the Jesuits, increased education, and built hospitals and spread courtesy and politeness, they have five or six years of war and revolutions and kill off twenty million people.

This knowledge of death is one of the few certain benefits that an experience of Europe gives to those Jews who survive it. What separates Artur Sammler from the American Jews who surround him in New York (and later unites him with the Israeli Jews who are otherwise so foreign to him) is a knowledge of what death is. By a kind of miracle, he had been saved from the Holocaust that engulfed everyone around him, saved not because he had any special merit or special knowledge of how to survive— "had the war lasted a few months more, he would have died like the rest"—but because he has been given a duty, an assignment: namely, to condense for others some essence of experience available only to those who have returned from the dead. *Mr. Sammler's Planet* is precisely an attempt to imagine and capture this essence.

The novel begins with an account and discussion of two crimes, two criminals, two forms of "explanation" (a pejorative word throughout the book) for their acts. Since the two crimes, one the massive one of Adolf Eichmann in transporting Jews to the gas chambers, the other that of a black pickpocket in Manhattan who also assaults Sammler, are recalled again and again throughout the book, it seems reasonable to suppose that in the relation between them lies at least a hint of the novel's significance.

The subject of the Holocaust is explicitly introduced into the novel by means of a fierce attack by the novel's protagonist on Hannah Arendt's thesis (set forth in her book of 1963)[2] that Eichmann was the most ordinary of men, a sort of cliché endowed with arms, legs, and a mouth, and that the perpetrators of the unspeakable evil of the death camps were in general not great criminals but merely the petty bureaucrats everywhere produced in modern times by the principle of division of labor. Up until this point in the novel, we have learned that Mr. Sammler, who is over seventy, was in Poland during the war, that in 1940 he had lost his wife and lost an eye, and that in 1947 he and his daughter Shula had been located by relatives in a D.P. camp in Salzburg and brought to the United States by his nephew Elya Gruner, an abiding presence in the novel. Hannah Arendt's thesis about the "banality of evil" that prevailed in Nazi Germany is proposed to Sammler by his niece, Margotte.

Although Sammler has long since recognized the futility of arguing with his niece, his reply is passionate rather than perfunctory. Hannah Arendt, he says, has been duped, for the banality that she purports to discover in these murderers and their evil deeds was merely camouflage. " 'What better way to get the curse out of murder than to make it look ordinary, boring, or trite?' " Intellectuals with literary training expect every wicked hero to be like Richard

III, who steps to the front of the stage announcing "I am determined to be a villain." The Nazis, Sammler contends, never forgot their old, normal knowledge of what is meant by murder. " 'That is very old human knowledge. The best and purest human beings, from the beginning of time, have understood that life is sacred. To defy that old understanding is not banality. There was a conspiracy against the sacredness of life.' " No one, he maintains, can believe that the abolition of conscience is a trivial or banal matter unless she believes that human life itself is trivial. Hannah Arendt stands accused of " 'making use of a tragic history to promote the foolish ideas of Weimar intellectuals.' "[3]

To what uses, then, Bellow is asking, should that "tragic history" be put? The novel has already raised, in connection with a much smaller crime, the question of whether the notion that we learn things from suffering is anything more than cant. The problem of crime is much in Sammler's mind when we first meet him because he has been observing a black pickpocket regularly at work on the Riverside Drive bus and has made a futile effort to interest police in the matter. But in liberal and enlightened New York, interest in such criminals, he recognizes, comes mainly from people like his young relative, Angela Gruner, who is attracted by "the romance of the outlaw" and sends her rich father's money to defense funds for black murderers and rapists. Angela, like Margotte and Shula and several others in the novel, holds the liberal view that everyone is guilty of a crime except the person who has actually committed it. Their typical concern is not with that abstraction called justice or with upholding the honor of the victim, but with such "explanatory" questions as: "Who was this black? What were his origins, his class or racial attitudes, his psychological views, his true emotions, his aesthetic, his political ideas?"

Sammler himself is repelled by the notion that style, art, and meaning attach to criminals and inhere in their crimes. He recognizes that modern artists, like liberal intellectuals, respond to a sense of affinity between themselves and the criminal classes. Thus it is no accident that the most memorable moment in *Crime and Punishment* is the instant when Raskolnikov crushes the old woman's head with an ax. "Horror, crime, murder, did vivify all the phenomena, the most ordinary details of experience. In evil as in art there was illumination." His daughter stoutly declares, " 'For the creative there are no crimes.' " But was there, wonders Sammler, any crime or (significant alteration) sin that was not committed for the highest motives? "Was there any sinner who did not sin *pro bono publico*? So great was the evil of helplessness, and so immense the liberal spirit of explanation." Since the Enlightenment, there had been a tremendous attention paid to the "significance" of prisons, yet (perhaps paradoxically, perhaps as the working out of inner logic) "where liberty had been promised most, they had the biggest, worst prisons."

The liberalism whose inanities are mocked throughout *Mr. Sammler's Planet* has been for over a century the most widely embraced ideology of Western intellectuals. As long ago as 1864, John Henry Newman had written that "the Liberalism which gives a colour to society now, is very different from that character of thought which bore the name thirty or forty years ago. Now it is scarcely a party: it is the educated lay world."[4] But liberalism shares with other offspring of the Enlightenment—egalitarianism, socialism, communism—certain assumptions about the world, the mind, and society that are Bellow's ultimate targets: naturalism, monism, relativism, worship of Mankind (rather than God), social utopianism, and revolutionism. The fact that liberals, socialists, and communists are so often at each others' throats does not blind Bellow to the fact that they have a common ancestor, for he is keenly aware of the implications of the remark of Robespierre's henchman St. Just, who, when asked to define the Revolution, said that it was the destruction of whatever the Revolution was not. Thus a recent critic of the Enlightenment shrewdly observes that "enlighteners have spent the past two centuries seeking out what they oppose, and, in quiet times, studying ways to turn the instruments of attack into philosophies in order to discover what it is they favor."[5]

Mr. Sammler's Manhattan is one of the great modern temples of Enlightenment worship. There he is daily witness to "the increasing triumph of Enlightenment—Liberty, Fraternity, Equality, Adultery! Enlightenment, universal education, universal suffrage, the rights of the majority acknowledged . . . , the rights of women, the rights of children, the rights of criminals. . . ." If the Enlightenment is indeed an exploded dream, news of the fact has not yet reached to New York, has not reached either to the "mental masses" or to "the worst enemies of civilization . . . its petted intellectuals who attacked it at its weakest moments—attacked it in the name of proletarian revolution, in the name of reason, and in the name of irrationality." Having set out to abolish the ancient privileges of aristocracy, the Enlightenment succeeded only in democratizing and universalizing them, so that now virtually nobody was willing to leave the earth unsatiated. Carlyle, one of the earliest critics of the Enlightenment world-view, had predicted that "the whole Finance Ministers and Upholsterers and Confectioners of modern Europe" could not contrive to make one shoeblack happy, and declared that *the Fraction of Life can be increased in value not so much by increasing your Numerator as by lessening your Denominator.*[6] The crises of the modern world were proving him right. Everywhere he looks Sammler sees "limitless demand—insatiability . . . Non-negotiable. Recognizing no scarcity of supply in any human department. Enlightenment? Marvelous! But out of hand, wasn't it?"

There follows upon these reflections, and by way of illustration of their validity, one of the most spectacular incidents of the novel, and one in which the athletic energy of Bellow's prose and imagination is most intense. Sammler has been persuaded by a young friend named Lionel Feffer to lecture at Columbia University on his recollections of English intellectual life in the thirties, which he had experienced firsthand during his residence in Bloomsbury. All the students in the audience are humorless, most are bored, and some are in an ugly mood to start with because Feffer has misled them into thinking they are going to hear a lecture on "Sorel and Modern Violence." (Feffer later justifies his chicanery by saying that the occasion was, after all, a benefit for black children.) Sammler quickly offends the revolutionary pieties of the students by quoting George Orwell's remark that British radicals were comfortably protected by the Royal Navy. One member of the audience, particularly sensitive to anything that calls into question the perfections of Communism, regales Sammler with the sexual-excremental rhetoric of left-wing militancy. " 'That's a lot of shit. . . . Orwell was a fink. He was a sick counterrevolutionary. It's a good thing he died when he did. And what you are saying is shit.' Turning to the audience, extending violent arms and raising his palms like a Greek dancer, he said, 'Why do you listen to this effete old shit? What has he got to tell you? His balls are dry. He's dead. He can't come.' " This, Sammler reflects as he is bundled out of the auditorium, is just the way it was in the Weimar Republic. The official bastions of sweetness and light yielded most eagerly to their seeming opposites, irrationality and barbarism. Instead of routing the demons from their entrenched strongholds, Enlightenment and rationalism invite them into the sanctuary. It is only later that Sammler learns that his assailant was " 'a poor man's Jean Genet' " who believed in the achievement of sainthood through murder and homosexuality. This, too, is a legacy from Voltaire and Rousseau, for " 'the Marquis de Sade in his crazy way was an Enlightenment philosophe.' "

No sooner has Sammler escaped from what Matthew Arnold, surveying another university, once called "our young barbarians all at play,"[7] than he is subjected to another version of the *argumentum ab genitalibus*. The pickpocket, noticing that Sammler has observed him, follows the old man into the lobby of his building and forces him to contemplate his exposed and brandished penis. No warning or threat, or indeed speech of any kind, is deemed necessary by the black man. He, like the Columbia students, has invoked the irrefutable modern argument. "Then it was returned to the trousers. *Quod erat demonstrandum.*" When he recovers sufficiently from the shock of this experience,

Sammler views it as the existential realization of the philosophy of naturalism, the philosophical doctrine that reached full flowering in the Enlightenment, whose luminaries proclaimed that there is only one order of being, that nothing in reality has a supernatural significance, and that miracles are impossible. To speak, as Spinoza and later Voltaire had done, of a God who was indistinguishable from nature was to involve oneself in a contradiction and to lead others astray in the direction of idolatry. "Make Nature your God, elevate creatureliness, and you can count on gross results."

Sammler had not always known this. But since the Holocaust, since his return from the grave, he cared only for the spirit, for God. He wished to be "a soul released from Nature." Naturalism not only gave a false account of the world, it was incompatible with Judaism, a religion in which the prohibition against idolatry is primary. Sammler senses this during his trying conversations with his oversexed young relative Angela Gruner, the daughter of Elya. Angela is another of the novel's many characters caught up by the sexual madness overwhelming the Western world. She tirelessly regales poor Sammler with tales of her sexual exploits, and succeeds only in reminding him that the propensity of numerous Jews for pagan idol-worship, for playing the harlot, as Jeremiah (3:1) says, with many lovers, cannot alter the fact that the Torah forbids worship of stocks and stones. "Somewhere he doubted the fitness of these Jews for this erotic Roman voodoo primitivism. He questioned whether release from long Jewish mental discipline, hereditary training in lawful control, was obtainable upon individual application." Typical of Angela's shallowness is her merely naturalistic conception of what it means to be human. She cannot understand why Sammler should praise her dying father for being a man. " 'I thought everybody was born human,' " she says. But Sammler replies, " 'It's not a natural gift at all. Only the capacity is natural.' " Sammler recognizes clearly that, as his unloved Hannah Arendt liked to point out, "man's 'nature' is only 'human' insofar as it opens up to

man the possibility of becoming something highly un-
natural, that is, a man."[8]

Having barely survived the day's encounters with the
revolution in its various guises, Sammler returns home to
find what looks like a providential message in the form of a
manuscript, filched by his daughter from an Indian
professor at Columbia, entitled *The Future of the Moon*. Its
first sentence leaps out at Sammler: "How long will this
earth remain the only home of Man?" To what looks very
like a hint from a realm beyond human experience,
Sammler responds with alacrity. "How long? Oh, Lord, you
bet! Wasn't it the time—the very hour to go? For every
purpose under heaven. A time to gather stones together, a
time to cast away stones. Considering the earth itself not as
a stone cast but as something to cast oneself from—to be
divested of. To blow this great blue, white, green planet, or
to be blown from it."

Before Sammler can think very deeply about the
implications of Dr. Lal's plans for colonizing the moon, his
visit to his dying nephew Elya carries his mind back to a
world that had indeed been a different planet: wartime
Poland. At first he thinks of his period of hiding in the
mausoleum of a family called Mezvinski. During a whole
summer and part of autumn, he had sought metaphysical
meanings—the very meanings that according to naturalism and monism do not exist—in a piece of straw, a
spider thread, a beetle, or a sparrow. But there was either no
meaning or else a meaning impossible to live with. Viewed
in retrospect, his residence in the mausoleum foreshadowed
a kind of living death that was to be his only future. The
yellow light of Polish summer that filtered through the
mausoleum door is no different from the light penetrating
his Manhattan apartment now; it is a light that does not
measure growth or change but, rather, accompanies
"endless literal hours in which one is internally eaten up.
Eaten because coherence is lacking. Perhaps as a punishment for having failed to find coherence."

We are nearly a third of the way into the novel before
Bellow reveals to us the experiences that have made Artur

Sammler repudiate both the premises and hopes of the Enlightenment. The reason why coherence and sacredness have been eluding Sammler since he entered the mausoleum, as well as the reason why he continues to pursue nothing but them, is revealed in his recollection of the open-air killing center to which he and his wife had been taken:

> Yes, go and find it [sacredness] when everyone is murdering everyone. When Antonina was murdered. When he himself underwent murder beside her. When he and sixty or seventy others, all stripped naked and having dug their own grave, were fired upon and fell in. Bodies upon his own body. Crushing. His dead wife nearby somewhere. Struggling out much later from the weight of corpses, crawling out of the loose soil. Scraping on his belly. Hiding in a shed. Finding a rag to wear. Lying in the woods many days.

This is the bedrock of Sammler's experience, the anchor of his imagination and intellect. The immediacy of his recollection of the death camps restrains him from those "fantasies of vaulting into higher states" that are the characteristic delusion of utopians and revolutionaries.

Having already returned from a different planet, Sammler approaches with caution and skepticism schemes to transport man to still another one, whether through science or revolution. In modern intellectual circles, "if your theme was social justice and your ideas were radical you were rewarded by wealth, fame, and influence." But Sammler cannot forget that Hitler was the century's most daring and successful revolutionary, and one whose incorporation of the word *socialism* in his public program was no accident. Neither can it be merely coincidental that every revolution that followed upon the French model ended up in the hands of murderers. This, in fact, was what the second term of the Enlightenment triad—equality—meant. You redistributed the aristocratic privilege of murder among the people and persuaded them (with the help of such modern French enlighteners as Jean-Paul Sartre) that they could recover or establish their identity by killing and thus becoming equal to the greatest. "What did equality mean? Did it mean all men were friends and brothers? No, it meant that all belonged to the elite. Killing was an ancient privilege. This was why revolutions plunged into blood. Guillotines? Terror? Only a beginning—nothing." Under the guise of "rights," the privileges of barbarism were doled out to the populace.

It was true that the planet did seem more and more intolerable, madness and poison more and more ubiquitous. But would escape to other worlds help much? Was it really plausible to believe with Dr. Lal that " 'access to central data mechanisms may foster a new Adam' "? Sammler has learned the folly of supposing that every social shortcoming is a sickness capable of remedy. "Nonsense. Change Sin to Sickness, a change of words . . . , and then enlightened doctors would stamp the sickness out." When this failed, the intellectuals who had preempted the privileges once reserved for God despaired of man altogether and "their man-disappointed minds" sought refuge in madness or in utopias of various kinds. Utopianism, that search for the heavenly city on earth that characterized the *philosophes*, is for Sammler and his creator invariably a sign not of love but of hatred for humanity. "Always a certain despair underlining pleasure, death seated inside the health-capsule, steering it, and darkness winking at you from the golden utopian sun." Dr. Lal "must have been sick of earth to begin with if he had such expectations of the moon." Wells, we recall, who envisioned the heavenly city *on* earth, "could in the end only blast and curse everyone." Sammler, by no means satisfied with present social arrangements, and very much inclined to think that New York is a modern re-creation of Sodom and Gomorrah, nevertheless accepts the fact that anomalies and inequities are necessary accompaniments of the human condition, evils only to be removed by a much greater evil. "When he tried to imagine a just social order, he could not do it. A noncorrupt society? He could not do that either. There were no revolutions that he could remember which had not been made for justice, freedom, and pure goodness. Their last state was always more nihilistic than the first."

Sammler, unlike the utopian improvers and friends of the species who surround him, recognizes that the human mind, if it is ever to rise into the skies and conquer new worlds, must begin with the resolve to stoop to the horrors that already have existed, and see the worst of them in their stubborn, maniacal permanence. " 'My travels,' he says, 'are over. . . . I seem to be a depth man rather than a height man.' " This is why, no matter how deeply buried within his subconscious life, the experience of the Holocaust keeps asserting itself as the chief determinant of what life is left to Sammler after twice escaping his doom. Half-way through the novel, we learn the details of his journey to the underworld of the killing centers and even of his own temporary marriage with the god of darkness who ruled there. We learn that after he escaped from under the mountain of corpses in the mass grave, Sammler had become something other than the victim, had shed that role to which Jewish history in Europe traditionally assigned him. He became a partisan in the Zamosht forest, where he and other starving men chewed at roots and grasses to stay alive, and also exploded bridges, unseated rails, and killed German stragglers in the dark of night. In the forest, he had discovered a German soldier and twice shot the man through the head as he pleaded for mercy and told Sammler he had children. Sammler had then stood at the place of last resort in the human soul, a place to which the appeal from another human being cannot reach. More important, he had shut his ears to the tempting voice of Jewish ethical "idealism" that congratulated the Jew for two thousand years of not picking up the gun (the gun that, of course, he had no chance to decline because it was never available to him). He admits to himself that he even derived pleasure and joy from killing the German. Indeed, his own survival— spiritual, not merely physical—was contingent on this act of violence. "You would call it a dark action? On the contrary, it was also a bright one. It was mainly bright. When he fired his gun, Sammler, himself nearly a corpse, burst into life. Freezing in Zamosht Forest, he had often dreamed of being near a fire. Well, this was more sumptuous than fire. His heart felt lined with brilliant, rapturous satin."

All this must be kept in mind as the necessary

background for understanding Sammler's reaction, in May 1967, to the news that Nasser had closed the Straits of Tiran and Arab armies were encircling Israel while announcing their intention to reduce the country to sandy wastes. For Sammler, this is a historical repetition that confirms the permanence of evil and therefore, by logical necessity, the precariousness of Jewish life. Sammler has not only seen but experienced it all before: "For the second time in twenty-five years the same people were threatened by extermination: the so-called powers letting things drift toward disaster; men armed for a massacre." In such circumstances, Sammler could not merely sit in New York reading the world press and listening to his young relatives—like the pro-Arab Wallace Gruner—of the leftist persuasion "explaining" the psychological necessity which drove the Arabs to war. He gets himself an assignment as a journalist so that he may be *there*, in Israel, "to send reports, to do something, perhaps to die in the massacre."

This reaction by Sammler, who is no Zionist and has not been much of a Jew either, can be explained only by what he has learned from the Holocaust. Sammler, twice excused from death, was "sent back again to the end of the line" so that he might distill for others, "in a Testament," the essence of experience. Up until the age of forty, he had been "simply an Anglophile intellectual Polish Jew and person of culture—relatively useless." But that was before he was arrested, struck in the eye by a gun butt, and thrown into a mass grave. Forever after, he was a one-eyed man: " 'Of course, since Poland, nineteen thirty-nine, my judgments are different. Altered. Like my eyesight.' " John Stuart Mill once said, figuratively, that he had "a large tolerance for one-eyed men, provided their one eye is a penetrating one: if they saw more, they probably would not see so keenly. . . ."[9] Sammler's experience may have blinded him to certain possibilities of human life, to visions of new worlds and fresh beginnings, but it has enabled him to penetrate to a level of reality that will remain forever hidden from a new generation of "Bohemian adolescents, narcotized, beflowered, and 'whole.' " Sammler recognizes that cant may lurk in the idea of learning through suffering, and is capable of much irony toward the notion that the Holocaust was a rich and rewarding educational experience—"I did not want to fall into the Grand Canyon. Nice not to have died? Nicer not to have fallen in. Too many inside things were ruptured. To some people, true enough, experience seemed wealth. Misery worth a lot. Horror a fortune." Nevertheless, Sammler does believe that he has been preserved for the completion of some unfinished business, which is connected with what he has experienced and learned during the Holocaust.

It is no accident that at the one point in the book where Sammler seems in danger of forgetting this experience and its lessons, he is reminded of them by his half-mad Israeli son-in-law, Eisen. Late in the novel, Sammler, racing to the hospital to see the dying Gruner, sees his old persecutor, the black pickpocket, thrashing Lionel Feffer, whose boundless liberal curiosity about criminals had led him to the imprudent act of photographing the pickpocket at work. A large crowd watches the action, but—after the accepted fashion of New Yorkers—does nothing to interfere to save Feffer. The seventy-two-year-old Sammler, frustrated by his feebleness, spots Eisen in the crowd and pleads with this powerful man (a foundry worker) to intervene. Finally, after some minutes, he stirs Eisen into action, violent and potent action. Eisen pounds the black man with blow after blow, until Sammler begs him to desist from what a moment before he had begged him to do. " 'You'll murder him. Do you want to beat out his brains? . . . I didn't say to hit him at all. You're crazy, Eisen, crazy enough to murder him.' " But the retort of this Israeli is devastating to Sammler because it wrenches him back to the painful truth he had learned in the Holocaust and remembered at the time of the Six-Day War. " 'You can't hit a man like this just once. When you hit him you must really hit him. Otherwise he'll kill you. You know. We both fought in the war. You were a Partisan. You had a gun. So don't you know?' " Josephine Knopp, in a very intelligent essay on Bellow, argues that Sammler's wish to save the pickpocket from Eisen's blows shows his moral evolution since he killed the German soldier.[10] I think that, on the contrary, Eisen's retort recalls Sammler to awareness of the hard choices of survival and explains why Sammler's identification with Israel extends beyond May 1967 when she was the potential victim of a massacre to June 1967 when she had won a decisive victory over those would have killed her if she had not.

Ten years after the Six-Day War, Saul Bellow, writing from Israel, reminded his readers that "the Jews, because they are Jews, have never been able to take the right to live as a natural right."[11] The reason why Sammler should identify himself with Israel at all is that the Holocaust had proved to him that the Enlightenment's conception of natural, human rights would, in time of crisis, do nothing to save those Jews who did not have national rights as well. This becomes clear during Sammler's great aria of the novel, his confession of faith delivered (after some coaxing) to Shula, Margotte, and Dr. Lal, who have insisted on hearing his "views" on life in general. Skeptical, as always, of "explanations," he prefers to convey his idea of modern history through the story—a true one—of Chaim Rumkowski, the mad Jewish king of the Lodz ghetto. This failed businessman, " 'a noisy individual, corrupt, director of an orphanage, . . . a bad actor, a distasteful fun-figure in the Jewish community,' " was installed by the Nazis as *Judenältester* (senior Jew) of the ghetto. While the Nazis carried on their customary depredations, Rumkowski was enabled to flourish as a king. He had his court, printed money and stamps carrying his picture, royal robes, pageants and plays in his honor; and he enforced a reign of terror over his own people.

Sammler returns obsessively in his thoughts and conversation to the subject of the theatrical forms that the striving for personal definition has taken ever since the Enlightenment and the French Revolution "liberated" men from their inherited identities into individuality. The theatricality of the French Revolution itself, the subject of a number of books,[12] was the earliest indication of the desperate, individual forms that spiritual striving would take in the new era. No sooner were men freed and enjoined to define themselves instead of accepting a preimposed identity than they lost themselves and took, in consequence, to play-acting. The reason why this should have been so was given by one of the earliest critics of the Enlightenment and the French Revolution, Edmund Burke: "We are afraid," he wrote, "to put men to live and trade each on his own private stock of reason; because we suspect that this stock in each man is small, and that the individuals would do better to avail themselves of the general bank and capital of nations, and of ages."[13]

The Nazis understood that the well-known desire of certain Jews to become distinguished "individuals" in non-Jewish society could be put to German advantage. Sammler's choice of Rumkowski, a Jew, as the extreme version of the hopeless search for noble individuality affords a striking insight into the link between antisemitism and the psychic development of post-Enlightenment Europe. Sammler, liberated—though at a terrible price—from liberalism and relativism, declares that " 'individualism is of no interest whatever if it does not extend truth.' " But to many of the Jews of the nineteenth century, who no longer believed in truth, individualism offered the greater temptation of "emancipation" through the granting of equality and human rights. Both proved to be illusory and to involve Jews in yet greater dangers than those from which their seeming liberators promised to free them.

In her study of antisemitism, Hannah Arendt pointed out that once equality is declared individuals and groups actually become more unequal than they had ever been before because it is more difficult to understand and explain why, with equal conditions, differences should exist between people. This was especially the case with the Jews, who first gained equality with the triumph of the French Revolution, and yet continued to be "different" from the rest of society. In consequence, those Jews who entered gentile society—whether as pariahs or as parvenus—were looked upon as actors, admitted and admired, yet denied and feared. [14] Enlightened Europe had opened society's doors to certain Jews, but by the Nazi era, " 'the door had been shut against these Jews: they belonged to the category written off.' "

Why were those "rights," which, as Sammler observes frequently, are the most lavishly dispensed gift of the enlightened world, of so little use to the Jews of Europe when the Germans decided to destroy them? Here again Burke offers an explanation. Burke had argued, in *Reflections on the Revolution in France* (1790), that the human rights "granted" by the French Revolution's Declaration of the Rights of Man were a mere abstraction of far less value than "the rights of an Englishman" (or, by implication, those of a Frenchman or a German.) "It has been the uniform policy of our constitution," he wrote, "to claim and assert our liberties, as an *entailed inheritance* derived to us from our forefathers, and to be transmitted to our posterity."[15] According to Hannah Arendt (who may be Sammler's aversion but was Bellow's colleague at the University of Chicago), the Holocaust confirmed the soundness of Burke's critique. "Not only did loss of national rights in all instances entail the loss of human rights; the restoration of human rights, as the . . . recent example of the State of Israel proves, has been achieved so far only through the restoration or the establishment of national rights. The conception of human rights, based upon the assumed existence of a human being as such, broke down at the very moment when those who professed to believe in it were for the first time confronted with people who had indeed lost all other qualities and specific relationships—except that they were still human. The world found nothing sacred in the abstract nakedness of being human."[16] It was, moreover, in just those countries where the Jews had been most determined to ingratiate themselves with their neighbors as "men" rather than as "Jews"—"Be a man in the street and a Jew at home" was the assimilationist slogan—that the population responded most readily to the allegation that the Jews were not human beings at all.

Sammler instinctively identifies his own fate and that of

the Jewish people with Israel because he recognizes the preferability of national to natural rights. He does so partly because of his experience, partly because he has given up his naturalism for supernaturalism, which makes him mindful, if only in the most nebulous way, of the "entailed inheritance" which the Jews derive from *their* forefathers, and transmit to *their* posterity: namely, their religion built on the idea of a covenant between God and man.

The search for sacredness that began for Sammler only after he had been rescued from Europe has certainly not led him in a straight line to the Torah. He is more confident of what "the main thing" is not than of what it is. It is certainly not "the expulsion of . . . demons and spirits from the air, where they had always been, by enlightenment and rationalism." His reading, in his seventies, has narrowed to Meister Eckhardt and the Bible, because he is convinced that a man who has been killed and buried should have no other interest but God and the spirit. He is "given to praying . . . often addressed God." This God is not recognizable as the Jewish one, yet Sammler's "religion" has at least two distinctly Jewish characteristics. It is prophetic rather than apocalyptic, and it is predicated on the assumption that the very condition of virtuous states is that they are not pleasant, for morality is essentially made up of "thou shalt nots," is a bridle rather than a spur.

Now that most forms of individualism have been discredited, says Sammler, people begin to wonder why they were born and even long for nonbeing. " 'Why should they be human?' " In such a mood, they contemplate apocalyptic answers, and yearn toward that leap into chaos which they believe the prerequisite to construction of a new cosmos. But Sammler " 'always hated people who declared that it was the end. What did they know about the end? From personal experience, from the grave if I may say so, *I* knew something about it.' " What he knew about it was precisely that it was *not* the end, for he had received, from a realm beyond human experience, the message that there is in man "something . . . which he feels it important to continue. Something that deserves to go on." If modern sensibility indulges in the cheap luxury of apocalyptic emotion, thought, and utterance, that is because "Humankind had lost its old patience." Although Sammler has actually experienced death and rebirth, his "entailed inheritance" is a Jewish wisdom that stresses not death and rebirth but survival and recovery.[17] He is a descendant of the beggar who is described at a party in Bellow's early novel *The Victim* (1947):

> "They tell a story about a little town in the old country. It was out of the way, in a valley, so the Jews were afraid the Messiah would come and miss them, and they built a high tower and hired one of the town beggars to sit in it all day long. A friend of his meets this beggar and he says, 'How do you like your job, Baruch?' So he says, 'It doesn't pay much, but I think it's steady work.' "

The idea of the ethical life set forth in *Mr. Sammler's Planet* is not based on reason and is not directed toward amelioration of the social order. Since a just social order is unattainable, perhaps, muses Sammler, " 'the best is to have some order within oneself.' " This is old advice, and distinctly unappealing in apocalyptic times. " 'A few may comprehend that it is the strength to do one's duty daily and promptly that makes saints and heroes. Not many. Most have fantasies of vaulting into higher states. . . .' " If justice does not reign on this planet, neither movement to another nor bloody revolution here will remedy the situation, for the failure is one of will and not of ignorance. Every man, from Cain to Eichmann, has known the difference between a just and an unjust act. If duty is the stupidest virtue—Dr. Lal calls it hateful and oppressive—it is also the most indispensable. " 'The pain of duty,' replies Sammler, 'makes the creature upright, and this uprightness is no negligible thing.' "

The concluding passage of the book is Sammler's prayer for the soul of Elya Gruner. Although Elya has participated in much of the corruption that characterizes life in the modern American city, he has also met the terms of his contract, has accepted and fulfilled his "assignment" even though he disliked it. Gruner, the character in the novel whose being is most thoroughly entangled in the Jewish world of his fathers and their fathers before them, had rescued Sammler and Shula after the war, and provided them money with which to live. For Sammler, he represents the unspectacular but essential virtues of the ordinary life lived according to custom, tradition, duty. "He did what he disliked. . . . Elya, by sentimental repetition and by formulas . . . has accomplished something good." From the "entailed inheritance" of his ancestors—"He knew there had been good men before him, and that there were good men to come, and he wanted to be one of them."—Gruner had received a knowledge of what it means to be human that could never be provided by Enlightenment epistemology and ontology. With a defiant final flourish, Sammler (and Bellow) celebrate in this eulogy over Gruner the ancient idea that virtue has a covenantal basis, that between man and God there exists a reciprocal agreement whose terms have a clarity and irresistibility unimaginable in a Social Contract: " 'He was aware that he must meet, and he did meet—through all the confusion and degraded clowning of this life through which we are speeding—he did meet the terms of his contract. The terms which, in his inmost heart, each man knows. As I know mine. As all know. For that is the truth of it—that we all know, God, that we know, that we know, we know, we know.' "

Given the extraordinary attachment of Jews to the Enlightenment and its various offspring, the still more extraordinary phenomenon of Jewish attempts to prove that Judaism is itself the epitome of Enlightenment secularism and universalism, *Mr. Sammler's Planet* gains its importance precisely as a Jewish repudiation of the Enlightenment. By the end of the novel, we understand so fully how the Revolution that promised to the Jews as Jews nothing but to the Jews as men everything deprived Jews of their humanity and their birthright that we wonder how anybody ever missed so obvious a truth. It may at first seem odd that, in a novel so overwhelmingly dedicated to showing how untenable, how false, how mischievous are the philosophical premises of the Enlightenment after the destruction of European Jewry, we should hear relatively little of an explicit nature about the special harmfulness of Enlightenment premises to Jews and Judaism, and nothing at all about the fact that, as Bellow readily remarks in another book, "The intellectual leaders of the Enlightenment were decidedly anti-Semitic." Marxism, for example, is treated as the most destructive modern offspring of the Enlightenment, but no mention is made of Marxism's uninterrupted tradition of Jew-hatred or of the fact that Sammler and all his ancestors, that is to say, the impoverished Polish Jews, were vilified by Marx himself as "this filthiest of all races."[18] Bellow may have wished to protect himself from allegations of ad hominem condemnation and contemptible parochialism. More likely, he wished to rest his case on the reader's ability to recognize that if monism and naturalism are baneful to mankind as a whole, they must be particularly so to that people whose religion makes the sharpest distinction between human and divine, and most resolutely prohibits worship of the former because it knows that an idol cannot respect a covenant with God.

1. Irving Howe, *The Critical Point* (New York: Delta, 1975), p. 133.

2. Hannah Arendt, *Eichmann in Jerusalem* (New York: Viking Press, 1963).

3. Mr. Sammler's severity with Arendt causes him partially to misrepresent her views. What she says, in *Eichmann in Jerusalem,* is not that the Nazi system kept people like Eichmann ignorant of what they were doing but that it kept them from equating what they were doing with their old, "normal" knowledge of murder.

4. John Henry Newman, *Apologia Pro Vita Sua* (1864).

5. Robert J. Loewenberg, "The Theft of Liberalism: A Jewish Problem,"*Midstream* 28 (May 1977): 24.

6. Thomas Carlyle, *Sartor Resartus* (1833), book second, chapter 9.

7. Preface to *Essays in Criticism* (1865).

8. Hannah Arendt, *The Origins of Totalitarianism,* 3 vols. (New York: Harcourt, Brace & World, 1951), 3:153.

9. J.S. Mill, *Mill on Bentham and Coleridge*, ed. F.R. Leavis (London: Chatto & Windus, 1959), p. 65.

10. Josephine Knopp, *The Trial of Judaism in Contemporary Jewish Writing* (Urbana: University of Illinois Press, 1975), p. 142.

11. Saul Bellow, *To Jerusalem and Back* (New York: Viking Press, 1976), p. 26.

12. See, e.g., Marvin Carlson, *Theater of the Revolution* (Ithaca, N.Y.: Cornell University Press, 1966).

13. "Reflections on the Revolution in France," *Works of Edmund Burke* (London: Bohn edition, 1909-12), 2:366.

14. *The Origins of Totalitarianism*, 1:54, 66-67.

15. "Reflections on the Revolution in France," p. 306.

16. *The Origins of Totalitarianism*, 2:179.

17. This point has been very effectively made, with respect to Bellow's earlier novels, by J. C. Levenson, "Bellow's Dangling Men," *Critique* 3 (Summer 1960): 5.

18. See the conclusion of the articles by Marx and Engels on the Polish question, in the *Neue Rheinische Zeitung*, 29 April 1849.

If thou will not observe to do all the words of this law that are written in this book, that thou mayest fear this glorious and awful Name, the LORD thy God; then the LORD will make thy plagues wonderful, and the plagues of thy seed. . . . And ye shall be left few in number, whereas ye were as the stars of heaven for multitude; because thou didst not hearken unto the voice of the LORD thy God. And it shall come to pass, that as the LORD rejoiced over you to do you good, and to multiply you; so the LORD will rejoice over you to cause you to perish, and to destroy you; and ye shall be plucked from off the land whither thou goest in to possess it. And the LORD shall scatter thee among all peoples, from the one end of the earth even unto the other end of the earth; and there thou shalt serve other gods, which thou hast not known, thou nor thy fathers, even wood and stone. And among these nations shalt thou have no repose, and there shall be no rest for the sole of thy foot; but the LORD shall give thee there a trembling heart, and failing of eyes, and languishing of soul. . . . These are the words of the covenant which the LORD commanded Moses to make with the children of Israel in the land of Moab.—Deuteronomy 28:58–69*

A remnant shall return, even the remnant of Jacob, unto God the Mighty. For though thy people, O Israel, be as the sand of the sea, only a remnant of them shall return; an extermination is determined, overflowing with righteousness. For an extermination wholly determined shall the LORD, the GOD of hosts, make in the midst of all the earth.—Isaiah 10:21-23*

You only have I known among all the families of the earth; therefore, I will visit upon you all your iniquities.—Amos 3:2*

chapter 7

The Holocaust and the God of Israel

In the mind of the believing Jew, the tragic paradox of the Holocaust must be that it was not the denial but the fulfillment of the divine promise, as set forth in every elucidation of the Covenant in the Bible. To the skeptic, the destruction of European Jewry makes a mockery of the sentences in the Jewish daily prayer book: "With abundant love hast Thou loved us, O Lord." "With everlasting love hast Thou loved the house of Israel." To the skeptic, including the Jewish skeptic, who surveys Jewish life from the outside, the contradiction between God's professions of love for His Chosen People and the way in which these people are tortured and killed must be complete. But the believing Jew has accepted a structure of relations between the Chosen People and God in which love and chastisement are inseparable from each other. He has traditionally acknowledged that the Covenant contained a curse as well as a blessing. The Jews have been chosen to receive the Law, but if they lust instead after idols and so violate the Covenant, they will be cursed and exiled and destroyed. But the destruction will never be total, for that would constitute God's violation of His own Covenant. Despite the endless transgressions of the people of Israel, "when they are in the land of their enemies, I will not reject them, neither will I abhor them, to destroy them utterly, and to break My covenant with them. . . ." The Jews' destiny, moreover, is in their own control and not in that of the nations of the earth. The God of Israel is the god of all mankind, but the nations of the world are instruments of the Lord in His dramatic struggle with His refractory people. In His lawsuit against His people, God calls heaven and earth to witness against His beloved adversary that "I have set before thee life and death, the blessing and the curse. . . ."

The whole structure of Jewish religious life was

predicated on acceptance of responsibility for the Exile and its endless humiliations and oppressions. These had been brought upon the Jews not by Assyrians or Babylonians or Romans or Crusaders or Cossacks but, ultimately, by their own transgressions. Regularly, in his festival prayers, the Jew acknowledged his responsibility for his condition of exile and debasement: "Because of our sins, we were exiled from our land and removed far away from our country." This very act, moreover, of blaming their fate on their own sins tended to reenforce the Jews' belief in their chosenness because it enabled them to survive when other peoples, who had also suffered expulsion from their homelands and oppression in the lands of strangers, were disappearing. These peoples came to the outwardly sensible and reasonable conclusion that their miserable fate proved the inefficacy of their national god, whom they abandoned in order to worship the gods of their new neighbors; thus were they assimilated, thus did they disappear. The Jews, persistently interpreting their misery as divine punishment for their sins, clung to their God and to the promise of the Covenant, and so survived, albeit in ever diminishing numbers. "Except the LORD of hosts / Had left unto us a very small remnant, / We should have been as Sodom, / We should have been like unto Gomorrah" (Isaiah, 1:9).

The structure of the covenantal relation between God and the Jewish people was so pervasive in Jewish life and in the Jewish imagination that it could withstand and accommodate a considerable amount of resistance and rebellion from within. What is the book of Job but an instance of such rebellion and accommodation? It takes the traditional form of the lawsuit between the two partners to the Covenant, with enumeration of curses, invocation of witnesses, professions of innocence, and allegations of guilt. Job desires "to reason with God" (13:3), to justify himself. Yet even at the height of his rebellion, when he insists "I will argue my ways before Him," he submits to the inherited structure of faith: "Though He slay me, yet will I trust in Him." Death itself, however seemingly undeserved and unjust, becomes an aspect of endurance if it is acknowledged as a chastisement from God. This covenantal structure took such hold of Jewish life that it can still today provide a framework for modern Jewish poets and novelists of a secular cast of mind whose instinctive reaction to the Holocaust is, not to reject God, but to accuse and curse Him.

The inherited structure of covenantal relations had to endure unprecedented strains during the Holocaust. For the first time in modern history, the Jews faced an enemy in no way respectful of, or leavened by, the Jews' own sacred texts. From the point of view of Judaism—though not, to be sure, of most emancipated Jews—Christianity was preferable to paganism because it had several drops of Torah mixed in with all its Greek mystery religion. Therefore, it acknowledged that the Jews had once received the divine election (even if they no longer had it), and that their Scriptures were a true, if partial, revelation of the Divine Will. But for the Nazis (as for Voltaire), Judaism represented evil incarnate, and Jews had inherited in their genes a plague that could not be cured, but only extirpated. Modern Jews, for their part, had been trying in every way to slough off their covenantal chosenness and all its signs. But now they found the ancient doctrine that they were indeed the Chosen People spuriously confirmed by their most determined enemies.

Chaim Kaplan: Warsaw Diary

The paradoxes with which the Holocaust assaulted the mind of a religious Jew are conveyed with great immediacy in Chaim Kaplan's *Warsaw Diary*. If we would anchor in actuality our discussion of the imaginative literature that seeks out the role of God in the Holocaust, we cannot do better than to begin with this remarkable book. For it foreshadows many of the purely literary treatments of the Holocaust we shall examine, from Glatstein to Rawicz, in that its search for a principle by which to impose order on a phenomenon that is the embodiment of chaos is a literary quest that can succeed only through a resort to religious beliefs that the author resents but cannot reject. Kaplan kept his Warsaw Diary from 1 September 1939, when

Germany invaded Poland, until 4 August 1942, when he and his wife were transported to the death factory in Treblinka. His very first entry expresses doubt that they will survive the carnage. He also knows, as the severity of German restrictions on Jewish activity increases, that he literally risks his life by continuing to write. Yet even as late as 2 August 1942, when he feels himself overwhelmed as a writer by the incoherent horror of events, and as a man by the imminence of starvation or deportation, his utmost concern is for hiding his diary, so that he may fulfill his "sacred task" of recording for future generations the unimaginable crimes of the Germans. His last recorded thought was: "If my life ends—what will become of my diary?"

Although Kaplan never speaks condescendingly of the literary aspect of his work, and even invites the application to it of literary standards, he was moved by transcendent reasons to keep his diary. According to the biblical promise, the destruction of the Jewish people would never be total; there would always be a remnant. It is to bear witness to this remnant of the destruction of European Jewry that Kaplan devotes himself to his diary. "O earth, cover not thou my blood!" he prays. He does not know whether anyone else in the ghetto is recording daily events, and is well aware that the conditions of life in the ghetto are not conducive to "literary labors," yet he senses that if there is such a thing as a vocation, a being summoned to one's destiny, then he has here received it: "I sense within me the magnitude of this hour, and my responsibility toward it, and I have an inner awareness that I am fulfilling a national obligation."

The tragic paradoxes of Jewish survival pervade Kaplan's diary. He is well aware that, according to classical Jewish tradition, redemption will not come except in association with catastrophe. The tenth chapter of the Tractate Sanhedrin states, "The Son of David will come only in a generation wholly guilty or a generation wholly innocent." Since simple observation suggests to Warsaw's Jews that few generations seem more likely than the generation of Hitler to fulfill the former condition, they give themselves over to messianic speculation. On 17 November 1939, Kaplan remarks, "The soil is ready even for religious

Messianism." His own reaction to such messianism is ambivalent, and he speaks of it with two voices. Sometimes, especially when the Jewish masses imagine that Stalin or Roosevelt is in fact the Messiah, Kaplan condemns messianic imagination as yet another form of Jewish fantasy and wish-fulfillment. Yet he also understands that it is precisely this faith in messianic truth and justice, this stupid hope, that has enabled the miracle of Jewish survival. "In actual reality," he writes in January 1940, "there is disappointment upon disappointment, yet hope flourishes. A nation which for thousands of years has said daily, 'And even if he tarries, I will await the coming of the Messiah every day,' will not weaken in its hope, which has been a balm of life."

From the very beginning of the German occupation of Warsaw, Kaplan had sought to control the disorder that assaulted his imagination by asking what role God was playing in this latest and perhaps final tragedy of His Chosen People. Month after month, year after year, he assails God with seemingly unanswerable questions: "Have we indeed sinned more than any other nation?" "Will the Eternal break His promise?" "Is this the way the Almighty looks after His dear ones?" "Why has a 'day of vengeance and retribution' not yet come for the murderers? Do not answer me with idle talk—I won't listen to you. Give me a logical reply!" Kaplan writes not as a skeptic questioning God's existence but as a believer openly quarreling with, and directly reproaching, a partner to an agreement who has failed to keep his side of the contract. As the German barbarities grow more unspeakable, the tone of reproach breaks free from mere questioning and becomes accusatory: "O Leader of the city, where are you? But he Who sits in Heaven laughs." It is not until July 1942, when Kaplan at last has full knowledge of the details of the "final solution" and watches the mass deportations from the ghetto, that he calls into question God's very existence: "In these two days the emptiness of the ghetto has been filled with cries and wails. If they found no way to the God of Israel it is a sign He doesn't exist."

But skepticism is merely a fleeting impulse in the diary.

What is far more difficult for Kaplan to assimilate to his imagination than the denial of some of God's promises is the confirmation and fulfillment of them, but in counterfeit forms. According to the Divine Promise (Deuteronomy 5:3), the Covenant was given not only to the Jews who stood at Horeb or Sinai but to all their descendants as well, to all those generations of Jews who were not physically present to receive the Law. This promise, it strikes Kaplan, is confirmed in the ghetto, albeit spuriously and with the assistance of the Nazis. Since the destruction of Judaism entailed, according to Nazi racial ideology, destruction of all who could by any stretch of the imagination be thought to belong to the Jewish people, the most senseless suffering depicted by Kaplan is that of marginal Jews or actual apostates or antisemites of Jewish descent. Among the diary's most powerful scenes are those showing Jewish apostates or their children, "the cream of Polish society, people who had always showed their hatred for the Jews," being dragged, literally and metaphysically, back into the ghetto. Kaplan freely admits that the misery of these people, whose suffering lacks even a human meaning for them, provides the first occasion in his life when he has derived pleasure from the distress of others. The reason why Kaplan should deal so harshly with these ex-Jews, half-Jews, and Jewish antisemites who must now bear the fate of real Jews, is not far to seek. It lies in his conviction that the Jews are still a covenanted people, with a fate that is collective not individual. "Who of them dreamed that his ancestors stood on Mount Sinai?" The ancient promise that all Jews, including those not yet born, received the Covenant and were not free to relinquish it is thus bizarrely confirmed.

Another spurious fulfillment of the Divine Promise is to be found in the signs of Jewish national rebirth in the ghetto. God had promised that only after the Jewish people had endured the punishment of its iniquities and nearly perished completely in the lands of its enemies would He remember his Covenant with them and remember the Land from which they had been exiled. For Kaplan, one of the most striking instances of the link between the symbols of destruction and restoration is the charade of a "Jewish kingdom" that the Nazis have established in the ghetto (for the purpose of conserving their manpower and facilitating the process of destruction): Jewish tax officials, Jewish public utility officials, Jewish housing officials. "In short, a Jewish state complete in every detail, but a closed, cramped one, imprisoned, mummified within its narrow borders." Even the policemen, traditional symbols of gentile oppression in the Diaspora, have become Jews, to whom one can speak Yiddish. "The residents of the ghetto," remarks Kaplan, "are beginning to think they are in Tel Aviv." Kaplan sees only too clearly that this is all facade, and that the very logic of their situation may well make Jewish policemen even crueler than their gentile counterparts. Yet he perceived in the most visible symbol of Jewish degradation a sign, from a realm beyond human experience, of Jewish national rebirth. The Nazis order all the Jews of Warsaw to wear on their bodies and to display on their shops the Star of David, in the Jewish national colors of blue and white. "In the future," muses Kaplan, "everywhere we turn we shall feel as if we were in a Jewish kingdom. The national colors will flutter everywhere. From now on Jerusalem will not only crown our every joy, but also our ordinary weekdays, as we get up and as we lie down. . . ." The Ingathering of the Exiles, the dawn of deliverance— gifts of the Nazis! Kaplan's tone in such passages is a turbulent mixture of genuine emotion and corrosive irony.

The opposing voices of hope and despair, faith and doubt, the conflicting impulses toward belief in redemption and resignation to meaningless death, eventually became impossible for Kaplan to contain within his own mind and breast. In the depths of his agony, therefore, at the end of May 1942, he invented an alter ego named Hirsch, whose role in the diary is to reject altogether his creator's messianic hopes and to express the irredeemable gloom of the Jewish predicament. This literary device clarifies, but does not remove, the paradox. Thus, on 7 June 1942, Kaplan writes: "We were always a nation bound by hope—and so we shall remain. Jewish faith is marvelous; it can create states of mind that have nothing to do with reality. Like the believing Jewish grandfather who in anticipation of the Messiah always wore his Sabbath clothes, so we too await him, 'and though he tarry, I will wait daily for his coming!' " The belief in the imminent downfall of the Nazis and the hope for the physical and spiritual salvation of the Jews are shared at this point by everyone in Jewish Warsaw except for Kaplan's recently invented "wise friend" Hirsch. "He is the only one who sits like a mourner among bridegrooms. 'Idiots!' he shouts, and his face becomes red with anger. 'Your hope is vain; your trust a broken reed.' " Thus, the belief that because the world has grown thoroughly wicked and that because the Jews have at last been sufficiently punished the Messiah must be at hand, is at once embraced and ridiculed.

In Kaplan's imagination, it is the path of belief rather than that of skepticism and despair that requires courage. The shockingly intimate relation between the depths of Jewish degradation and the heights of Jewish aspiration is difficult to accept precisely because it appears to bear out the prophetic promise of God's active involvement in Jewish history and implicates God in the Holocaust. Yet it seems to him that just this belief enables the Jews to cling to life. According to the "laws of nature," which in perverted form are at the basis of Nazi racial doctrine, the Jews should already be dead, yet despite the frightful suffering in the ghetto, there are no suicides. Kaplan never ceases to marvel at this fact, or indeed at the fact that Jewish cultural and religious life continues in the midst of horror and degradation: "Nursery schools bring their infant charges to the gardens, and older children have their lessons there. . . . We are schooled in life, schooled in the art of living; it is like the words of the prophet: 'When thou walkest through the fire thou shalt not be burned; neither shall the flame kindle upon thee!' " Here was empirical evidence that even if millions of individuals were destroyed the Jewish people would survive. For all his resentment toward the God of Israel for being indifferent to the suffering of His people, Kaplan returns for sustenance to the inherited structure of belief, according to which God visits all their iniquities upon the People Israel exactly because He has made His Covenant with them alone among all the families of the earth.

Kaplan wrote in 1942 that what would be hardest about his impending death was the necessity for leaving the earth without knowing the final outcome of the struggle between giant adversaries: the Nazis against the Allies; the Nazi will to murder against the Jewish will to live; empirical despair against messianic hope. Kaplan, hesitatingly, bitterly, ironically, casts his lot with the God of Israel, who has been anything but loving to His people, but whose Covenant with them represents the only possibility of meaning in the midst of otherwise unfathomable suffering: "In these fateful hours, we long for life. 'Blessed is he who hopes, he will live to see the restoration of Israel!' "

Yiddish Holocaust Poetry

Just how irresistible was the inherited myth of the Covenant between God and his Chosen People may be seen in Yiddish Holocaust poetry, one of the most coherent and substantial bodies of writing on the subject. From its inception, in the nineteenth century, Yiddish poetry had been secular in idea and outlook. The idea that literature might be a profession suitable to a Jewish male was itself an act of defiance, so much so that Isaac Bashevis Singer recalls how his father "considered all the secular writers to be heretics, all unbelievers—. . . . To become a *literat* was to them almost as bad as becoming a *meshumed*, one who forsakes the faith. My father used to say that secular writers like Peretz were leading the Jews to heresy. He said everything they wrote was against God. . . . And from his point of view, he was right."[1] Although most writers of Yiddish literature considered themselves Jews, they were devoted to a secularization of Jewish culture. Moreover, many who came to prominence in the second and third decades of this century sought to reject the traditional subject of Yiddish literature, the fate of the Jewish people, sought to reject, that is, the chosenness of the Jewish people.

For why could not Yiddish writers, like their counterparts writing in French or German or English, range freely through the world for their subjects instead of being limited to the concerns of the collective body from which they had sprung? Thus, Jacob Glatstein wrote in 1920 of himself and his fellow poets in the Inzikh group: "We are Yiddish poets by virtue of the fact that we are Jews and write in Yiddish. Whatever a Yiddish poet may write about is *ipso facto* Yiddish. One does not need specifically Jewish themes. . . . "[2] But the Holocaust proved that the Jewish poet no more than the Jews themselves could become "normal." After the Holocaust, as Irving Howe has written, 'Yiddish poetry . . . returns . . . to its original concern with the collective destiny of the Jewish people. . . . In the desolation of memory, Yiddish poets find themselves turning back to the old Jewish God, . . . a God inseparable from Jewish fate, a God with whom one pleads and quarrels."[3]

In some of these Yiddish poems about the Holocaust, the tone of bitterness and reproach is dominant. This is not only because the poet has been dragged, kicking and screaming, back to the very subject he defiantly abandoned in his youth, before the deluge of the Holocaust. It is also because of a revulsion from the God who has done the Jews the dubious favor of choosing them without allowing them the option of surrendering their chosenness and so avoiding the sufferings specially reserved for God's servants. Perhaps the best-known single expression of outrage and resentment at the imposition of divine election is Kadia Molodowsky's poem "God of Mercy." Here the poet does not deny the chosenness of Israel, but declares that it has been always a curse, never a blessing:

> O God of Mercy
> For the time being
> Choose another people.
> We are tired of death, tired of corpses,
> We have no more prayers.
> For the time being
> Choose another people.

If a covenant there must be, let it descend upon some other people, for the Jews can no longer afford the price exacted by the Law they were chosen to receive:

God of Mercy
Sanctify another land
Another Sinai.
We have covered every field and stone
With ashes and holiness.
With our crones
With our young
With our infants
We have paid for each letter in your Commandments.

(Translated by Irving Howe)

What is still more remarkable about this poem than its bitterness and indignation against God is its entire indifference to the worldly aspect of "chosenness." Molodowsky writes with a secular animus, yet takes it for granted that both Jews and Germans were only puppets of God. She ends the poem with a plea to God to "Grant us one more blessing— / Take back the gift of our separateness." The fact that many Jews *had* in fact already given back that separateness when they were identified by the Nazis as Jews does not even enter into her vision of this ghastly drama. The poet rebels against God, yet never thinks to question either His existence or omnipotence.

In the poetry of Jacob Glatstein,* the Yiddish tradition of intimate quarrel and mutual reproach between the Jew and God is continued, but subjected to strains and storms that threaten to shatter the old framework. In the wake of the Holocaust, the poles of the ancient antithesis between suffering and faith, the terms of the paradox whereby the unending misery of the Jews is precisely a sign of the unending Covenant with God, move so far apart that their link is almost ruptured. Glatstein cannot fathom the Holocaust without viewing it as part of the ongoing quarrel

*Except where other names are given, all the translations are by Ruth Whitman, *The Selected Poems of Jacob Glatstein* (New York: October House, 1972). All other translations of Yiddish verse in this chapter come from *A Treasury of Yiddish Poetry*, ed. Irving Howe and Eliezer Greenberg (New York: Holt, Rinehart & Winston, 1969).

between God and His Chosen People. The Jews cannot be themselves without God, for "without our God / we have a funny look." Neither can God exist without the Jews, in whose post-Holocaust absence He is

> pursued, forsaken,
> wandering around,
> looking for a Jewish face,
> a hand to give you shalom:
> *Shalom aleichem*, Jewish God.

But neither, finally can Glatstein live with the horror of believing that the Holocaust *was* part of God's ongoing quarrel with the Jews:

> From the crematory flue
> A Jew aspires to the Holy One.
> And when the smoke of him is gone,
> His wife and children filter through.
>
> Above us, in the height of sky,
> Saintly billows weep and wait.
> God, wherever you may be,
> There all of us are also not.
>   (Translated by Chana Faerstein)

Any impulse toward locating the source of the unspeakable horror in God must mercilessly be squelched. If the God of history has indeed been involved in the Holocaust, then the Jews must sue for divorce from Him.

At times Glatstein sounds like the "radical" theologian Richard L. Rubenstein insisting that Jews cannot believe in a God who acts in history "without regarding Hitler and the SS as instruments of God's will."[4] But just as often he sounds like Emil L. Fackenheim refusing to abandon a God who is Lord of actual history and insisting that "in faithfulness to Judaism we must refuse to disconnect God from the holocaust."[5] Glatstein's Holocaust poetry is not informed by a consistent theology. Rather he seeks imaginatively to assimilate the Holocaust by perceiving it through the inherited myths of Jewish religion. He looks upon this religion to some extent as an outsider, one who has become alienated from its language and beliefs, and who revisits it nostalgically:

It's as hard to return to
old-fashioned words
as to sad synagogues,
those thresholds of faith.
You know exactly where they are.
Troubled, you can still hear their undertones.
Sometimes you come close and look longingly
at them through the windowpanes.

The world of his youth provides not so much truth as
warmth, familiarity, and shelter: "I love you, dead world of
my youth, / I command you, rise up, let your joy revive, /
come close, letter by letter, warm, pulsing, meaning
nothing." The religious myths that once provided the
shelter of a protective covering have now been hollowed out,
by intellect and by history. Yet still they seem to the poet the
only framework within which he can begin to make sense of
what has happened. Having been disillusioned by Western
culture, by its "Jesus-Marxes" and "weak-kneed democracy," the poet returns in imagination to his very beginnings in the ghetto and implores help from those whose
lives are still bound by the all-embracing myths of religion:
"You who still take your ease in the shadow of biblical
trees / O sing me the cool solace / of all you remember,
all that you know."

Glatstein conceived of his Holocaust poetry as a safeguar-
ding and even a resurrection of the dead. In a poem called
"Nightsong," he imagines the post-Holocaust imaginative
life of the Yiddish poet as a nightly stroll among the graves,
among the "valleys and hills and hidden twisted paths"
that have become the landscape of his mind. Here he
gathers to himself the whole vanished Jewish world, in a
heroic attempt to "grasp and take in / those destroyed
millions." If they are to be redeemed, it can henceforward—
such is the implication of the poem—only be through
literature. The appropriate language of the literature is
Yiddish, but its structure can be provided only by the myths
of religion, that is to say, by the world-view that Yiddish
literature, at its inception, was intended to erode and
supplant. Glatstein's work is pervaded by anger, but
especially by anger directed against himself for failing to

perceive, until both Jewry and Yiddish were virtually destroyed, that neither Yiddish literature nor Jewish life could survive without in some way incorporating the religious heritage. Amidst the wreckage of European Jewry, the lesson was now brutally clear: Yiddish, once the language of militant secularists, had suddenly become a "dead" language whose only future was as the sacred tongue of martyrdom: "Poet, take the faintest Yiddish speech, / fill it with faith, make it holy again."

A short poem entitled "My Father Isaac"* illustrates Glatstein's habit of lending significance—albeit ironic significance—to his experience of the Holocaust by casting it within the framework of biblical story. The poem gains its power at once from the sense of timeless and inescapable repetition of a pattern, and from a striking departure from it. The Isaac to be sacrificed here by the Nazis is, unlike the biblical Isaac, a father (the poet's father) rather than a son, an old man rather than a young one. He is thoroughly accustomed to the procedure, as if he were the descendant of untold Isaacs who have been chosen by God and know that, unlike the Isaac of the Bible, they will *not* be rescued by a good angel from the sharpened blade. "Isaac, old, was not deceived / as when he'd been that lad from Genesis; / he knew that there would be no lamb." Always he speaks in "a tired voice," as if wearied of the process of being chosen and being sacrificed, and knowing better than to expect rescue from a God who has done nothing to rescue his Isaacs since the original binding told in Genesis. Indeed, the poem implies that the Genesis story is an archetype of Jewish experience except for its ending, which is not to be believed. But this ancient Isaac, having long ago learned not to expect mercy and rescue from this God, submissively goes to the altar:

> and as he smelled the searing fumes,
> he spoke his mind thus:
> "God will not interrupt this slaughter!"
> He called out in a tired voice:
> "Here I am—prepared to be your ram."

*Translated by Etta Blum.

Several of Glatstein's Holocaust poems take the form of a dialogue between the poet who presents the accusations of his people and the Jewish God who tries to justify His action or inaction during the great destruction. In "My Brother Refugee," Glatstein appears at first to be sacrificing God's power in order to rescue the belief in His goodness. In the first part of the poem, God is presented as just another powerless, persecuted Jew, in fact a "brother refugee." The poet discovers new fellowship with so miserable a character, and wonders how he could in olden times have expended so much energy in profaning the words and blaspheming the person of so helpless and pitiful a creature. But is this "human" and lovable God really the God of the Jews, of Abraham, Isaac, and Jacob? Glatstein's mixture of skepticism and belief, of aggression and reconciliation, is conveyed in the declaration "The God of my unbelief is magnificent."

This God, when His turn comes to speak, is in no mood to make great claims for Himself. In fact, He acknowledges that the Jews (whose faithfulness to Him has, after all, been greater than His to them) have now become, by virtue of their unprecedented *"wallowing in dust," "godlier than I am,"* and predicts that the nations *"will yet bow / to their anguish."* But here the poet's irony and bitterness overcome his newfound affection. Who needed, who requested, such exaltation?

> But God, my brother,
> why have you exalted my people like this,
> constellating their misfortune
> across the whole sky?

God comes up with an extraordinary, and perhaps desperate answer that says, in effect, that since the Christian version of the Messiah—"a childish fable with foolish words"—left the world just as it had always been, He decided to crucify the whole Jewish people, thus "constellating their misfortune across the whole sky." No sooner does Glatstein allow himself to imagine a God with the power to act in history, than he imagines a God implicated in monstrosity, who confirms the election of His people through eternity by decimating them, and dreams that His people "will bloom / crucified forever on a shining tree." The poem ends, therefore, with Glatstein's retreat into the image of a very small, childlike, helpless God, entirely dependent on the few remaining Jews willing to dream Him into existence.

In another poem, Glatstein states boldly yet with inescapable logic that "Without Jews there is no Jewish God. / If we leave this world / The light will go out in your tent." If God's ultimate purposes for the universe required the creation and election of the Jewish people, how can God condone the extinction of that people? The removal of any member of the family of nations is a crime against humanity, against human diversity and the nature of mankind. The removal of this particular member, however, must constitute God's self-destruction. Without Jews,

> Who will dream you?
> Who will remember you?
> Who deny you?
> Who yearn for you?
> Who, on a lonely bridge,
> Will leave you—in order to return?
>
> (Translated by Nathan Halper)

These lines are not only an expression of the peculiarly intimate relation between the Jews and their God, or a skeptic's suggestion that God's existence is merely subjective, the creation of human minds, but a recognition that God had made the Jews the special instrument for the achievement of His purposes and their life His chief interest. The death of the Jews means the death of God: "The Jewish hour is guttering. / Jewish God! / You are almost gone."

More than any other Jewish myth, however, the Covenant between God and the Jewish people is for Glatstein the locus for his paradoxical mixture of faith and denial, submission and outrage. "Dead Men Don't Praise God," one of Glatstein's most ambitious poems, is based entirely on the idea that the Jews as a people have been called into existence to serve God's purpose in the world, and that they were created by His special act of Covenant. It depends especially on the doctrine, whose use we have already noted in Kaplan's diary, that Jews of all generations were potentially present at Sinai, and were as much recipients of the Torah as those physically there. But it treats the Holocaust too as an event of more than human significance, whose full implications for Jewish existence can be fathomed only if it is understood in precisely the way we have traditionally understood the Covenant, of which it is at once a validation and a denial:

> We received the Torah on Sinai
> and in Lublin we gave it back.
> Dead men don't praise God,
> the Torah was given to the living.
> And just as we all stood together
> at the giving of the Torah,
> so did we all die together at Lublin.

If the gift of life at Sinai was a collective one to every generation of Jews, then the plague of death at Lublin-Maidanek (and all the other death factories for which it stands) must also implicate every Jew; if all stood at Sinai, then all fell in the slaughter at Lublin:

The souls of those who had lived out their lives, of those who had
   died young,
of those who were tortured, tested in every fire,
of those who were not yet born,
and of all the dead Jews from great grandfather Abraham down.

That Moses, Aaron, King David, and the multitudes already dead should come to die again at Lublin perversely confirms the logic of the Covenant. What they were given at Sinai was not physical but spiritual life; if they were indeed being required to return the Covenant, then their souls must be killed as well as their bodies. What better place for such a second death than Lublin?

That the Jews of all generations should congregate for death in the Holocaust in the same way that they had congregated for life in the Covenant shows the continuity between Sinai and Lublin and the unity of the Jewish people—in both cases, a kind of arbitrariness visited upon all individual Jews, whether they liked it or not, and whether they "deserved" it or not, the collective fate of the Chosen People. But this continuity of chosenness is threatened by the discontinuity between the old and the new covenants. The pain and suffering that devolve upon the Chosen People may themselves be a sign of their invisible destiny, but the Holocaust, far from bringing a voice of redemption, seems to drown out the redeeming voice of Sinai. "Above the gas chambers / and the holy dead souls, / a forsaken abandoned Mount Sinai veiled itself in smoke." The Sinai Covenant makes its presence felt above Lublin, but the smoke of the death factories blackens and conceals Sinai itself. The new covenant obliterates the original one, for if *all* Jews are present to be killed at Lublin, then the new covenant is none other than a covenant for death; if all Jews have been done to death at Lublin, then it logically follows that the Torah has been returned: "Dead men don't praise God, / The Torah was given to the living."

Whereas Glatstein's anguish moved him, again and again, to resort to traditional structures of religious meaning only to fill those structures with a body of experience that seemed at once to make sense only within them and to defy all sense whatever, Aaron Zeitlin stood virtually alone among Yiddish poets in viewing the Holocaust of the Jewish people not only within the confines of, but as a terrifying testimony to, the truths of orthodox Jewish religion.* He was among the few who claimed to hear a redeeming voice from Auschwitz, and who refused to back away from the recognition that God, if He is indeed the traditional Jewish God who acts within history, must be the God of the Holocaust as well as the God of Sinai. He may also be the hidden God of Isaiah, but he cannot be the reduced, powerless God sometimes imagined by Glatstein.

Zeitlin was saved by an accident of fate from perishing in the Holocaust. He had written a play about German militarism called *In Keynems Land* (*In No Man's Land*)

* All Zeitlin translations are by Robert Friend.

that opened in Warsaw in 1938. In the spring of 1939, he was invited by Maurice Schwartz to New York for the Yiddish Art Theatre's premiere of his play. While he was in New York, the war broke out and prevented his return to his family, all of whom were murdered by the Nazis. The Holocaust came to occupy the center of his emotional, poetic, and religious life. Unlike Glatstein, he wrote from the compulsion of religious conscience, rather than from the impulse to memorialize and resurrect the dead through art. In fact, the Holocaust seemed to him to have rendered the whole literary enterprise frivolous: "Were Jeremiah to sit by the ashes of Israel today, he would not cry out a lamentation, nor would he drown the desolate places with his tears. The Almighty Himself would be powerless to open up his well of tears. He would maintain a deep silence. For even an outcry is now a lie, even tears are mere literature, even prayers are false."[6] It was a religious, not a literary, impulse that moved Zeitlin to the composition of his two-volume justification of the ways of God to men: "I Believe."

Belief pervades the poem, since for Zeitlin the beginning of inquiry is not "If there be a God, how could the Holocaust have been permitted to happen?" but "Since there is a God, what does the Holocaust mean?" The aggression directed toward God in other Yiddish poems on this subject is here directed primarily toward competing religions that claim to derive from Judaism. "Should I believe in Spinoza's geometric god?" he asks. This is a god "without horror or miracle," to be sure, but also without relation to men in general or Jews in particular. There is an intentional ambiguity in Zeitlin's reference to this monistic and naturalistic god as "a distant relative / who won't acknowledge me as his relation." The "me" refers not only to humanity at large but to Zeitlin's Jewish identity; and Spinoza's god is a kind of snobbish relative because he was conceived by a Dutch Jew yet explicitly rejected the election of the Jews acknowledged by Christianity itself. Rather than believe in this utterly detached and indifferent god of nature Zeitlin would "willingly believe in Satan and damnation."

Christianity too is objectionable both for its general inadequacy to the human condition—its location of human guilt and divine mystery in the wrong places—and for its need to affirm itself through the denial of Torah, to found its life on Jewish death.

> Should I believe in the redeemer who never redeems,
> the dreamed-up god who dangles on all the crosses,
> . . . the god of cloister bells
> whom the dark dreams
> of sadists bleed and kill
> with the deliberate will
> to torture my truth with his lie?

Zeitlin here means to call up the centuries-old invocation of alleged Jewish guilt for the death of Jesus as a license to kill Jesus (over and over again) and the Jews at once. How trivial, in any case, does the Christian mystery of a god become a man appear when viewed by a generation that has experienced the reality, and the mystery, of Hitler,

> a devil who became a man,
> who lived with us here upon earth,
> lived and was seen, lived and was heard,
> and—incinerating, gassing—crucified
> a people.

Here are transformations enough to satisfy the most voracious appetite for mysteries. Yet it is clear that the Christian myth evokes something more than vituperation from Zeitlin. Like Glatstein, Zeitlin is ensnared by a certain morbid fascination for the very Christian image that he excoriates into imagining the whole Jewish nation as a crucified people. By so doing, he claims (again like Glatstein) to be giving to a literary fable the moral significance that always inhered in it, but that was never fully realized until the Holocaust. (Neither of these Yiddish poets seems aware of the fact that by the very act of insisting that the murder of six million Jews is the true crucifixion, they are endorsing the very Christian scheme that they derogate, which claims that the conformity between the Cross and the suffering of all mankind is precisely what makes innocent suffering bearable.)

Having disposed of the claims of the Spinozistic and Christian rivals to Judaism as untenable in the aftermath of the Holocaust, Zeitlin dismisses modern secular ideologies and man-made religions with a mere wave of the hand as "More hollow than ever . . . / After the all-destroying flames." Whatever cries of rebellion arise from the Holocaust can be flung only at the one God who could have ordained the Holocaust. What but an orthodox structure can make rebellion meaningful?

> Who would rebel against pale Jesuses?
> And who would rage
> against a Spinozan god,
> a nonbeing being?

Zeitlin feels himself and his God to be locked into a pattern from which there can be no escape except at the price of denying one's principle of being. "One is—what one is. / I am Jew as He is God." Zeitlin's must be a living God; and since He is living, He is of necessity and unavoidably the God of cataclysm, the God of the Holocaust.

Zeitlin's voice is as a rule far more personal, far less representative and collective than that of other Yiddish Holocaust poets. He typically uses "I" rather than "we." Yet in the most deeply felt passages expressing the irrevocability of the covenantal relationship between the Divine Father and the favored but chastised child, Zeitlin is forced to link himself with all the others who are no more, and without whose tacit consent he could not with any decency accept justification or consolation for their suffering.

> Can I then choose not to believe
> in that living God whose purposes
> when He destroys, seeming to forsake me,
> I cannot conceive;
> choose not to believe in Him
> Who having turned my body to fine ash
> begins once more to wake me?

The pressure of emotion obliges Zeitlin, without ever forsaking the singular pronoun, to join himself with the body of the Jewish people whom God has burned in order to reawaken. That "aspiration" to the Holy One through the crematory flue which provoked bitter irony in Glatstein becomes a declaration of faith—albeit tragic and paradoxical faith—in Zeitlin. Although he uses the Yiddish word *Khurbn*, for Zeitlin the idea behind the English word Holocaust retains its full, original meaning, derived through the Greek *holokauston* from the Hebrew *olah*, "an offering made by fire unto the Lord."[7]

Although Zeitlin does not hesitate to involve God totally in the Holocaust and to profess faith that the burning and the awakening are part of a single process, he gives no indication of where the signs of new life are to be found in this world. That so much suffering is even more difficult to conceive without God than with Him, that "even my pain confirms Him," that without God our cries are like dead letters reaching nowhere: all this is convincingly expressed. But that there is in truth a divine rationale for what the poet has himself labeled the devil's destructiveness remains an article of faith, a willed belief sustained by no evidence:

> I believe God gives
> His inconceivable hells
> because somewhere else
> His eye surmises
> Inconceivable paradises
> for his slaughtered fugitives.

That "somewhere" has, to the mind of anyone but an orthodox believer, a fatal vagueness; for Zeitlin, however, it is the next world, whose standards are simply incommensurable with our own and can therefore hardly be conveyed through human language.

Whereas Glatstein thought that the Covenant granted at Sinai was dissolved by the great slaughter at Lublin-Maidanek, Zeitlin insists that God's presence manifested itself in both places: "Who so volcanic as my God? / If He is Sinai to me, / He is Maidanek as well." Maidanek too confirms the covenantal relationship between God and the Jews, who are depicted by Zeitlin as locked into a fatal embrace from which there is no escape but through death. "We cannot let go / of each other, / not He of me, nor I of

Him." A secular poet like Yehuda Amichai can respond to such a recognition with the ironic "My God, my God, / Why have you not forsaken me!?" But for Zeitlin the death that is the price of the Covenant is a death that breaks through the limits of this world to a new life. The Holocaust is for him nothing less than the biblically promised destruction of the world by fire, as well as the catastrophe that according to Jewish tradition must precede the messianic deliverance. So far is Zeitlin from the view that Auschwitz and Maidanek represented a radical evil, wholly divorced from God's purposes, that he repeatedly, even compulsively, refers to God's "experiments" in the Holocaust, "experiments on me, / experiments in fire." He knows that no other word so effectively calls up the obscene, cold cruelty of the Germans' treatment of people they had relegated to the status of laboratory rats. No other word could serve to involve the Jewish God so totally in the depredations visited upon His people, and thereby give credence to the blasphemous view of the skeptical writer (see, e.g., the Israeli novelist Kaniuk) that the God who willingly presided over Auschwitz must himself be a Nazi.

Few readers, whatever their religious convictions, are likely to give intellectual assent to Zeitlin's defiant affirmations. But they can hardly fail to be awed by so passionate a commitment to the biblical promise of consolation, and so complete an expression of the experience of loss and gain, curse and blessing. Far from being suppressed, the pattern of violent oscillation between love and chastisement in God's tragic relationship with the Jews is the cornerstone of Zeitlin's faith:

> He lets no one go under,
> as He lets me go under,
> lets no one be
> so utterly
> a paradigm in fire.
> There is no one He will equally desire
> to find, to lose.
> And I for my part find and lose Him, too,
> lose Him and find Him,
> an interchange of beatitude and law,
> lamentations and the Song of Songs.

"The Last of the Just" and "Blood from the Sky"

There is no coherent and connected body of fiction about the Holocaust that has the weight and impressiveness and unity of theme of Holocaust poetry. A poet facing a world emptied of his people and his God can make of those very absences his subject. This is particularly true of the postwar Yiddish poets. For them, as Glatstein wrote, "earth and heaven [were] wiped bare"; the Yiddish-speaking world that was their subject and their potential audience no longer existed. Their poetry became an extended elegy for what was no more and a reproach to, and quarrel, with, the God who was, whether by inadvertence or design, responsible for the disappearance of the Jewish world.

For a writer of fiction, it is far less easy to find a sufficient subject in deploring the absence of his proper subject, or to make his art solely a vehicle for accusing God of having emptied the world of meaning, of words, of the Covenant itself. Yet novelists too, albeit with greater indirection, have assaulted the heavens with question and challenge, and have sought to define the religious dimensions of the Holocaust, sometimes against the background of Jewish history, sometimes through an apocalyptic mode that makes Jewish experience the instrument for revelation of the darkest universal truths. Andre Schwarz-Bart's *The Last of the Just* (1959) provides a representative example of the first approach, and Piotr Rawicz's *Blood from the Sky* (1961) of the second.

For writers whose primary quandaries about the Holocaust are religious in nature, the long continuance of Jewish suffering over thousands of years appears in a double aspect. On the one hand, the endless persecutions and hideous massacres seem a blatant contradiction of God's love and concern for His Chosen People. As an old Eastern European Jewish quip, half-Hebrew, half-Yiddish, puts it:

אתה בחרתנו מכל העמים: וואָס האָסטו
געוואָלט פון דיין פאָלק ישראל?

Thou hast chosen us from among all the nations; why did you have to pick on the Jews?[8]

But on the other hand, the endurance of the Jewish people in spite of suffering and loss, its ability to survive long after its most potent enemies and overlords had disappeared from the face of the earth, to survive against all odds, seemed inexplicable except by miraculous causes, and specifically by a God whose chastisement of the Jews was inseparable from the desire to fulfill His purposes through them. The very decision to view the Nazis as descendants of Haman and Pharaoh, to see the Holocaust as an event of Jewish history, the latest and culminating disaster in an ancient series, would seem likely to predispose an author to imply an element of supernatural design in even the most dismal universe, a promise of continuance even after the impending cataclysm.

In Schwarz-Bart's *The Last of the Just*, these opposing attitudes (or conflicting emotions) coexist in uneasy tension with one another. The book traces the history of a family named Levy from the York massacre of 1185, "a minor episode in a history overstocked with martyrs," through its apparent extinction in the gas chambers of Auschwitz. The thread that links the many generations of the family is not only persecution and suffering—the "holocaust" that is said to have afflicted the Jews "since the beginning of time"—but their possession, in every generation, of a Lamed-Vovnik, one of the thirty-six Just Men upon whom, according to Jewish tradition, the world reposes. It does so because the Lamed-Vovnik takes everyone's suffering upon himself and " 'raises it to heaven and sets it at the feet of the Lord—who forgives.' " Schwarz-Bart's history of the Levy family is a dismal record of frightful persecution, but it is also a chronicle of noble heroisms and, above all, of miraculous survival. The original Just Man of the Levys went to his martyr's death convinced that he was the last of his line and his generation, the last of the Jews. So too did many of his successors through the centuries. But they were mistaken; always a remnant remained. Consequently, that part of the novel which carries us from the twelfth to the twentieth century beautifully celebrates what Simon Rawidowicz once called the phenomenon of Israel as the ever-dying people: "a phenomenon which has almost no parallel in mankind's story: a nation that has been disappearing constantly for the last two thousand years, exterminated in dozens of lands all over the globe, reduced to half or third of its population by tyrants ancient and modern—and yet it still exists. . . . "9

The largest segment of the novel is devoted to the story of Ernie Levy, who learns at an early age that he is destined to be the Just Man of the Levy tradition in the era of Nazi domination over Europe. The fate of the Jews throughout history and now under the Nazis moves Ernie to curse and blaspheme God, between whom and himself "there was an unbreachable wall . . . of Jewish lamentations." Yet as the Nazi net closes upon his people, and he moves to fulfill his inherited role of comforter and martyr, finally turning himself in voluntarily to the Germans at Drancy, Ernie becomes a believer in precisely the God who has been the author of Jewish misfortune through millennia. En route to the gas chambers with a group of Jewish children who have come to think of him as their "rabbi," Ernie prays: " 'O Lord, we went forth like this thousands of years ago. We walked across arid deserts and the blood-red Red Sea in a flood of salt, bitter tears. We are very old. We are still walking. Oh, let us arrive, finally!' " From such passages, in which Ernie's experience fits into an assigned place as the culmination of a series of like events in Jewish history, one could indeed conclude with Rawidowicz: "A nation dying for thousands of years means a living nation. Our incessant dying means uninterrupted living, rising, standing up, beginning anew. . . . If we are the last—let us be the last as our fathers and forefathers were. Let us prepare the ground for the last Jews who will come after us, and for the last Jews who will rise after them, and so on until the end of days."10

But there is another, contrary movement of the novel, in which Schwarz-Bart uses Jewish history only to repudiate it, and to deny the consolation implicit in the old affirmation, periodically made after Jewish populations were decimated: "the *people* Israel lives." The segment of the novel that describes Ernie's journey into death really does insist that he is indeed the *last* of the Just, that he will be survived by none, and that this is final death for him and his people. "Ernie realized clearly that he was entering the last circle of the Levys' hell." In the camp, he does fulfill his historically prescribed role as Just Man by offering to the children the consolation of new life to come in the "Kingdom of Israel," but it is a false consolation, a lie that he dispenses because " 'there is no room for truth here.' " Not in his words, but in his face "the death of the Jewish people . . . was written clearly." In the moments before death, "it seemed to him that an eternal silence was closing down upon the Jewish breed marching to slaughter—that no heir, no memory would supervene to prolong the silent parade of victims." In all these passages, the novelist appears to say that the Holocaust was truly the end of the Jewish people and even to warn that longevity, which may cultivate its own illusions and complacency, is no guarantee of permanence.

The tension between the impulse to see the Holocaust as another tragic event within the history of an ever dying and therefore eternally Chosen People and the contrary impulse to see it as the end of Jewish history and a denial of the Jewish God continues to the end of the novel, and beyond it. A moment before his death by gas, Ernie recalls the legend of a rabbinical ancestor who, martyred by Roman fire while wrapped in the scrolls of the Torah, told his people with his last breath that although the Torah parchment was burning, its letters were taking wing. " '*Ah, yes, surely, the letters are taking wing*,' Ernie repeated as the flame blazing in his chest rose suddenly to his head." But whatever of affirmation is to be found in Ernie's final revelation of Jewish continuance is turned to mockery by the blasphemous concluding prayer of the narrator himself:

> And praised. *Auschwitz*. Be. *Maidanek*. The Lord. *Treblinka*.
> And praised. *Buchenwald*. Be. *Mauthausen*. The Lord. *Belzec*.
> And praised. *Sobibor*. Be. *Chelmno*. The Lord. *Ponary*. And
> praised. . . .

Earlier in the novel, an elderly Jew in Paris had called God to account for His unending punishment of the Jews for their iniquities by warning: " *'We Jews will soon sleep in the dust, and one day you will seek us . . . and we will no longer exist.'* " By finally identifying himself with this reproach to God, even Schwarz-Bart—a writer with only the vaguest idea of the meaning of the Jewish Covenant, and with an abundant hostility toward the Jewish God—finds himself, like Glatstein and Molodowsky, partner to an ancient quarrel that confirms the very attachment it wishes to deny.

Two years after *The Last of the Just* appeared, another French-Jewish writer of East European background, Piotr Rawicz, published a novel also in the tradition of the Jewish quarrel with God, but much more profoundly aware of the paradox of chosenness that is at its base. *Blood from the Sky* (1961) is at once more nihilistic and more mystical than Schwarz-Bart's book. Its innumerable "excursions into ontology" generally terminate in the conclusion that Being is "a foul-smelling dough in a kneading machine" and that "the only enemy of beings is Being." After watching the Germans, in scenes of unbearable horror, cut out the tongue of a Jewish boy and the eyes of a Jewish girl, the narrator sees in the monstrosity before him, "the belly of the Universe, the belly of Existence . . . gaping open, and its filthy intestines invading the room." This is taken as irrefutable proof that "God is mad, stark raving mad. . . . " If He exists at all, He should create only atheists. But alongside the nausea and cosmic disgust that reverberate through the book, there is another impulse, which must be responsible for the fact that the book exists at all, since one target of its metaphysical fury is literature itself, "anti-dignity exalted to a system." The novel's narrator and protagonist is a Ukrainian Jew named Boris, whose story and reflections and poetic fragments are framed by the editorial comments of the author Rawicz, who claims he has had to do much cutting and reshaping to give some coherence to Boris' outpourings. Boris, in his grim and peculiar fashion, is a continuator of the tradition of a rabbi among his ancestors who had pleaded on behalf of the Jewish people against God. This rabbi had readily acknowledged his own sins and those of his brethren, but had challenged God to say what *He* would do " 'If You were the permanent target of every kind of mockery and cruelty and yet, in the teeth of it, had to survive? To survive, not because You love life . . . but from a sense of duty, so that someone survived by whom Your Law would be more or less rigorously observed?' " Boris, witness and victim of more terrible mockery and cruelty than his grandfather's generation had ever known, flings his people's reproach against a God who now threatens not only Jewish existence but, through His punishment of His wayward people, the ground of all being and the meaning of existence itself.

Jewish history exists in *Blood from the Sky* primarily as an aspect of the mental world of its protagonist, who comes to view the Holocaust as both a collapsed history of the Jewish people and a test of whether that history had ultimate meaning. Boris senses that this long history and the ordering it gave to human experience may now be not merely ended but rendered absurd by the new barbarism. All of Jewish history was now being relived within a few years and "was possibly about to be extinguished before our eyes, and together with us." Both the horrible events recounted in the novel and the concurrent story of the narrator's attempt to impose coherence on them by writing a "composition on the subject of decomposition" call into question the power of Jewish history to provide a meaningful background to the Holocaust. One character asserts that "both past and future must be destroyed so that they may be integrated in the solely existing present." Rawicz, unlike Schwarz-Bart, does not believe that the destruction of European Jewry can be presented or contained within the historical mode because it is an apocalyptic event. His postscript to the novel insists that *"this book is not a historical record."* Elsewhere he has maintained that in his writing he is less concerned with the historical than with the psychological, the metaphysical, "above all the ontological aspects" of the Holocaust. "I believe that the fate and condition of the Jewish people are the very essence of the human condition—the furthest borders of human destiny. And the fate of the 'Holocaust Jew,' . . . is . . . the ontological essence of that ontological essence."[11] Yet the ontological revelation toward which the novel strives would be meaningless if it did not provide an answer to the question of whether Jewish history pointed beyond itself to the relation between the Jewish God and all mankind. The novel's implicit claim to greatness depends upon its ability to demonstrate Emil Fackenheim's assertion that, precisely because the Germans cut off Jews from humanity and denied them the right to exist, Jews have since Auschwitz come to "represent all humanity when they affirm their Jewishness and deny the Nazi denial."[12] Boris, in his most desperate moments of imprisonment and torture, declares that "the body of History [is] attacked by cockroaches . . . but they will not devour it. . . ."

The paradox of chosenness whereby the gift of the Covenant that the Jews were singularly privileged to receive became the single reason for their persecution and murder is the pivot on which the novel's action turns. Boris, the hero and narrator, at first speaks ironically of a certain unwillingness to escape from the fate of his fellow Jews because " 'I have the feeling it would be a cheap way out not to pay for all that I have received from my God.' " In fact, Boris has many traits that would aid his escape from the Nazis and their Ukrainian helpers. He is fair-haired, he speaks excellent German, he has mastered Ukrainian history and literature, and he has managed to obtain a Christian birth certificate. Only one thing can keep him from passing as a non-Jew: "The sign of the Covenant, inscribed in my body long ago, as it had been inscribed in the bodies of my forefathers and THEIR forefathers, could be made out all too plainly by those taking part in the hunt that was going on in our town. It was within the capacity of the dimmest oaf from Bavaria to interpret this hieroglyph. . . ."

It is not too much to say that in this book not only Jewish history but the nature of literature and ultimately the whole of the universe converge on the circumcision as sign of the Covenant. From the outset of the book the ultimate meaning of the Covenant, the question of whether Boris can ever become sufficiently attached to life to prefer it to death, and the ability of Boris (or anyone else) to compose a work of literature about the Holocaust are intertwined. Of the novel's three parts, the first and the third make explicit reference to the mysterious link between the circumcision by which the Jew is distinguished from the gentile and the metaphorical habit whereby writers discover surprising similarities between things apparently dissimilar: Part One is called "The Tool and the Art of Comparison," Part Three, "The Tool and the Thwarting of Comparisons." From the outset, the novel asks whether the paradigm for the writer's act of creation is supplied by God or by the Nazis. There seems a deliberate ambiguity in Boris's reference to the yellow stars that the Jews must wear in accordance with Nazi decree as "yellow stars of the Poet-King." This would seem to be a reference to the God of the Covenant, but when Boris's madly brilliant friend Leo L. contemplates the Germans' impending sweep through the town, he calls them "destroying angels" and says that it is they, not the Jewish God, who hold the key to the whole cosmic drama, since " 'this Performance of Nothingness . . . is less misleading than everything else. . . . ' " When the Germans, having already "chosen" the whole Jewish people to be murdered, are contemplating those Jews from whom they will select the first group to be murdered, Boris describes the moment as one of "vibrant complicity that arises between artist and raw material before the act of creation begins."

Before the town was destroyed, Leo L., though cynical about all else, had spoken to Boris of "the vocation to be witness," the only vocation that could ever again matter. But when, after his survival, Boris turns to the task of bearing witness to the saving remnant of the Jewish people, he finds that both the town and its memory are dead, that the "I" who lived in the town and who then survived prison and torture hardly exists in the man who puts pen to paper. "When a whirlwind comes along, one must make the most of it, exploit it, start writing at once, lying at once." But the difficulty of ascertaining any substantial relationship between the events of the Holocaust and the literature that describes them is only the beginning of the conundrum. After the Holocaust, "the 'literary manner' is an obscenity by definition." Rawicz's own dilemma in re-creating and interpreting the cosmic catastrophe that he survived is made a main subject of the novel itself. *Blood from the Sky* deplores, in every conceivable way, on the suggestive as well as the discursive level, the paralysis of language and imagination caused by this crime of unprecedented magnitude against the Jewish people and the human condition itself. "One by one," complains Boris, "words—all the words of the human language—wilt and grow too weak to bear a meaning. And then they fall away, like dead scales. All meanings evaporate." If this happens to the writer, he must cease to be one. The novel is therefore filled with would-be writers searching out ways to continue to write in a universe emptied of meaning. One madman named David G. keeps a diary that after the war becomes the basis for a widely popular novel. Its idea of "constructive action" in modern literature is to "spit on everything." At one point when Boris is masquerading as a Ukrainian, he is obliged to listen to a story composed by a Nazi second lieutenant of literary inclinations while outside the window the heads of five Jewish men who have been buried, alive, upright in a garden are being licked and chewed by pigs. At least this Nazi litterateur remains untroubled by the inadequacies of naturalism, for his sole subject is cockroaches killing other cockroaches.

It is this very image of the cockroach, almost compulsive in the novel, that invades Boris's thoughts after he is arrested and asked to drop his trousers, revealing the penis. "On it, the sign of the Covenant is inscribed in indelible lettering, all too easy for these bustling men to read. The tool and the art of comparison." Henceforward, his "dreams could not possibly come under any heading but entomology. Cockroaches' dreams." Since their escape from the Ukrainian Jewish town, Boris and his mistress Naomi had attached themselves, however precariously, to life not only through guile and luck but through their shared sexual passion. Now the tool of passion that had kept alive in Boris at least the illusion of meaning in life becomes the means of flinging him back among the members of the Jewish community covenanted to death. He wishes to pass as a Ukrainian among his gentile fellow prisoners, but they single him out in the shower by pointing to his circumcised tool:

> Boris would stare at the subject of contention: so this was the instrument, the poor instrument, of all his past metaphysics? Of all his metaphysics which in the past had seemed so personal, so exceptional, and which today were no more peculiar to him, no more "individual," than are the entrails of one squashed cockroach as compared to the entrails of another?

The book's most daring exercise of that "art of comparison" with which the "tool" is consistently linked either by similarity or contrast comes at the conclusion of part one. The Germans have just made an abattoir of a Jewish kindergarten, mutilating but not murdering the children. Two hours after the Germans leave, Boris manages to return to the scene with a nurse, who carries a syringe. "Several mutilated children were still suffering. The nurse went around distributing death, like portions of ginger-bread stuffed with darkness. For they do exist, Boris assures us, cakes stuffed with darkness. He also compares the nurse to the gardener who fulfills the destiny of the flowers and the sunshine by picking them." Here the art of comparison exemplifies literature's ability to assimilate new realms of experience to the imagination by linking disparate sensations through the bond of simile and metaphor. This is an artistic triumph of sorts, and yet it fills the author with revulsion rather than pride, for either it admits us into a world it would be better never to have known or deludes us into thinking we can know this world through words. Not long afterward, therefore, Boris, about to succumb to the temptation to compare each of the millennia that have elapsed or are yet to come to a squashed bedbug, resolves "to kill comparisons, to expunge them all, to exterminate the whole tribe, the whole pernicious breed." He must reluctantly admit, of course, that if figures of speech are killed forever, nothing is left to the writer but "mere recounting, mere enumeration, so pullulating, and so ugly . . . worthy only of a storekeeper."

What then is the connection between Boris's revulsion from the Covenant and his revulsion from literature? If the genocidal extermination of the Jewish people as if they were bedbugs or cockroaches has spread its poison even to "the Throne of God, who lay in a swoon . . . surrounded by His own vomit," then it has also transformed literature into "the art, occasionally remunerative, of rummaging in vomit." It is absurd and irrational that the sign of the Covenant, a mere detail of physiognomy, should, despite all one's talents and cleverness and acquirement, make him indistinguishable as an individual from all other Jewish males and obliterate every distinction except that between Jew and gentile. But if it is so, fears Boris, then the German aspirant to literature who writes exclusively about cockroaches killing other cockroaches is the real master of the old art of comparison. Everything hinges on the question of whether the Jews have been chosen by God or only by the world.

Finally, Boris's sixty-six days in prison, during which time he tries to persuade his captors that, despite his circumcision, he is a Ukrainian and not a Jew, reveal to him the true connection between the Covenant and creation, both literary and biological. Just prior to, and again during, his interrogation by the S.S., Boris perceives the Sign of Terrestrial Life, "a transverse line giving rise to three stems, each surmounted by a small flame." He had first learned to recognize this pattern when he was nearing his thirteenth year, the age of ritual maturity in Jewish males, and was being initiated into the mysteries of the Book of Creation. He had been visited by it on three subsequent occasions. Now, in its crucial visit to Boris, the Sign of Life drives all developments and phenomena "back to their point of departure, back to their seed and even to the seed of their seed." The Sign brings Boris to the recognition that the Covenant, which has come to him, like life itself, from his ancestors, is exactly the Word become flesh. The Sign of Life brings him to awareness of the implications of the fact that his tool, "this factory for producing metaphysics," has come through the shipwreck of everything else still alive, still responding, still capable of creation. "And there he was, unbuttoning his trousers with his manacled hands and baring, yet again, the organ on which the sign of the Covenant had been inscribed years before. Did this door still open onto God? Did it at least open onto the Divine . . . ? Dull rites, dull symbols, and those which are less so: are the Covenant with God and physical passion, sharing the same site and founded in the same crucible, the same thing . . . ? Could the Biblical patriarch, that forefather clad in the red desert and resonant dust, have foreseen this thought of mine? Did he set me a playful riddle, one that I am succeeding in solving after thousands of years —at the LAST moment?" This is as close as Rawicz and Boris will bring us to unraveling the mysterious connection between the Jewish Covenant and the creative act that underlies not merely literature but the universe itself. Less mysterious is the revelation to Boris that from a moral point of view there is one fate worse than being circumcised: namely, being uncircumcised. For no sooner is Boris accepted by his fellow prisoners as (what he is not) a gentile than he receives membership in the society of those Czeslaw Milosz called the "uncircumcised, the associates of death."

Blood from the Sky is built upon two enormous paradoxes. It asserts in a variety of ways that the Holocaust cannot be assimilated by the artistic imagination, and that "man never so much resembles an insect as when he engages in the activity of writing." But its intellectual brilliance admits us to a realm beyond grief and so belies the very paralysis that it deplores. It gains its unique power from Rawicz's ability to "constellate [Jewish] misfortune across the whole sky," as Glatstein would say, and to show how the destruction of the Jews has permanently disarranged the universe and altered the human condition. Yet Rawicz has placed himself firmly within the Jewish tradition that pleads on behalf of His people against the God who has chosen them. Cynical as he is about the universe and the powers alleged to control it, Boris argues that the Jews, "by dint of strange and inhumanly systematized meditations, had succeeded in approaching what was godlike in the human condition as no one else had ever done. . . . " With bitterness and cynicism, Rawicz reduces the Covenant from the spiritual to the merely physical; then, with resentment and grudging respect, he admits that only the Covenant is metaphysically capacious enough to contain the storms of his imagination and the meaning of the Holocaust.

I am grateful to Harcourt Brace Jovanovich, Inc., for permission to quote from *Blood from the Sky*, by Piotr Rawicz.

1. *Critical Views of Isaac Bashevis Singer*, ed. Irving Malin (New York: New York University Press, 1969), p. 15.

2. Quoted by Irving Howe in "Journey of a Poet," *Commentary* 53 (January 1972): 76.

3. *A Treasury of Yiddish Poetry*, ed. Irving Howe and Eliezer Greenberg (New York: Holt, Rinehart & Winston, 1969), pp. 52–53.

4. Richard L. Rubenstein, *After Auschwitz: Radical Theology and Contemporary Judaism* (Indianapolis: Bobbs-Merrill, 1966), p. 153.

5. Emil L. Fackenheim, *God's Presence in History: Jewish Affirmations and Philosophical Reflections* (New York: New York University Press, 1970), p. 76.

6. *A Treasury of Yiddish Poetry*, p. 53.

7. Lucy Dawidowicz, *The War Against the Jews: 1933-1945* (New York: Holt, Rinehart & Winston, 1975), p. xv.

8. Ruth R. Wisse, *The Schlemiel as Modern Hero* (Chicago: University of Chicago Press, 1971), p. 47.

9. Simon Rawidowicz, "Israel the Ever-Dying People," in *Modern Jewish Thought: A Source Reader*, ed. Nahum N. Glatzer (New York: Schocken Books, 1977), p. 140.

10. Ibid., pp. 140, 142.

11. *From Bergen-Belsen to Jerusalem: Contemporary Implications of the Holocaust*, ed. Emil L. Fackenheim (Jerusalem: Institute of Contemporary Jewry, 1975), p. 25.

12. Emil L. Fackenheim, *God's Presence in History*, p. 86.

We make out of the quarrel with others, rhetoric, but of the quarrel with ourselves, poetry.—William Butler Yeats, *Per Amica Silentia Lunae*

chapter 8

A Dialogue of the Mind with Itself
Chaim Grade's Quarrel with Hersh Rasseyner

If we had not long ago grown accustomed to the fact that Yiddish literature, apart from the work of I. B. Singer, remains *terra incognita* for most American and English readers, it would be a cause of some astonishment that Chaim Grade's novella *My Quarrel with Hersh Rasseyner* has not established itself as a minor classic of modern literature. It is both a great and a grandly representative story because it presents with tremendous dramatic force the most terrifying quandaries of our time in the special shape and with the compelling urgency that they have received from the cataclysms of twentieth-century history and particularly from the destruction of European Jewry. If we had to select a single work to stand as a paradigm of all Holocaust literature, a work of sufficient generalizing power to contain within itself not only most of the religious, philosophical, and artistic questions that the Holocaust raises but also the whole range of conflicting answers to them, we could not do better than to rely on Grade's story.[1]

My Quarrel with Hersh Rasseyner is told in the first person by a character named Chaim, who seems to be the author Chaim Grade, thinly disguised for fictional purposes. In the course of describing his quarrel, or rather series of quarrels, with his former Mussarist[2] schoolmate Hersh Rasseyner, Chaim creates a philosophical dialogue between the elements of faith and of doubt in his own soul. In the novella, Hersh Rasseyner, who never departs from orthodoxy, speaks for religious faith, and Chaim, the former yeshiva student turned writer, for religious skepticism; but in truth the voices we hear in this dialogue are the accusing and self-accusing voices of the author himself. In fact, the mental processes underlying the story's composition are made transparent toward the end when

Chaim says to his philosophical adversary: " 'Reb Hersh . . . as I sat here listening to you, I sometimes thought I was listening to myself. And since it's harder to lie to yourself than to someone else, I will answer you as though you were my own conscience. . . .' "

Chaim begins his story in 1937 at a point when he had already separated himself from the Mussarists and their unworldly ways. He is giving a lecture—apparently on a literary subject, for he is derisively referred to by Hersh as a writer of "godless verses"—in Bialystok near the yeshiva in which he had been a student seven years earlier. Some of his former schoolmates, in defiance of the yeshiva's prohibition against secular learning, attend his lecture, and others visit him secretly. But the one former schoolmate whom Chaim truly desires to see again does not appear; and that is Hersh Rasseyner. Nor is this surprising, for whereas many of the other Mussarists chafe under the severe religious discipline that binds them, Hersh thrives upon it and seems never to be tempted by the lures of secular knowledge or the pleasures of the world outside of the shtetl.

Chaim and Hersh do, however, meet unexpectedly in the street and at once discover that they already speak different languages. Chaim has so far forgotten his religious training that he unthinkingly greets Hersh with the modish "How are you?", a question that in the yeshiva means "What is the state of your religious life?" Hersh does not lose the opportunity to remind his lapsed brother that his frivolous social use of what is still for others the most compelling of questions reveals the diminution of life that attends the lapse from piety: " 'And how are you, Chaim Vilner?[3] My question, you see, is more important.' " Hersh then proceeds, in the middle of the street, with a sublime indifference to social decorum that shocks the assimilated narrator, to reproach Chaim for having allowed himself to be lured from a religious life into the "enlightened" world of Western Europe and to warn him that all his successes in the secular world will leave him less happy than he would have been had he remained in the yeshiva. The life of piety, he asserts, is validated by God; the life of letters by literary critics. " 'You write godless verses and they reward you by patting you on the cheek. Now they're stuffing you with applause as they stuff a goose with grain. But later you'll see, when you've begun to go to their school, oh, won't the worldly ones beat you! Which of you isn't hurt by criticism? Is there one of you really so self-confident that he doesn't go around begging for some authority's approval? Is there one of you who's prepared to publish his book anonymously?[4] The big thing with you people is that your name should be seen and known. You have given up our tranquillity of spirit for what? For passions you will never be able to satisfy and for doubts you will never be able to answer, no matter how much you suffer.' "

Chaim, for his part, accuses his pious friend of the sin of pride, for there is such a thing as pride in one's modesty and humility. Whereas Hersh alleges that the appetite for pleasure can never be satiated because it grows by what it feeds on, Chaim replies that in those people for whom pleasure and fame offer no temptation, what looks to the world like self-denial is really self-indulgence. Besides, Chaim denies that he himself has become a mere pleasure-seeker; accused of running away from the religious life, he maintains that he has actually returned to his proper home among the common people who in the shtetl were expected to support the very religious scholars (like Hersh) who deplored their worldliness and impiety.

To these arguments Hersh does not condescend to reply. But the argument has already proceeded far enough to assure the narrator of the correctness of his decision to leave the yeshiva. Or was it his decision? Ironically, he wants to believe both that the decision was the correct one and that *he* did not make it. "If at the time, I said to myself, I didn't know why and where I was going, someone else thought it out for me, someone stronger than I. That someone else was—my generation and my environment." It is the feeblest of faiths, and like all faiths in a generation, youthful or decrepit, it does not long survive the test of experience.

The second part of the story commences two years later,

when the generation and environment in which the emancipated Chaim had put his faith had produced, among other things, the two great revolutionary powers of the modern European world, the Soviet Union and Nazi Germany. It is 1939, they are carving up Eastern Europe between them, and the Soviets are in control of Vilna. "Hunger raged in the city. Every face was clouded with fear of the arrests carried out at night by NKVD agents. My heart was heavy. Once, standing in line for a ration of bread, I suddenly saw Hersh Rasseyner." For the Soviet domination of Vilna, Hersh (now a married man)[5] holds Chaim partly responsible. The Soviet Union had, of course, been the great, almost messianic, hope of secular progressives, and in Hersh's view such idol-worship is the logical culmination of the sentimental idolatry of the proletariat that Chaim had expressed to him in 1937. But Chaim is as little willing to accept responsibility for the Soviet occupation of Vilna as he had been for his own departure from piety into secularism. He disavows all responsibility for secular progressivism gone wrong by telling Hersh, " 'I bear no more responsibility for all that than you do for me.' " But the analogy is imprudently chosen, for it is precisely Hersh's point that under God every man is his brother's keeper and that human beings are so interconnected that no one may evade responsibility for his acts: " 'You're wrong, Chaim. I do bear responsibility for you.' He retreated a few steps and motioned with his eyes to the Red Army soldiers, as though to say, 'And you for them.' " Chaim's willingness to read even in Hersh's physical movements a reproach to himself is a reminder that although the story is written, literally and figuratively, from Chaim's point of view, it is eminently a dialogue of the mind with itself.

The next meeting between the two men takes place on our side of the great divide of twentieth-century history, the Holocaust in which six million Jews were murdered. The scene is Paris, 1948, and the two old friends, who have by now become rather old antagonists, meet on the Métro. The narrator has spent the war years wandering across Russia,

Poland, and Western Europe; Hersh Rasseyner has been in a concentration camp in Latvia, and is now the head of a yeshiva in Salzheim, Germany. The men greet each other affectionately, and when Hersh asks Chaim "How are you?" he no longer asks in derision but in the genuine Mussarist way, out of concern for the well-being of his friend. Soon, however, Chaim senses that Hersh's warmth flows from his assumption that no sane man, in the aftermath of the Holocaust, can believe in worldly ex- pedients for human and social redemption. Ironically, each man virtually takes it for granted that the Holocaust has destroyed the foundations upon which the other's life had until then been based. If Hersh assumes that anyone with eyes in his head can now see that to depend upon man-made ethical systems, works of art, and social machinery to transform the human condition is like relying on razor blades to hew down giant oak trees, then Chaim for his part assumes that no sane man can still believe in a God who presides over concentration camps and crematoria. Chaim is astounded that anyone can wring some affirmation of God's existence out of the concentration camps; and Hersh asserts that life is for him, in the post-Holocaust world, impossible without God: " 'How could I stand it without Him in this murderous world?' "

For the debate that ensues over the relative merits of faith in God and faith in the world in a universe that has been harrowed by the Holocaust, the Paris setting is peculiarly appropriate. Paris, after all, had once been the scene of the most gigantic and conscious attempt of modern times to realize a wholly secular faith. It was in Paris that the altar was replaced by the scaffold, the priest by the executioner, the congregation by a howling mob thirsting for *human* blood, the crucifix that had once been worn on the breasts of the citizenry by a miniature replica of the guillotine. The Enlightenment's dream of making man the sole idol to which he would himself bow down found its existential realization in the French Revolution and the Reign of Terror.

Hersh Rasseyner never even participated in this dream,

and so it is all the more incredible to him that his friend Chaim should continue to cling to it after the Holocaust. He looks at the statues in the niches of the walls of the Hôtel de Ville representing the great statesmen, heroes, scholars, and artists of modern France and pointedly asks his emancipated and worldly friend, " 'Who are those idols?' " From Hersh's point of view, Chaim has forsaken God only to seek objects of worship among these icons of mere human beings. In defense of these statues and of his reverence for their originals, Chaim praises the power of art to induce imaginative sympathy. He singles out from among the various statues those of poets and trots out for his benighted religious friend the *apologia* for literature as the great instrument of moral imagination that was first articulated by Shelley and De Quincey, then given canonical status by George Eliot. But is it good enough in the aftermath of the Holocaust? Hersh does not think so. Besides, the vaunted sympathy of artists and poets with lustful and wicked people arises from the fact that they recognize themselves in such people; hence what looks like sympathetic tolerance is only self-pity.

The Parisian setting of the argument over the meaning of the Holocaust is also used by Grade to emphasize an important difference in the personalities of the protagonists that was touched on briefly in the opening section of the story. As the argument becomes more heated, Hersh becomes more emotional and Chaim becomes—more embarrassed. A bearded Jew is shaking his finger at the sculptures of the Hôtel de Ville, and passing Parisians have begun to stop and stare. "Hersh did not so much as notice the passers-by. I felt embarrassed in the face of these Frenchmen, smiling and looking at us curiously." Apparently the vindication of God is a more engrossing activity than the vindication of literature. Later in the story, Hersh suggests that the extreme form of the worldly man's concern about what other people will think of him is the European practice of dueling. " 'Think of it! For a word they didn't like they used to fight with swords or shoot one another. To keep public opinion from sneering or a fool from calling them coward, though they trembled at the thought of dying, they went to their death.' "

Once he has got over his embarrassment at Hersh's shouting and gesticulating and long-beardedness, Chaim turns to the question of what, if anything, the Holocaust meant. Some of his remarks reenforce our uneasiness over the whole enterprise of trying to assign meaning to a moral debacle that defies it, for Chaim has a tendency to speak of the concentration camps as an educational "experience." He asserts that not even the camps could change men from what they were; nevertheless " 'in the crisis men saw themselves and others undisguised.' " Hersh, for his part, wonders why Chaim should even think it worthy of remark that suffering produced neither wisdom nor sanctity in men who did not possess them before entering the camps. Man is indeed capable of transformation, he argues, but only through religion. Hersh himself, in espousing asceticism and piety, had not been following the path of least resistance but of greatest blessedness, for his lusts and obstinacies had been, he maintains, as strong as those of any man. But he had accepted, as his enlightened friend had not, the fact that there are certain human impulses that require not mere enlightenment, improving, and perfuming, but uprooting; and that rebirth is a painful process because its prerequisite is the death of the old self. Rebirth, however, can be effected only through religion. If religion cannot transform man, nothing can; worldly, human instruments—art, politics, science, philosophy—can never raise man above himself for the simple reason that they originate with man.

In the face of this argument, Chaim nevertheless clings to the rhetoric of enlightenment: " 'You can't banish shadows with a broom, only with a lighted lamp.' " His invocation of enlightenment and its apostles enshrined in the Hôtel de Ville provokes Hersh to a long and moving discourse on the impassable gulf between knowledge and goodness, a gulf that he had grasped intellectually in his yeshiva study, but that was fully revealed to him only in the concentration camps. He recalls to Chaim that the Germans, who are always reminding people of the fact, have produced at least as many great men worthy of niches in the Hôtel de Ville as have the French, and in the realm of moral philosophy have produced more than the French. But did those moral philosophers influence the German people to become better? Or were the philosophers themselves good men? In the concentration camps, Hersh had for the first time come in contact with men—presumably assimilated Jews—who had been trained in the great German universities, and for the first time felt the power and even majesty of secular knowledge. Yet he was not tempted by it away from piety because he concluded from what he saw in the camps that the moral philosophers of Western Europe are men who say, and do not. " 'Occasionally I found in their writings as much talent and depth as in our own Holy Books, if the two may be mentioned in one breath. But they are satisfied with talk! And I want you to believe me when I say that I concede that their poets and scientists wanted to be good. Only— only they weren't able to. And if some did have good qualities, they were exceptions. The masses and even their wise men didn't go any farther than fine talk. As far as talking is concerned, they talk more beautifully than we do.' " A philosophical morality, Hersh implies, looks good in fair weather, but in concentration camps sterner stuff is required.

For one schooled in the yeshiva, Hersh shows a remarkable familiarity with enlightenment principles and rhetoric. He says that the reason why the moral philosophers were incapable of becoming better in action than they were was that they were committed to the pursuit of pleasure. The pursuit of pleasure or joy or happiness has been enjoined on Western man in a variety of forms from Epicurus (and it is worthy of note that the Yiddish word for heretic is *apikoyres*, derived from Epicurean) through the Declaration of Independence (where we are pledged to "the pursuit of happiness"). But according to Hersh the most enlightened and philosophical nation in Europe failed to achieve the goodness of which it wrote so eloquently because " 'pleasure is not something that can be had by itself, [therefore] murder arose among them—the pleasure of murder.' " The dream that worldly wisdom, as distinct from religious piety, could be a guarantee of sanctity, came to its end—or should have—in the concentration camps. " 'All the days of my youth I kept my eyes on the earth, without looking at the world. Then came the German. He took me by my Jewish beard, yanked my head up, and told me to look him straight in the eyes. So I had to look into his evil eyes, and into the eyes of the whole world as well. And I saw, Chaim, I saw—you know what I saw. Now I can look at all the idols and read all the forbidden impurities and contemplate all the pleasures of life, and it won't tempt me any more because now I know the true face of the world.' "

Hersh keeps referring to his own experience to reenforce his arguments, but his primary concern is the desire to secure the well-being of his friend by persuading him to forsake the world and return to the Jewish fold. This is what gives the story its dramatic force and makes it much more than a Voltairean philosophical dialogue. Feeling responsible for his secularized friend, Hersh must prove to Chaim that the world that he supposed was striving to improve itself was striving only for blood, and that it *could* not transform itself for good because its ethical systems were worked out by human minds, and no stream can rise higher than its source. The secular philosophers of Western Europe " 'trusted their reasoned assumptions as men trust the ice of a frozen river in winter. Then came Hitler and put his weight on the wisdom of the wise men of the nations. The ice of their slippery reasoning burst, and all their goodness was drowned.' " Centuries of the most highly refined hair-splitting and logic-chopping on every conceivable moral question had their conclusion in this: " 'there came in the West a booted ruler with a little mustache, and in the East a booted ruler with a big mustache, and both of them together struck the wise man to the ground, and he sank into the mud.' "

By this stage in the argument, Hersh is once again excited to the point where he is shouting. But now Chaim is less concerned about Parisian passersby because he has come to understand that Hersh is shouting in order to reach that buried self of his old friend which has retreated into the depths of his subconsciousness as into an infinitely distant land. "He shouted at me as though I were a dark cellar and he was calling to someone hiding in me." Hersh's passion does not affect his fluency because, as he now reveals, he has during all the long years in the concentration camp rehearsed his argument for faith in the hope that he might be able one day to use it on his heretical friend, who is fixed in his mind's eye as the representative of secularized Jews in general.

Although Hersh's argument, like the story itself, pivots on the question of how to respond to the Holocaust, he is also trying to demonstrate that the Holocaust is only the most devilish of all the human enterprises that engage the energies of those who desert the community of God because they would become like gods themselves. The enlightened Jew, according to Hersh, separated himself from piety because he wished to distinguish himself as an individual, to be acclaimed in life and remembered after death not as a member of the Community of Israel but as a great scientist, thinker, or writer. " 'You didn't violate the commandment against idolatry. Of course not! You were your own gods. You prophesied, "Man will be a god." So naturally he became a devil.' " Movements of religious reform, which seek to lighten the burden of the Law on the individual, are in Hersh's view as futile and unending as the pursuit of happiness; for in religious matters the lighter the burden is made, the harder is it to bear. The man who fasts twice a week does so without difficulty; the man who fasts once a year finds the task so difficult that he soon ceases to fast altogether. And here again the belief that Hersh had long entertained as to the folly of the Jew trying to assimilate himself into the nations and to become like his oppressors, was proved upon his pulses in the concentration camps:

> "I lay on the earth and was trampled by the German in his hobnailed boots. Well, suppose that an angel of God had come to me then, that he had bent down and whispered into my ear, 'Hersh, in the twinkling of an eye I will turn you into the

German. I will put his coat on you and give you his murderous face; and he will be you. Say the word and the miracle will come to pass.' If the angel had asked me—do you hear, Chaim?—I would not have agreed at all. Not for one minute would I have consented to be the other, the German, my torturer. I want the justice of law. . . . With the Almighty's help I could stand the German's boots on my throat, but if I had had to put on his mask, his murderous face, I would have been smothered as though I had been gassed. And when the German shouted at me, 'You are a slave of slaves,' I answered through my wounded lips, 'Thou hast chosen me.' "

To be murdered and mutilated as the member of a people chosen by God is a better, a more sanctified fate than to survive as a murderer—and certainly a better fate than to be murdered and mutilated in the act of aping the morality and the manners of one's murderer.

Hersh's final plea to his old yeshiva schoolmate is made on behalf of the six million who have been murdered. All Jews, he admits, mourn the third of their people who have been martyred, but not every Jew seems to be aware, of what must surely be true, that " 'it was not a third of the House of Israel that was destroyed, but a third of himself, of his body, his soul.' " From Hersh's point of view, every Jew living in the aftermath of the Holocaust lives with a part of his soul in the grave; and it is therefore incomprehensible to him that Chaim, who is by no means the least sensitive of Jews, should eat and sleep and laugh and dress quite as if nothing had happened, quite as if the values of the secular world in which he had placed his faith had not collapsed in ruins. For Hersh, nothing seems more luminously self-evident than that after Auschwitz nothing is left to us except God, to whom we must cry out, in desperate emulation of those who were slaughtered, " 'For Thy sake are we killed all the day.' "

When Hersh concludes his impassioned plea, the sky is growing darker and the stone figures around the Hôtel de Ville have shrunk, "as though frightened by what Hersh Rasseyner had said, and quietly burrowed deeper into the walls." Chaim, who has been relatively silent for some time apart from an occasional demurrer, now must respond to the challenge thrown down by his quarrelsome friend. Grade has given ample opportunity to the spokesman for his anti-self to state the best case that could be made for faith in the wake of the Holocaust; and it would be hard to find a literary work that gave fuller credence to the ancient theory that a devil's advocate must be admitted into the midst of one's dearest convictions if they are to become sufficiently resilient to survive. Only here the devil's advocate is the advocate of the angels and at times comes so near to speaking with the tongue of an angel that it is not easy to resist him.

That Grade does intend us finally to resist him we can hardly doubt, although the question of "intention" in literature is always a highly problematical one. If, despite Grade's apparent intentions, we find that Hersh gets out of his creator's control and moves us far more powerfully than does Chaim, we must remember that, as Charlotte Brontë said when she was trying to puzzle out how her sister had come to create Heathcliff, "the writer who possesses the creative gift owns something of which he is not always master—something that at times strangely wills and works for itself."[6]

Chaim is given the last word in the story, and it is a fairly lengthy last word, though not as lengthy as the argument just delivered by Chaim's adversary. The gist of Chaim's rebuttal may be summarized fairly briefly, for it is doctrine that is far more familiar in our age than is Hersh Rasseyner's. As a liberal, Chaim reiterates the doctrine of nineteenth-century liberalism that doubt is not a bad thing, that intellectual heroism consists in being able to live with it, and that revealed truth, by definition, cannot be true for the individual since he has not discovered it but received it ready-made. As an enlightened Jew, Chaim takes pride in shouldering a double responsibility: toward Jewish tradition as well as toward secular culture; and he rejects the attempt of the pious to declare all the species of those who worship man rather than God fundamentally indistinguishable from one another within the vast genus of idolators. As free-willed individualist, Chaim refuses to be lumped together with murderers, and insists that there are humane secularists and atheists as well as monstrous ones; but as sociological determinist he places the blame for his abandonment of Jewish tradition on precisians like Hersh whose rigid insistence on the narrowest path of piety drove those with more worldly inclinations into outright apostasy. " 'If we have abandoned Jewish tradition, it's your fault.' "

But the most terrifying accusation that Hersh has laid against secularized Jews is that their distraction from the Community of Israel made their suffering and their dying in the camps pointless, and that Chaim's continued separation from the Community of Israel prevents him from ascribing even a posthumous meaning to all that suffering. Chaim's indignant reply to this accusation is not, it must be admitted, very convincing. He answers that the Germans were not mistaken in taking the secularized Jews for complete Jews, and that if the world defines the Jew in this liberal and inclusive way, so too must the Master of the World. Otherwise, Hersh would have been incorrect to say that one third of the Jewish people perished in the Holocaust, for large numbers of the victims were, according to Hersh's strict definition, merely quarter-Jews or tenth-Jews, or less. " 'The gist of what you say . . . is that anyone who isn't your kind of Jew is not a Jew at all. Doesn't that mean that there were more bodies burned than Jews murdered?' " Outraged as Chaim is at Hersh's attempt to assign a religious meaning to what has happened—" 'Even if we were devils,' he shouts, 'we couldn't have sinned enough for our just punishment to be a million murdered children.' "—it is clear that he himself is absolutely resistant to the " 'despairing belief that the world has no sense or meaning.' " Yet he refuses the religious meaning that Hersh finds in the suffering of those who believed themselves to be sanctifying the name of God because it would consign the suffering of all the others to the shadowy realm of non-meaning.

Chaim's quarrel with Hersh Rasseyner has now come to an end, and in the closing paragraphs of the story, Chaim speaks no longer as an adversary but as a reconciler. In other words, the author himself has now directly intervened in the attempt to make peace between the two halves of himself that have been in conflict. Speaking through the mouth of his fictional creation, and speaking explicitly as a writer, he prays for a binding together of the religious and secular strands of the Jewish tradition and claims that in the very cries against God that are uttered by the secular Jewish writers there is yet concealed " 'a quiet prayer for the Divine Presence, or for the countenance of those destroyed in the flames, to rest on the alienated Jews.' " The Jewish writer who survived the Holocaust bears the same burden of suffering as does the believing Jew who communes through God with that segment of the Community of Israel and of his own soul that lies in the grave; but the writer, lacking Hersh Rasseyner's faith, can commune with his people only through the " 'travail of creation.' "

Chaim Grade's *Quarrel with Hersh Rasseyner* is one remarkable product of such travail. Matthew Arnold, who was deeply concerned with the meaning of "adequacy" in literature, once said that the most inadequate of all kinds of literature was "the dialogue of the mind with itself." It was inadequate for purposes of inspiriting and rejoicing readers because it dwelt on suffering which finds no vent in action and represented a "continuous state of mental distress . . . unrelieved by incident, hope, or resistance; in which there is everything to be endured, nothing to be done."[7] But Arnold forgot that there may be subjects that readers would be loath to see used as occasions for the exercise of art's capacity to bring joy out of suffering, and quandaries that readers do not want solved but only imagined and expressed. That is why Grade's story, which is precisely a "dialogue of the mind with itself," is able to involve us so deeply. It seems to be the perfect dramatic articulation, rather than the philosophic resolution, of doubts and difficulties that now beset all of us.

1. Chaim Grade was born in Vilna, Poland, in 1910 and spent his

youthful years in yeshiva study. He published his first book of poems in 1936, escaped to the Soviet Union in 1941, and reached New York in 1948.

2.   Mussarists are an ascetic Jewish sect, to which Grade himself belonged in his youth. In biblical Hebrew *musar* means "chastisement" and hence "instruction" as to right conduct; by extension it may be said to comprise the ascetic and devotional element of religious ethics.

3.   Since surnames have no functional existence in the shtetl, a man may be identified by the place from which he comes, in this case Vilna.

4.   Hersh's acerbity on this point has a foundation in Jewish tradition. In the world of talmudic scholarship, it is the name of an author's work and not his personal name that identifies him.

5.   His marriage is not to be interpreted as a concession to the flesh except insofar as, in the shtetl, boys destined to study the Law were married early so that their needs would be satisfied and they would be able to concentrate on their books.

6.   Editor's Preface to *Wuthering Heights*. Charlotte Bronte wrote this preface to the 1850 edition of her sister's novel.

7.   Matthew Arnold, Preface to First Edition of *Poems* (1853).

Selected Bibliography

Alter, Robert. *After the Tradition: Essays on Modern Jewish Writing.* New York: E. P. Dutton, 1969.

Amichai, Yehuda. *Not of This Time, Not of This Place.* Translated from the Hebrew by Shlomo Katz. New York and Evanston: Harper and Row, 1968.

Arendt, Hannah. *Eichmann in Jerusalem: A Report on the Banality of Evil.* New York: Viking, 1963.

――――. *The Origins of Totalitarianism.* New York: Harcourt, Brace, and World, 1951.

Bartov, Hanoch. *The Brigade.* Translated from the Hebrew by David S. Segal. New York: Holt, Rinehart, and Winston, 1968. (Original Hebrew edition, 1965.)

Bauer, Yehuda. *Flight and Rescue: Brichah.* New York: Random House, 1970.

――――. "Holocaust—Past and present." *Al Hamishmar* (in Hebrew), 18 January 1974.

――――. "The Holocaust and the Struggle of the *Yishuv* as Factors in the Establishment of the State of Israel." In *Holocaust and Rebirth.* Jerusalem: Yad Vashem, 1974.

――――. "Rescue." In *Holocaust.* Jerusalem: Keter, 1974.

――――. "When Did They Know?" *Midstream* 14 (April 1968): 51-56.

Bellow, Saul. *Mr. Sammler's Planet.* New York: Viking, 1970.

――――. *To Jerusalem and Back: A Personal Account.* New York: Viking, 1976.

Ben Amotz, Dahn. *To Remember, to Forget.* Translated from the Hebrew by Zeva Shapiro. Philadelphia: Jewish Publication Society, 1973. (Original Hebrew edition, 1968.)

Bercovitch, Sacvan. "Wine from a Broken Vessel." *Judaism* 20 (Spring 1971): 236-41.

Berkovits, Eliezer. *Faith after the Holocaust.* New York: KTAV, 1973.

Bettelheim, Bruno. "Reflections: Surviving." *New Yorker,* 2 August 1976, pp. 31-52.

Cohen, Arthur A. *In the Days of Simon Stern.* New York: Random House, 1973.

Dan, Joseph. "Will the Jewish People Exist in the 21st Century?" *Forum* 23 (Spring 1975): 61-67.

Dawidowicz, Lucy S. *The Golden Tradition: Jewish Life and Thought in Eastern Europe.* Boston: Beacon Press, 1967.

————. *The War against the Jews: 1933–1945*. New York: Holt, Rinehart, and Winston, 1975.

Des Pres, Terrence. *The Survivor: An Anatomy of Life in the Death Camps*. New York: Oxford University Press, 1976.

Donat, Alexander. *The Holocaust Kingdom: A Memoir*. New York: Holt, Rinehart, and Winston, 1965.

Ellmann, Mary D. "The Piety of Things in *The Manor*." In *The Achievement of Isaac Bashevis Singer*, ed. Marcia Allentuck. Carbondale: Southern Illinois University Press, 1969.

Elman, Richard M. *The 28th Day of Elul*. New York: Charles Scribner's Sons, 1967.

Ezrahi, Sidra. "Holocaust Literature in European Languages." In *Encyclopedia Judaica Year Book*, 1973, pp. 106–19.

Fackenheim, Emil L. *From Bergen-Belsen to Jerusalem: Contemporary Implications of the Holocaust*. Jerusalem: World Jewish Congress and Institute of Contemporary Jewry, 1975.

————. *God's Presence in History: Jewish Affirmations and Philosophical Reflections*. New York: New York University Press, 1970.

Faerstein, Chana. "Jacob Glatstein: The Literary Uses of Jewishness." *Judaism* 14 (1965): 414–31.

Feldman, Irving. *The Pripet Marshes*. New York: Viking, 1965.

————. *Works and Days*. Boston: Little, Brown, 1961.

Flinker, Moshe. *Young Moshe's Diary: The Spiritual Torment of a Jewish Boy in Nazi Europe*. Jerusalem: Yad Vashem, 1971. (Original Hebrew edition, 1958.)

Gouri, Haim. *The Chocolate Deal*. New York: Holt, Rinehart, and Winston, 1968. (Original Hebrew edition, 1965.)

Grade, Chaim. "My Quarrel with Hersh Rasseyner." Translated from the Yiddish by Milton Himmelfarb, in *The Seven Little Lanes*. New York and Tel Aviv: Bergen Belsen Memorial Press, 1972.

Halkin, Hillel. *Letters to an American Jewish Friend*. Philadelphia: Jewish Publication Society, 1977.

Halperin, Irving. *Messengers from the Dead: Literature of the Holocaust*. Philadelphia: Westminster Press, 1970.

Hazaz, Haim. "The Sermon." In *Modern Hebrew Literature*, ed. Robert Alter. New York: Behrman House, 1975.

Herman, Simon. *Israelis and Jews: The Continuity of an Identity*. Philadelphia: Jewish Publication Society, 1971.

Heyman, Eva. *The Diary of Eva Heyman*. Jerusalem: Yad Vashem, 1974.

Hilberg, Raul. *The Destruction of the European Jews*. Chicago: Quadrangle Books, 1961.

Howe, Irving. *The Critical Point*. New York: Delta, 1975.

————. "Journey of a Poet." *Commentary* 53 (January 1972): 75–77.

————. *World of Our Fathers*. New York and London: Harcourt Brace Jovanovich, 1976.

————, and Eliezer Greenberg, eds. *A Treasury of Yiddish Poetry*. New York: Holt, Rinehart, and Winston, 1969.

———, and Eliezer Greenberg, eds. *A Treasury of Yiddish Stories*. New York: Viking, 1953.

Kaniuk, Yoram. *Adam Resurrected*. Translated from the Hebrew by Seymour Simckes. New York: Atheneum, 1971.

Kaplan, Chaim. *The Warsaw Diary of Chaim Kaplan*. Translated from the Hebrew and edited by Abraham I. Katsh. New York: Collier, 1973.

Katz, Jacob. "Zionism and Jewish Identity." *Commentary* 63 (May 1977): 48–52.

Katznelson, Yitzhak. *Vittel Diary*. Translated from the Hebrew by Myer Cohen. Beit Lohamei Hagettaot, Israel: Hakibbutz Hameuchad Publishing House, 1972.

Kaufman, Shirley. Introduction to Abba Kovner, *A Canopy in the Desert*. Pittsburgh: University of Pittsburgh Press, 1973.

Knopp, Josephine Z. *The Trial of Judaism in Contemporary Jewish Writing*. Urbana: University of Illinois Press, 1975.

Koestler, Arthur. "On Disbelieving Atrocities." In *The Yogi and the Commissar*. London: Hutchinson, 1965.

Kovner, Abba. *A Canopy in the Desert*. Translated from the Hebrew by Shirley Kaufman. Pittsburgh: University of Pittsburgh Press, 1973.

Langer, Lawrence L. *The Holocaust and the Literary Imagination*. New Haven: Yale University Press, 1975.

Loewenberg, Robert J. "The Theft of Liberalism: A Jewish Problem." *Midstream* 28 (May 1977): 19–33.

Malamud, Bernard. *The Magic Barrel*. New York: Farrar, Straus, and Cudahy, 1958.

Ozick, Cynthia. "America: Toward Yavneh." *Judaism* 19 (Summer 1970): 264–82.

———. "Envy; or, Yiddish in America." *Commentary* 48 (November 1969): 33–52.

Rawicz, Piotr. *Blood from the Sky*. London: Secker and Warburg, 1964. (Originally published in French as *Le Sang du Ciel*, 1961.)

Rawidowicz, Simon. "Israel: The Ever-Dying People." *Judaism* 16 (1967): 423–33.

Ringelblum, Emmanuel. *Notes from the Warsaw Ghetto: The Journal of Emmanuel Ringelblum*, ed. Jacob Sloan. New York: Schocken Books, 1974.

Rosen, Norma. "The Holocaust and the American-Jewish Novelist." *Midstream* 20 (October 1974): 54–62.

———. *Touching Evil*. New York: Harcourt Brace Jovanovich, 1969.

Rosenfeld, Alvin H. "The Poetry of Nelly Sachs." *Judaism* 20 (Summer 1971): 356–64.

Rubenstein, Richard L. *After Auschwitz*. Indianapolis: Bobbs-Merrill, 1966.

Sachs, Nelly. *O the Chimneys*. New York: Farrar, Straus, and Giroux, 1967.

———. *The Seeker*. New York: Farrar, Straus, and Giroux, 1970.

Schaeffer, Susan F. *Anya*. New York: Macmillan. 1974.

Scholem, Gershom. *The Messianic Idea in Judaism.* New York: Schocken, 1971.

——. "Reflections on the Possibility of Jewish Mysticism in Our Time." *Ariel* 26 (Spring 1970): 46.

Schwarz-Bart, Andre. *The Last of the Just.* New York: Atheneum, 1960. (Originally published in French as *Le Dernier des Justes*, 1959.)

The Seventh Day: Soldiers' Talk About the Six-Day War. Recorded and edited by a group of young Kibbutz members. Harmondsworth, Middlesex, England: Penguin Books, 1971.

Singer, Isaac Bashevis. *Enemies: A Love Story.* New York: Farrar, Straus, and Giroux, 1972.

——. *The Estate.* New York: Farrar, Straus, and Giroux, 1969.

——. *The Family Moskat.* New York: Alfred A. Knopf, 1950.

——. *The Manor.* New York: Farrar, Straus, and Giroux, 1967.

——, and Irving Howe. "Yiddish Tradition vs. Jewish Tradition: A Dialogue." *Midstream* 19 (June/July 1973): 33-38.

——. "Yiddish, The Language of Exile." *Judaica Book News,* Spring/Summer, 1976, pp. 22-27.

——. *Satan in Goray.* New York: Noonday Press, 1955.

——. *The Seance and Other Stories.* New York: Farrar, Straus, and Giroux, 1968.

——. *The Slave.* New York: Farrar, Straus, and Cudahy, 1962.

Steiner, George. *Language and Silence: Essays 1958-1966.* London: Faber and Faber, 1967.

Syrkin, Marie. "The Literature of the Holocaust." *Midstream* 12 (May 1966): 3-20.

Talmage, Frank. "Christianity and the Jewish People. "*Commentary* 59 (February 1975): 57-62.

Talmon, J. L. "European History—Seedbed of the Holocaust." *Midstream* 19 (May 1973): 3-25.

Voegelin, Eric. *Science, Politics, and Gnosticism.* Chicago: Henry Regnery Co., 1968.

Wallant, Edward. *The Pawnbroker.* New York: Harcourt, Brace and World, Inc., 1961.

Wiesel, Elie. *Night.* New York: Hill and Wang, 1961. (Originally published in French, 1958.)

——. *One Generation After.* New York: Avon Books, 1972.

Wisse, Ruth R. *The Schlemiel as Modern Hero.* Chicago: University of Chicago Press, 1971.

Yudkin, Leon. *Escape into Siege: A Survey of Israeli Literature Today.* London: Routledge and Kegan Paul, 1974.

Index